Social Studies for Young Children

Third Edition

Social Studies for Young Children

Preschool and Primary Curriculum Anchor

Gayle Mindes and Mark Newman

ROWMAN & LITTLEFIELD

Lanham • Boulder • New York • London

Published by Rowman & Littlefield
An imprint of The Rowman & Littlefield Publishing Group, Inc.
4501 Forbes Boulevard, Suite 200, Lanham, Maryland 20706
www.rowman.com

86-90 Paul Street, London EC2A 4NE

British Library Cataloguing in Publication Information Available

Library of Congress Cataloging-in-Publication Data

Names: Mindes, Gayle, editor. | Newman, Mark, 1948– editor.
Title: Social studies for young children : preschool and primary curriculum anchor / [edited by] Gayle Mindes and Mark Newman.
Description: Third edition. | Lanham, Maryland : Rowman & Littlefield, 2021. | Includes bibliographical references and index.
Identifiers: LCCN 2021017402 (print) | LCCN 2021017403 (ebook) | ISBN 9781538140055 (cloth) | ISBN 9781538140062 (paperback) | ISBN 9781538140079 (epub)
Subjects: LCSH: Social sciences—Study and teaching (Early childhood)
Classification: LCC LB1140.5.S6 S64 2021 (print) | LCC LB1140.5.S6 (ebook) | DDC 372.83/044—dc23
LC record available at https://lccn.loc.gov/2021017402
LC ebook record available at https://lccn.loc.gov/2021017403

Brief Contents

Contents

2   How Are Literacy and Social Studies Inextricably Linked?   25
Marie Ann Donovan, Ed.D., and Gayle Mindes, Ed.D.

7 How Are We Including and Supporting All Children, Helping All Children Thrive? 143

Michelle Parker-Katz, Ph.D., and Amanda Passmore, Ph.D.

Figures

Tables and Textboxes

Tables

Textboxes

Foreword

Dominic F. Gullo, Ph.D.
Drexel University, Philadelphia

Children are born into social studies (Mindes, 2005). I am sure that Gayle did not realize how astute or how visionary this statement would be, written fifteen years before she would prepare the third edition of *Social Studies for Young Children*. As an early childhood professor and researcher, I have benefitted from Gayle's and my discussions and collaborations regarding young children's development and learning within their understanding of the world context. Young children's perspectives in these matters are quite interesting. It is a fascinating world in which they live and learn. Knowing this not only benefits children, but it also benefits the adults, as the significant adults in their lives structure their interactions with them based on this knowledge. By recognizing, appreciating, and considering children's personal and societal perspectives, adults benefit by increasing their understanding of how children explore and discover things in their world. Gayle and the chapter authors have used this to skillfully construct a volume that reflects their valuing of children, their views, and their circumstances.

This updated edition provides the backdrop for examining children's societal views within the framework of contemporary national circumstances difficult for us to have imagined when the second edition of this book was published in 2014: a pandemic, societal brutality, reemerging racial bias and inequality, insurrection against the US government, all in the face of a threatened democracy. When this volume was last published, the political and cultural landscapes of the times did not transform children's day-to-day living experiences as drastically as they do today: virtual schooling, lack of or severely diminished peer socialization, wearing face coverings, and more. This makes it even more important for teachers of young children to be able to adroitly prepare learning environments with thoughtful understanding and evidenced-based practices so that children can gain an understanding of their world in ways that are meaningful and useful. This volume accomplishes these goals and more.

The National Council for the Social Studies (NCSS) defines social studies as "the integrated study of the social sciences and humanities to promote civic competence."

It includes subject matter content such as history, geography, sociology, psychology, as well as appropriate content from the humanities. While this volume addresses all the usual elements associated with the teaching and learning of social studies in the early childhood classroom, it goes beyond merely a subject matter approach. It accomplishes this by integrating discussions of teaching strategies that make the content meaningful for all young children, taking into account how individual children distinctively and characteristically process information around them, construct new knowledge and problem-solve. In short, the authors of this book's chapters have striven to emphasize the necessity of teaching social studies in such a way that it becomes alive for young children. Throughout the book they interweave evidence for and examples of the necessity for pedagogical practices that are anchored in children's inquiry, citing the importance of children's learning through "projects with themes to guide the integration of knowledge." Collectively, the chapters construct a multidimensional cultural lens through which social studies is taught and learned. There is emphasis on pedagogical routines that will ensure that all young children, regardless of ethnicity, socioeconomic background, and cultural or religious orientation, receive instruction in social studies that is culturally relevant, individually appropriate, and developmentally reactive.

The NCSS (2019) early childhood position statement asserts that young children show a natural interest in the world in which they live. This book is a testament to this. Each chapter reflects that social studies is more than merely subject matter to be learned. It emphasizes the importance of social studies understanding for establishing the foundation for the formation of good citizenship. Yes, "children are born into social studies," but only through living social studies can children *know* social studies.

At birth, young children begin the exploration of their social world. As infants, toddlers, preschoolers, and young school-agers, they interact with people and the environment to learn about the world and their places in it. Gradually, they become community members and acquire the skills to be effective citizens in a democratic society. The precise nature of their learnings and the ways in which they learn about the social world, with its customs and rules for engagement, depend on the developmental stage, as well as the cultural, family, childcare, and school environment. However, all young children will face the demand of policymakers, who require an enlightened citizenship equipped with the tools for problem-solving in the twenty-first century.

Using the inquiry process of social studies, teachers facilitate the acquisition of the tools and concepts appropriate for learning the social studies to serve young learners lifelong. Such tools include raising questions as well as gathering, analyzing, discussing, and displaying data. These are the open-ended, inquiry-based learning strategies ideally suited for child investigations of topics and projects that are appealing to young children. The exploration works best when it is based around problems as defined by the young learners. Of course, teacher guidance facilitates the actual learning project activities in conjunction with the aims of the school and children's understanding of their social world.

So, part of social studies is the academic content of the social studies, which includes the traditional fields of civics, economics, geography, and history. Investigations through project-based learning foster the inquiry process, a key to social studies as of today. Using the academic tools appropriate for the ages of the children, teachers provide learning environments and activities enhancing their understanding of the fundamental questions they raise. In the pages that follow, this curricular approach is described and applied. As well, the book illustrates the development of citizenship and civic action for young children at school and in their communities. Intertwined throughout are respect for cultural diversity, collaboration with families, the development of citizenship ideals, and a focus upon civic engagement.

This text pulls together the disparate but intertwined content of the social studies and discusses the processes of social studies that promote social learning, self-concept development, character development, and emotional intelligence. Issues of culture, classroom community development, and family collaboration are vital aspects of the social studies discussed. The book offers an integration of this content and a significant examination of issues underpinning it to provide a whole-child orientation to the curricular area of social studies for young children. The approach recognizes the view of literacy as the way children learn about their worlds from multiple dimensions and child-constructed meaning to support the acquisition of the required academic material proposed by state and national standards. Finally, culture and community are inextricably linked to the teaching and learning of social studies.

New to This Edition

Since the last edition, the National Council for the Social Studies responded to the imperatives of the Common Core State Standards to create the C3 Framework (https://www.socialstudies.org/standards/c3) with standards to guide the instruction of social studies understandings. These standards are similar in philosophy to the Council of Chief State School Officers and the National Governors Association Common Core State Standards (2010) adopted by most states to guide the instruction of math and English Language Arts. This edition places particular emphasis on cultural diversity in non-simplistic ways with attention to using the social studies to understand our global and multicultural orientation to schooling, considering the funds of knowledge children bring to the table. Digital media and social media are tools reshaping our world and offering opportunities for new approaches to teaching and learning so all young learners may be successful.

All these changes in the world of education and the world at large are incorporated in this edition. In addition, the content of all chapters is updated while maintaining the focus on best early childhood education practice, as reflected in the latest position statement on Developmentally Appropriate Practice from the National Association for the Education of Young Children (2020). Integrated throughout the chapters is the idea of linking social-emotional learning as an integral part of the social studies. The book includes special foci on emerging English learners, history and implication of institutionalized racism throughout education and our thinking about it, and respect for cultural and individual diversity. Each chapter has at its core a focus on the principles of democracy and an engaged citizenry.

Key Features of the Text

- focus questions, study questions, reflection prompts
- suggested further readings
- Internet resources to support teacher and child learning
- integrated approach to social-emotional learning and social studies education
- examples of holistic instructional approaches

Acknowledgments

A book always requires the support and contributions of many friends and colleagues: I thrive on their challenges, conversations, and advice. For this edition, Mark Newman provided important understandings from the perspective of the National Council for Social Studies, as well as his view of the needs of teacher candidates. We collaborated on the development of the revised chapter lineup. Xiaoning Chen, Amy Clark, Marie Donovan, Iheoma U. Iruka, Michelle Parker-Katz, Amanda Passmore, and Megan Schumaker-Murphy all added specific expertise to enhance the perspective of social studies as the central curricular focus in the lives of young children.

In this edition, I am particularly indebted to Derry Koralek who helped me think about solutions to chapter quandaries. Her thoughtful perspective permitted me to consider alternatives and solutions to writing; I am very grateful for her assistance. I appreciate very much the contributions of Bridget Amory who provided real examples based on her work in the Milford, Delaware School District. She provided editorial comments to drafts in process and brought the perspective of her many years of teaching and leading in early childhood. Megan Schumaker-Murphy read early chapter drafts, contributing her thoughts on issues from an East Coast perspective and based on her commitment to anti-racist education for teacher candidates and in classrooms for young children. Amy Clark delivered outstanding examples for planning in short order and was much appreciated. Besides contributing to writing for this edition, Marie Donovan added crucial connections from her work with the International Baccalaureate Program and her experiences in field-based education for teacher candidates, where her heart is always. She was very helpful in reading drafts of other portions of the manuscript; her critical editorial comments were very important. Sarah Bright read earlier versions of the literacy chapter and contributed her expertise in digital media literacy and skill from her perspective as a writer, providing helpful guidance to the revision process. Karen Monkman and Kathy Sheridan provided general support as I faced a few writer's blocks as well as giving me encouragement to persevere. George Morrison always lends a perspective from the world of early childhood education teacher candidate preparation and the dilemmas of writing textbooks; I am indebted to him for professional advice and friendship. Of course, the children, teacher candidates, and school, college, and childcare professionals influence my thinking and add to my understanding of the dilemmas in today's classrooms. Finally, I am indebted to the support and encouragement of my son, Jonathan, for his critical review of sections of the book and his perspective as a writer and editor. He is unfailing in his encouragement of my efforts and always willing to listen.

Mark Newman wants to thank Gayle for the opportunity to collaborate on this book. He also thanks all the chapter authors whose contributions have increased the richness of the content. Mark wants to thank his wife, Kim, who was a preschool teacher for many years. Much of what he learned about young children's education came from dinner conversations over the years. He also thanks her for reviewing chapters and offering advice from a real-world classroom, and her and Kitty Culbert for sharing their work on the around-the-world project context.

Lastly, we appreciate the support and care of Mark Kerr, Courtney Packard, Jehanne Schweitzer and others behind the scenes at Rowman & Littlefield.

Xiaoning Chen, Ph.D., is assistant professor at the National College of Education, National Louis University (NLU). She teaches English as a Second Language and Bilingual Education courses. Dr. Chen's research interests include multicultural children's literature, visual literacy, and the impact of digital technology on literacy development. Published articles, book chapters, and presentations include foci on English Language Learners' (ELLs) identity construction and literacy development; the quality of bilingual children's books; the impact of technology on multimodal design in digital books; visual literacy and ELLs. Currently, she serves as a board member of the International Visual Literacy Association and as an assistant editor for the *International Visual Literacy Association Book of the Selected Readings*.

Amy Clark, Ph.D., is currently visiting faculty, professional lecturer in the Department of Teacher Education at DePaul University. Her research focuses on bilingual and biliteracy development and culturally sustaining pedagogy in early childhood education. Previously she was a first-grade dual language teacher in Chicago Public Schools for more than a decade. Her work has been published in the *Bilingual Research Journal: The Journal of the National Association for Bilingual Education* and *Reading Horizons*.

Marie Ann Donovan, Ed.D., is associate professor of teacher education at DePaul University. She anchors courses in early reading and children's literature. Her research focuses on professional identity development in vocational education settings, as well as early childhood professional education pathways across two- and four-year degree programs. She serves as an associate editor for the *Illinois Reading Council Journal*, coauthoring its column on the intersection of classroom and school libraries in fostering children's literacy. She also serves as the program director for Early Childhood Education at DePaul and is immediate past chair of the Faculty Advisory Council to the Illinois Board of Higher Education.

Dominic F. Gullo, Ph.D., is professor of early childhood development and education. He has worked in the profession for over thirty-five years as a Head Start and public school classroom teacher as well as a university professor and researcher. Dom's areas of specialization and research include early childhood curriculum and assessment, school readiness, risk and resiliency in early childhood, and early childhood school reform. Dom has held many leadership positions in the field with professional associations and has consulted widely with schools throughout the United States and abroad. He has published widely and presented his work both nationally and internationally.

Iheoma U. Iruka, Ph.D., is research professor in the Department of Public Policy, a Fellow at the Frank Porter Graham Child Development Institute (FPG), and the founding director of the Equity Research Action Coalition at FPG at the University of North Carolina at Chapel Hill. Dr. Iruka's work focuses on family engagement and support, quality rating and improvement systems, and early care and education systems and programs. She focuses on ensuring excellence for young diverse learners, especially Black children and their families, through the intersection of anti-bias/anti-racist research, program, and policy. Dr. Iruka serves or has served on numerous national and local boards and committees, including the National Academies of Sciences, Engineering, and Medicine committees on Supporting Parents of Young Children and Applying Neurobiological and Socio-behavioral Sciences from Prenatal through Early Childhood Development: A Health Equity Approach, as well as the American Psychological Association's Board of Educational Affairs Racial Disparities in PreK–12 Education.

Gayle Mindes, Ed.D., professor of education emerita, is a DePaul faculty member of twenty-five years. Mindes served as associate dean, acting dean, and chair of the Teacher Education Department. She is the author of *Assessing Young Children*; *Social Studies for Young Children: Preschool and Primary Curriculum Anchor, 2nd Ed.*; editor of *Teaching Young Children with Challenging Behavior*; and editor of *Contemporary Challenges in Teaching Young Children: Meeting the Needs of All Students*, 2020. Mindes earned a B.S. in Elementary Education from the University of Kansas, an M.S. in Counseling and Behavioral Disabilities from the University of Wisconsin, and an Ed.D. in Curriculum and Early Childhood (Erikson Institute) from Loyola University of Chicago.

Mark Newman, Ph.D., is professor of social studies education at National Louis University. He has written and edited articles and books on maps, photographs, primary sources, and various historical and geographical topics. He is coauthor of a book on visual literacy. Newman has been awarded several National Endowment for the Humanities grants and was director of a Library of Congress Teaching with Primary Sources project. In 2016, he won the National Louis University Distinguished Teaching Award.

Michelle Parker-Katz, Ph.D., is clinical professor in the Department of Special Education at the University of Illinois at Chicago, where she also coordinates the master's programs and clinical fieldwork and teaches courses to undergraduates and graduate students. Her research focuses on teacher inquiry and participation in authentic urban collaborative engagement amongst educators, students, families, and a range of community members. She also focuses on how teachers develop cultural competencies and literacies related to their students.

Amanda Passmore, Ph.D., has experience as an instructional coach for special education and early childhood teachers. Amanda has worked to build educators' capacity in instruction, social-emotional learning, and lesson planning through in-person support and professional learning facilitation. Amanda is an Assistant Professor of special education at Purdue University Northwest. Her research interests include using play to support the social-emotional learning needs of students with disabilities within inclusive early childhood settings.

Megan Schumaker-Murphy, Ed.D., assistant professor, Salem State University, has experience across early childhood settings including preschool special education teacher, early intervention provider, and teacher coach. Dr. Schumaker-Murphy's research focuses on how educators can engage in more equitable practices across early childhood settings. Published in 2019, her dissertation, "Fathers' Experiences in Early Intervention: Marooned in the Kitchen or Member of the Team," informed practitioner workshops for the Virginia Early Intervention Professional Development Program. Dr. Schumaker-Murphy's current work relates to the impact of COVID-19 on early intervention services. Results from this study are included in the State of Virginia's 2020 annual early intervention report for the Office of Special Education Programs (OSEP). Dr. Schumaker-Murphy is also engaged in ongoing work to address racial equity in teacher preparation programs. She is part of the team that presented the paper "'Capital'izing on Cultural Wealth and Sense of Belonging: Narratives of Successful Students of Color in a Teacher Preparation Program" for the AERA in 2021.

An Introduction to the Book

Why Should Social Studies Be the Curricula Anchor for Young Children?

Gayle Mindes, Ed.D.

> You may not divide the seamless cloak of learning. There is only one subject matter for education and that is Life in all its manifestations.
>
> —*Alfred North Whitehead*

Over the years (most recently in 2015), I have written about the importance of the social studies education for young children. It is my passionate belief that the social studies should be the basis upon which curricula are built. For it is through the classroom community that young children learn about themselves, how to function in a group, and ways to understand others. Thus do they begin to acquire the requisite skills of citizenship in a democratic society. Curiosity leads young children to ask questions, to discover more about the world they live in—the children and school. They are developing a school self, an identity as a learner, where they will answer immediate curiosities and develop relationships and academic skills.

It is from the questions of children that a skilled teacher can implement appropriate exploratory strategies for children to seek answers to immediate questions and then lead young children to greater investigative depths. Teachers can think of ways to align the questions to curricular objectives, state standards, and other school priorities. For the questions of social studies are broad, offering many opportunities for teachers to shepherd the inquiry to address child curiosity and accomplish curricular goals.

Where, Then, Do Standards, Assessments, and Local, State, and National Priorities Fit in Deciding What to Teach and How?

As we know, in public schools and federally funded childcare settings, our programs have the requirement to meet standards and to document accomplishment with assessment measures. While the standards movement began as a goal to provide fair and equitable education across the nation, it became corrupted by the zeal to prove with numbers that all children were learning, according to predetermined standards. Well-meaning citizens, philanthropists, and politicians assumed what could be quantified would determine that young children were learning. The standards movement and accountability requirements always have been idealistically and politically motivated and ironically not evidence-based (Mindes, 2016).

In the face of the standardized accountability movement, the Common Core State Standards (2010) took the ideal, shared by many, to emphasize college and career readiness, outlining standards based on problem-solving and reflective thinking skills—necessary skills in both math and English language arts. Following the CCSS, other national professional associations quickly created standards to guide curricular development and instructional delivery. First were the Next Generation Science Standards (2013), based on an inquiry approach to education, and the National Council for the Social Studies, with the C3 Framework (2013), also with the focus on inquiry.

Although each of these efforts for guiding curriculum development emphasizes critical thinking and holistic teaching, an inquiry approach, such broad foci do not easily lead to quantification in assessment. Not to simplify assessment, but it can be done in a holistic manner to create the accountability school boards, community, and families need and want. In fact, early childhood educators have long used formative assessment, such as child observation of behavior and learning situations, to document learning. One such system widely used in Head Start programs and other childcare situations is Teaching Strategies Gold® (2011). This is one of many systems that thoughtful educators have created to show progress using examples of children's work and skilled teacher observation. In the elementary school environment, to counter the narrow, quantified approach to accountability emphasized most notably with the No Child Left Behind Act of 2001, assessment research and policy practice have emphasized standards-based documentation and grading (cf. Guskey, 2001, 2020).

Living with Standards and Focusing on the Social Studies

Even though our programs often must meet accountability requirements, we can and want to document child progress on many important learning outcomes through a holistic approach to curriculum and teaching. Early education has always valued the play-based approach to learning in childcare and education situations (cf. Montesssori, Piaget, Vygotsky, Frobel, Dewey). With this history in mind, we turn to social studies as a central focus of curriculum. This is because the questions of social studies flow from the natural interests of children and can be investigated using observation, reflection, and hypothesis testing. Think of the four-year-old's eternal question: Why? This is one of the many ways of explaining the foundation for inquiry learning. Further, in their beginning years in care and education young children are learning how to be members of a social group. They learn to cooperate with their friends in the classroom, to appreciate individuality, and think critically through the big questions of the social studies. They are learning how to be members of a community and to become active, engaged citizens.

So in this edition of the book, you will find, from diverse perspectives, discussions of the importance of social studies, the ways in which it can anchor the curriculum, and opportunities to focus on the subject areas and skills of the social scientist. Because young children when first starting in school are learning the ropes of school itself, we can connect social studies to social-emotional learning, as well as the thinking skills and literacy development with the inquiry process. But young children don't learn everything from the social studies in their first years in the academy. They come to school with funds of knowledge from their families and communities; we explore with them ways to build upon their budding academic skills and social acumen.

While we are concerned with external guidance, such as state standards, school requirements, and educational philosophies, we think that beginning with civics and citizens' responsibilities and privileges offers a firm foundation for young children to acquire the skills of school. The authors in this volume share the ideal of meeting children where they are and taking them forward, starting where they begin and not where they should be by some arbitrary measure. This requires agile teachers, adept at individualizing instruction, appreciating diversity, and skillfully molding together a classroom community. So, the book starts from the idea that social studies is the center for curriculum offerings for young children. There are myriad possibilities for integration of all of the subject areas.

Welcome to the Third Edition of *Social Studies for Young Children*

This edition features more expert author voices, representing diverse perspectives in early care and education. With these important voices, you will acquire knowledge and tools to employ individually appropriate and culturally relevant pedagogy. As a whole, the book is designed to promote your reflections upon teaching from the perspective of developmentally appropriate practice for all young children.

Planned before the pandemic began, this edition evolved as we lived the project—just as your projects will evolve as you work with the children, families, and teachers in your future classroom. What began for us as a project to include new professional position statements, learning standards, and curricular priorities shifted as the implications of historic events unfolded: challenges to the ways in which we vote and how votes are counted; living in a country ill-prepared for a public health crisis of pandemic proportions; watching on our screens a steady churn of sickening incidences of racism, violence, and cruelty in our society; helplessly watching as families lost loved ones and economic stability, all of it laying bare the fundamental inequities that have always existed in our society—also protest, resistance, organizing, civil disobedience, heightened civic participation, and record voting levels.

Finally, while completing preparations for this new edition, we saw a breakdown of fundamental democratic institutions, a direct assault on the peaceful transition of power.

All of it was lived and watched too by the families and children of those we serve.

Yet we also saw in media, nationally and internationally, a call for improving the civic education of adults and children. One of these calls is illustrated with the remarks of Danielle Allen, director of the Edmond J. Safra Center for Ethics (October 8, 2020):

> We have really disinvested in civic education and social studies. You can see . . . in the comparison that we currently spend $54 per kid year of federal dollars on STEM education and only five cents per year per kid on civics . . . we have really ceased to lay the foundation in K–12 for young people to understand democracy, be motivated to participate in it, to have the skills and tools they need to participate effectively and as a result enjoy participation.

At the same time, we learned the importance of helping young children understand the messages of media. A recent report defines a concept known as "Truth Decay" (Rand, 2018).

Truth Decay is characterized by four trends:

1. increasing disagreement about facts
2. a blurring of the line between opinion and fact
3. the increasing relative volume and resulting influence of opinion over fact
4. declining trust in formerly respected sources of facts

Although we who teach young children are not preparing them for civics examinations, we can—must—prepare them to inquire and to appreciate the elements of citizenship in a free society. Thus, in each chapter, as a reader you will find illustrations of ways the authors approach inquiry and thoughtful reflection for facilitating young children's capacity to learn.

Chapter 1 addresses the social studies as they are defined today, with emphasis on why social studies is important today and the role the study has on the development of young citizens. Newman delineates the subject areas of the social studies: civics, economics, geography, and history. He connects these to the foundational method for teaching social studies: inquiry. Inquiry flows from a child's curiosity, where their knowledge begins, and the child then builds upon this base to expand their skills and knowledge.

Chapter 2 (by Donovan and Mindes) examines the fundamental ways children interrogate their worlds using their burgeoning literacy skills to access and develop the inquiry process. We take a broad view of literacy as the tools and processes we use to make sense of ourselves and our environment. The chapter illustrates the reciprocity between inquiry and literacy development, and how through planned inquiries, students deepen their content knowledge across subject areas while increasing their facility in using various literacies—listening, speaking, reading, writing, spatial, and digital. We also emphasize the critical link of inquiry to social-emotional learning in fostering young children's capacity as learners and citizens.

A central thesis of this book is that learning works best for young children when it focuses on projects with themes that frame the integration of knowledge, providing opportunities to anchor the larger curriculum. Thus, chapter 3 (by Mindes) focuses on how social studies content is the unifying element of all early childhood curricula. Social studies offers an opportunity for children to develop respectful peer relationships in the construction of the classroom as well as the larger school community. In these ways, all young children enhance the social-emotional skills necessary for becoming thoughtful, active citizens of school, community, and world. I examine curricular connections across science, the arts, and mathematical thinking through investigating the big questions of the social studies. I delineate developmentally appropriate practice and culturally responsive teaching principles in action, utilizing the formal subjects of civics, economics, geography, and history. Inquiry again is shown to be the central, natural way in which children learn.

Chapter 4 details the critical role that children's literature plays in developing young children's social studies understanding. Donovan guides the reader in seeing how the various forms of literature shared with children need to provide not only windows and mirrors on their lived experiences but also springboards for further discussion and collective inquiry. She explains how to find, choose, and use literature that is culturally responsive and academically sound. The chapter includes many practical tools to help you link the social studies with children's current lives and the goals of citizenship development.

Iruka's chapter (chapter 5) reminds us of institutionalized racism as it occurs in our history and in practice throughout early childhood care and education. Here the reader will find ample illustration of the total need for transforming the early childhood education profession. It is urgent and ethically imperative for our field that young children experience a curriculum and learning environment that meets their needs in the social studies and beyond. Iruka includes a plan for the future to fight against the legacy of racism and inequities so that we are mindful of the prejudices and discrimination of the past and present. With an emphasis on culturally responsive and grounded, developmentally appropriate practice and reflection upon the past, Iruka implores us to create and implement a curriculum that critically and thoughtfully respects all learners and their families. This chapter is built on understanding truly culturally responsive and grounded teaching and developmentally appropriate practices to meet the needs of all young learners.

Continuing in our efforts to assure fair and equitable learning opportunities for all young children, Chen examines the lives of young emergent bilinguals and their families in chapter 6. She identifies ways teachers can meet the families and children where they are and contribute to their developing fluency and understanding of English. Chen illustrates how families' funds of knowledge contribute to the development of their children's socialization in school, as well as their understanding of citizenship as young social studies learners. By learning children's traditional cultures and weaving them into the curricular fabric, early childhood teachers can increase all children's understanding of how people live in the United States.

Chapter 7 offers a variety of tools to work with diverse learners. Thoughtful teachers can draw on what they learn through observation and gathering data to do teacher research that informs their practice. Parker-Katz and Passmore advocate an approach to instruction centered on collaboration with families and others. Specifically, they focus on the first and fourth domains of the C3 Framework; that is, *developing questions and planning inquiries* and *communicating conclusions and taking informed action*. Thus, the focus is on the inclusion of all learners as a democratic principle, which is central and grounded in thoughtful reflection including all stakeholders. The chapter illustrates culturally responsive, individually appropriate, and developmentally appropriate practice.

In chapter 8, Newman distinguishes some early approaches to helping young children understand their roles as participatory citizens in our society, beginning with a focus on community. He contextualizes this process through a classroom example of young children learning about voting, and he situates learning principles in the disciplinary concepts of the social studies. The chapter shows how the concepts of community and citizenship contribute to learning development in young children.

Chapter 9 (by Mindes) concludes the book with a discussion of young children as engaged citizens. Roles they assume early in their young lives—acting locally. This chapter focuses on civics, honoring young learners demonstrating the capacity to function as citizens within a classroom, school, and larger community. I look at children's capacity to understand the complex issues of our time such as the pandemic, economic disadvantage, insurrection, and racism. The emphasis is on inquiry, informed discussion, respect for individual rights, and cultural diversity. Civic participation by an informed citizenry is the bedrock of democracy; with guidance from family and teachers, young children learn their privileges and responsibilities in a democratic society.

Overall, this edition further promotes the idea that literacy guides inquiry. Projects cement comprehension of fundamental social studies understandings. Responsiveness to individual children in partnership with their families now, during the early childhood years, assures an engaged, educated citizenry for tomorrow. This edition shows a view of early childhood practice history—highlighting the inequities of the past—and provides throughout a plan for our field's future use of the social studies to honor individuality, culture, and family partnerships in the best interest of young children—the citizens of tomorrow.

Our goal in constructing social studies curricula and practice as we have is simple: create a society of thinkers and doers unencumbered by old prejudices and discriminations. This approach requires teachers prepared to challenge the status quo, critical thinkers who are wholly dedicated to culturally responsive teaching. In times like these, the task of this revision was not only to address learning models but also the constant strain of our society's assumptions about the past and present. With each new day's events, we too are learning about our world and our roles in it, ever students of the social studies as well as teachers by way of trying to be good citizens. Our hope is that this edition reflects these ideals and principles in ways you may use as you begin or continue your personal practice on behalf of young children and their families.

Websites for Additional Information

- American Constitution Society https://www.acslaw.org/
- Constitutional Rights Foundation https://www.crf-usa.org/
- National Constitution Center https://constitutioncenter.org/

Chapter 1

Why Is Studying Social Studies Important for Young Learners?

Mark Newman, Ph.D.

Education is the most powerful weapon which you can use to change the world.

—Nelson Mandela

TERMS TO KNOW

citizenship	history
civics	inquiry
economics	social studies
geography	

Overview

The chapter begins by defining what social studies is and describing its component subject areas. Next, we examine why social studies is important for young learners. Connections are made between classroom learning, everyday life, and a child's development. The goal of social studies to develop competent citizens is also discussed. Third, the chapter explores how to teach social studies effectively, focusing on inquiry-based learning as a method that relates naturally to a young learner's curiosity.

Focus Questions

1. What is social studies?
2. Why is social studies important for young learners?
3. How can social studies be taught effectively to young learners?

In a PreK class in a private preschool, students planned and took a "trip around the world" in their classroom, as shown in figure 1.1. The unit took several weeks to plan and develop a re-creation of the world geared for young children. After learning about maps, geography, and aspects of various continents, with their teachers'

FIGURE 1.1   Our Trip Around the World. *Source*: Mark Newman.

help they transformed their classroom into their "world." The children helped create bulletin boards and presentations for all the continents. They drew, cut, and pasted construction-paper models of various animals and plants, such as ears of corn for North America and penguins for Antarctica. Three-dimensional representations of animals and fish hung from the ceiling.

After the world was finished, armed with passports, they toured each continent to complete a treasure hunt that was their summative assessment. The ten clues included:

1.   Find a famous building that is symmetrical. (Eiffel Tower)
2.   What animal never walks? (Kangaroo)
3.   Find a mountain with snow on top. (Mount Fuji)

In the process, the students learned about maps; continents, nations, and bodies of water; animals and plants from various regions; what a passport is; and foods from different places, among other things. They learned to read a visual (map, picture) and to plan a project. Various small motor skills were developed. The students worked together on certain aspects. They asked questions and sought answers. They made decisions about certain details of the project. They communicated what they learned orally and with their finished works. After they and their teachers completed building the world, they took the trip, "visiting" the places they had learned about in class. In addition, family members came to the classroom to tour the students' world.

The trip around the world touched upon almost all of the significant aspects of an effective social studies education. The planning, development, and participation in the project involved inquiry and developing visual literacy skills (reading, thinking, communicating), in part through the study of primary and secondary source documents and artifacts (Newman & Ogle, 2019). Learning about maps introduced the children to spatial thinking. Visual literacy skills were honed by reading maps, photographs, and other pictures. With the teachers facilitating, they also created a concept map for the project. The children learned not just to read an image but to comprehend it as well as to create a visual. They also gained a larger view of the world and recognized that geography affects how we live.

As such, they learned about themselves and their place in the world as well as about different global communities. The classroom was an interactive community geared to creating the project. Participation by the children was an exercise in citizenship that involved enjoying certain rights and having certain responsibilities, such as following rules and sharing. Working collaboratively in groups and as a whole class to create the finished product contributed to the young learners' social-emotional development. The content and skills learned applied not just to the classroom but also to the real world. In a nutshell, the project represented what social studies education is all about.

This chapter explores how social studies acts as a foundational element in education for grades PreK–3. As you read the chapter, our hope is you will see that at a basic level, social studies is the story of us. It examines who we are, where we came from, where we are today, and indicates where we are going in the future. It does so through the perspectives of the content areas that make up this subject, showing young children how what they are learning is relevant to their lives.

What Is Social Studies?

The name provides some clues to its meaning. **Social studies** explores the social aspects of human society so students can better understand the world (Gonser, 2018). "Social" is defined broadly as related to society. More specifically, social studies examines the interaction of people, places, and time in varying combinations. It could be studying the interaction of people in a single place or in different places at the same time or over time. Or, it could be the study of how and why people interacted with the environment in one place or many places during a specific period or over time.

The term "social" also indicates that the major emphasis is on community. Over the PreK–12 school levels, the focus shifts to include family, classroom, neighborhood, local community (city, suburb, rural area), state, region, nation, and world. What do children study about all these different types of community? They study:

1. Change and continuity: how and why certain aspects change and how and why some things remain the same or similar to what they were.
2. Cause and effect: a pivotal aspect of change and continuity.
3. Significance: the importance of what is being studied within the context of the study and to us today. A goal is to make all social studies learning relevant to the individual so children care about what they are learning.

What Is the Academic Content of Social Studies?

Because of the wide-ranging content of the subject area, we should remember that the term social studies is singular, not plural. Often it is called *the* social studies because it includes a number of academic subject areas in the humanities and social sciences:

- civics and political systems
- economics
- geography
- history
- social sciences such as anthropology, archaeology, psychology, and sociology

The National Council for the Social Studies (NCSS) has designated the first four subjects in the preceding list as core areas (C3 Framework, 2013). The social sciences are considered supplementary by the NCSS, though some states have not made that distinction.

The content of the subject areas is adapted to the grade levels where social studies is learned. The content for PreK–3 differs from that in grades 9–12. What students learn in the early grades provides the foundation for future learning. Figure 1.2 provides an overview of social studies. It contains a definition, two major themes, the content areas, and sample questions relevant to grades PreK–3.

Looking at figure 1.2, do you see the connection between the social studies curricula and the related disciplines? Examine the questions in the chart; how important is it for students to answers these queries? Equally important, how might these questions and answers change as students possess more knowledge and experience? What other questions does figure 1.2 raise?

Regarding subject area content, what is presented below is not comprehensive, but for our purposes, it is a start.

- **Civics** examines political systems, how we organize and maintain order in communities, and **citizenship**, meaning how and why we participate in our various communities (Center for Civics Education, n.d.).
- **Economics** explores how resources are created, distributed, and used; needs and wants; and financial literacy (American Economic Association, 2019).
- **Geography** uses a spatial perspective to study the natural and human-built environment, looking at location, place, region, movement, and how people interact with the environment (five major themes of geography) (Geography for Life, 2012).
- **History** employs a time perspective to study the past, present, and, at times, the future. It examines why the interaction of people, places, and events were significant in the past and why they are important today.
- **Social Sciences** examine aspects of society, culture, and behavior.

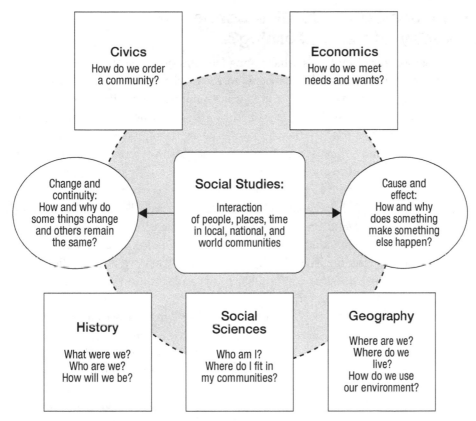

FIGURE 1.2 Social Studies in Perspective. *Source*: Mark Newman.

The overall idea is to provide as full-bodied and robust a study as possible. In grades PreK–3, the foundation of academic content and skills is laid. What ties everything together is citizenship. Helping young learners to become good citizens is a multifaceted task that helps children develop the abilities needed to productively participate in their family, school, community, and beyond. Effective citizens can read and think critically. They communicate clearly. Equally important, they can successfully function in varied social situations to contribute to the common good.

Why Is Social Studies Important for Young Learners?

Simply put, social studies is important because it helps young learners:

- develop understanding of self and where they fit in the world
- build interpersonal skills in diverse settings with others
- become productive citizens in school, community, and society

Social studies accomplishes these lofty goals by providing formative experiences that influence a child's views and actions regarding who they are and who they want to be. It helps them learn how to be citizens in their classroom, their school, and the surrounding community (NCSS, 2019). Equally important, social studies connects classroom learning to everyday life through the study of family, school, and community. Often this study involves working with others on projects.

How Does Social Studies Connect to Everyday Life and Learning?

In many ways, social studies is what young learners do when they are in the classroom. They apply social studies concepts to their behavior and learn social studies content, though often in an indirect manner. Young learners follow a routine when they are in the classroom that often is tied to a posted schedule of activities. They discuss these activities to help them know the what, when, where, and how of what to do and with whom they will be working. They also learn how the projects and other activities connect to social studies.

The "around the world" project shows how the classroom experience can be extended to a student's life outside school with family and friends, and in the neighborhood. This project could be adapted to focus on the countries or cultures represented in your class. One kindergarten class invited families to an evening potluck to share dishes representing their family background. Children and families became excited to learn more about the unfamiliar foods and traditions. This event led to a longer project-based unit on families.

In such projects, study becomes practice and practice leads to a greater understanding of the world as it expands children's lives from families to the community, school, and beyond. Knowing the relationship between social studies learning in school and in everyday life is an important first step in understanding what social studies is and why it is important.

Let's take a look at a common practice. When a teacher asks a question, how do students respond? Most likely, the teacher has set up a rule for answering questions. Students may raise their hands, signaling they want to be called upon to answer the query. Children embrace the rule by listening attentively and raising their hands to comment on their friend's idea, comment, or thought. The teacher also listens carefully to what the children are saying, offering comments as needed. The rule provides order, eliminating the possible chaos if everyone started talking at once. By raising their hands, students gain the right to be called on to answer the question.

There are likely many other rules that govern various aspects of student behavior, perhaps regarding what they do when they come into the classroom. They may go to the cubby, sit at a learning center to read a book, or talk to friends. When they leave, they may stand quietly by their table or desk. They may pack their backpack. And there are a host of other things that happen in between, such as going to the bathroom, washing hands, walking in the hall, or going to the park or playground.

In PreK–3 classrooms, students learn what rules are, how they work, and why they should follow them. In this way, early education acts as a training ground for learning about and following laws, which occur in later grades and in life. An important lesson is that following the rules gives students certain rights. They can be the line leader, line ender, table setter, calendar helper, and so on.

By following the classroom rules and other practices, students act as respectful, responsible members of the classroom community. In fact, their behavior helps build the classroom community of friends respecting each other. In part, society is based upon the idea that people have an identity as a member of a community. For children in the early years, this means becoming a "school citizen."

Membership involves certain rights and responsibilities. To enjoy their rights, citizens have to fulfill their responsibilities, such as obeying laws—or rules in school. Over time, young children learn what a community is and that their identity includes being a member of various communities. As such, the classroom acts as a training ground for students to be productive citizens now and in the future; the community of learners is a microcosm of our larger society.

What Is the Goal of Social Studies Education?

Learning to be a productive member of society is the aim of social studies. According to the NCSS, the primary purpose of social studies is to "help young people develop the ability to make informed and reasoned decisions for the public good as citizens of a culturally diverse, democratic society in an interdependent world" (NCSS, 2018). More simply put, the goal is to educate responsible, competent citizens who are informed and thoughtful. They appreciate the history of the United States and democracy and participate in their communities, exercising their rights and responsibilities. They also possess moral and civic virtues such as social responsibility, tolerance, and respect, and a belief they can make a difference (Golston, 2010).

The *Colorado Preschool Social Studies Academic Standards in High Quality Early Child Care and Education Settings* (2012) offers a good description of how social studies helps build citizenship:

> Ideas of citizenship are based upon meaningful daily events and a classroom environment that ensures that children are aware of and respect another person's interests, preferences and cultural background. When children participate in activities that bring the community into the classroom, they feel good about themselves and find out how different groups of children live. Teachers and family members who help children negotiate the rules, responsibilities and challenging issues that characterize a vibrant learning environment can expose children to a community based upon kindness, equality and justice.

So, how do we as teachers develop social studies curricula with our learners in a developmentally appropriate and culturally responsive way?

How Can Social Studies Be Taught Effectively to Young Learners?

Teaching and learning are two sides of the same coin. Asking how to teach effectively also means asking how social studies can be learned effectively. The natural bent of young learners to ask questions provides a simple answer to effective teaching and learning. As mandated by the NCSS and some state standards, inquiry-based learning provides a developmentally appropriate and perfect instructional approach that matches the natural curiosity of young learners (NCSS, 2019).

In this section, we will:

1. examine inquiry generally and specifically as it applies to grades PreK–3
2. explore unit and project planning to show how inquiry works in the PreK–3 grade levels

What Is Inquiry?

At the most basic level, **inquiry** is a versatile instructional method that can be used for varied activities from reading a picture or a document to project-based learning. No matter what the activity, the process generally involves:

- identifying a topic
- posing questions to explore the topic
- using the questions to access, examine, and manage information
- answering the questions
- communicating findings

Before going into more detail on inquiry and how it works as an effective teaching and learning method, perhaps we should briefly explain why it can be so effective. Building upon the innate curiosity of young learners and their inclination to ask questions, inquiry puts their interests at the center of instruction. Inquiry creates a question-and-answer pattern that engages students in learning social studies content relevant to them. In the process, it builds important literacy and other academic and social skills. The inquiry process does not depend exclusively on child-generated curiosities. Teachers can stimulate curiosity through props and materials provided to the community of learners.

Inquiry helps students connect what they are learning in the classroom to their everyday lives, which is why the projects can evolve from family and school to community topics. The questions and the pursuit of answers can allow students to draw upon their experiences as they look into various topics. For example, in their article "The Challenge of a Community Park," Cole and McGuire noted that kindergartners addressed such real-world problems as rules, graffiti, and bullying as they planned their mural depicting a community playground. The authors stressed that safety was an important issue for young learners (Cole & McGuire, 2011, p. 24).

Inquiry also supplies a method to have students collaborate in groups as they pose questions, look for answers, and make decisions, among other things. In both the "around the world" project described earlier and the planning of the community playground, success depended upon the students working together to meet common goals. As they progressed through the projects, the young learners practiced important social-emotional skills related to cooperation, respecting the opinions of others, and sharing, to name just a few. The group work helped students realize the value and benefits of collaboration.

How Does Inquiry Help Meet State Standards?

One way to show the importance of inquiry and to gain insight into how it works is to examine state standards. The Illinois Social Science Standards are divided into two categories: inquiry skills and subject area content. Table 1.1 shows the inquiry standards for grades K–2. They show not just what kindergarten students are expected to do; they also indicate where support should be provided. There are eight inquiry standards for grades K–12, but only six relate to grades K–2. Note that teachers may decide that some of the six listed may be introduced in one of the three grade levels, depending upon student competency. (The two standards not listed for K–2 are introduced in grades 3–5. They are not included in the table.)

TABLE 1.1   Illinois Inquiry Standards K–2

Standard	Disciplinary Concept	My Social World Standard
Developing Questions and Planning Inquiries	Constructing Essential Questions	**SS.IS.1.K-2:** Create questions to help guide inquiry about a topic with guidance from adults and/or peers
	Determining Helpful Sources	**SS.IS.2.K-2:** Explore facts from various sources that can be used to answer the developed questions
Evaluating Sources and Using Evidence	Gathering and Evaluating Sources	**SS.IS.3.K-2:** Gather information from one or two sources with guidance and support from adults and/or peers
	Developing Claims and Using Evidence	**SS.IS.4.K 2:** Evaluate a source by distinguishing between fact and opinion
Communicating Conclusions and Taking Informed Action	Communicating Conclusions	**SS.IS.5.K-2:** Ask and answer questions about arguments and explanations
	Taking Informed Action	**SS.IS.6K-2:** Use listening, consensus-building, and voting procedures to decide on and take action in their classrooms

As table 1.1 indicates, the inquiry standards focus on three tasks, each of which has two standards, that plot out the inquiry process. An important point is that two of the standards specifically state that adults and/or peers will help guide that aspect of the inquiry process. The help comments tell us that scaffolding likely will be necessary and that students may be working in groups. Simply put, in kindergarten, inquiry involves students (with help):

1. posing questions
2. exploring one to two sources to gather the information and facts to answer the questions
3. evaluating the source itself as being fact or opinion
4. asking and answering questions about any arguments or explanations to communicate conclusions
5. deciding on and taking action

The standards amply show that inquiry places students at the center of the learning experience, giving them a sense of ownership. It is their trip around the world or their community park mural because they planned and built it. The emphasis on questions helps motivate learning while the seeking of answers builds content mastery and skills. Equally important, a similar planning process is used for units and lessons.

Why Is Questioning a Key to Effective Inquiry Learning?

As our discussion so far hopefully indicates, questioning is the engine driving inquiry. There are two levels of questions. The compelling (also called essential) question is a big-picture query that probes into the entire topic from a certain perspective. For example, in a unit on community helpers, the compelling question might be why community helpers are important. To help answer the compelling question, supporting questions are asked. These are more narrowly defined and seek specific information. For community helpers, sample supporting questions could be:

1. Who are the community helpers?
2. What do community helpers do?
3. Where can you find a community helper?
4. If you need a community helper, what should you do?
5. How do you become a community helper?

The supporting questions play several roles in the inquiry process. They set the parameters for the inquiry, acting as a guide to identifying pertinent information. They provide the means to answer the compelling question and help focus the organization of information into categories. They also help organize the evidence used to support the answer to the compelling question. In PreK–3, some adjustments to the inquiry model may be necessary. For example, instead of compelling and supporting questions, the teacher might use big and small questions, distinctions that are more readily understood by preschoolers.

The success of inquiry depends upon posing questions that are clear, direct, and appropriate for the students. Especially for young learners, questions need to be brief, use vocabulary and sentence phrasing that the students understand, and get right to the point. Note that the questions above are simply phrased, and each question focuses on a single aspect largely defined by the who, what, when, where, why, and how questions. Most of the questions have four or five words. Only the query on getting help has an explanatory phrase that helps frame the question.

Depending upon the prior knowledge and experience of the students, the teacher poses questions, helps the students to create queries, or has students develop the questions. The hardest query to pose may be the compelling question, as it addresses the topic in a global fashion. Students may be more experienced and familiar with asking more direct questions that focus on the who, what, when, and where.

Equally important, students need to know how to examine a question so they understand how to construct it and they are clear on what they are being asked to do. Teachers can help by going over questions with students to identify the three major components that are basic to all questions:

- An interrogative (who, what, when, where, how, or why) identifies what the task is and what question will be answered.
- The topic (such as community helpers or immigration or my ancestors) is who or what we are investigating.
- Asking for examples (Who are the helpers in your community?) helps identify what aspects of the topic we are studying.

For instance, in the compelling question of why community helpers are important, the teacher could ask students what question they are being asked to answer, leading them to the why, the interrogative. Next, they can have students identify who the question is about so they identify community helpers as the topic. Last, they can ask what they are going to learn about community helpers so they see that the example is important. In questions 3, 4, and 5 at the start of this section, the example is personalized. Students are asked what they would do to find a community helper if they needed one, and how they would become a community helper.

In some cases, the topic is also the example. Community helpers are the topic as well as the example for the supporting question: Who are community helpers? In going over this question, teachers may just focus on having students identify the interrogative and the topic, as including the example may prove confusing in this case.

The last consideration for PreK–3 students is whether or not they can read. Especially in preschool but also for students with special needs or those for whom English is not their initial language, text may prove difficult. In these cases, the teacher can use pictures, props, or a mix of pictures, props, and words to help students pose or read the questions.

For community helpers, a prop may include a visit from the school resource officer or the school nurse. A project on recycling can use the class trash can as a prop. In those places where recycling is happening, questions may include: Why do we have the categories for recycling materials? In places where recycling is not happening, a question could be: Where does this stuff go? Often the term is placed under the picture so students can connect the two.

Because there are different categories of questions, it may help if the visual used for the interrogative helps students distinguish between the who, what, when, where, why, and how. Various methods exist to help students learn the different terms. For example, a graphic with six question marks, each one a different color, can be used. Each color would represent a different query, such as blue for what, yellow for when, and so on. The relevant term would be written under the appropriately colored question mark.

When posing queries, the teacher would point to the color column so students would know which interrogative to use. In the community helper unit, the colored question marks and a picture of a group of community workers (fire, police, postal, etc.) can help students construct or read the questions. Over time, the students would learn the terms so that the color coding could become unnecessary. Practice also helps students learn how to ask the questions. Understanding the role of questioning in inquiry is an important first step in planning an inquiry unit. There are other equally important considerations in unit planning. Those considerations are discussed next.

How Can an Inquiry Unit Be Developed?

Units tend to be the larger structure for inquiry-based learning. Such planning employs a skills-based strategy to study a content topic over a specified period of time. Units also provide an effective way to organize the study of a subject across a school year. Each unit focuses on a specific topic related to the subject. Lesson planning occurs within the context of a unit. The discussion below on units also applies to lessons with the distinction being the time frame. Lessons typically last for one day.

The inquiry approach allows students to practice the method over time so they can improve their skills and connect prior to new learning. As students become familiar and more proficient with the inquiry process, through the gradual release of responsibility they may be able to take more control over their learning. Yes, they are learning new content, but the process being used is familiar, as are the skills being developed.

There is a ton of literature on planning units and projects. Most focus on backward mapping, also called backward design and backward planning. The starting point often is with the goals or outcomes of what students will be able to do, using state standards as either the goals or guides for creating the goals (Wiggins & McTigue, 2005; Helm & Katz, 2016). In social studies, recent works have focused on adapting backward mapping by beginning with the compelling question before moving to standards (Swan et al., 2018, 2019). Some of these approaches are quite complex and involved. Often school districts or schools have required unit planning methods.

There are several factors that guide unit planning. They include class demographics, standards, the proposed length of the unit, and where the unit fits in the overall flow of learning across the school year. Prior learning is a major component of the last factor. What factors influence how you plan units? Are any of the above part of your planning process?

How Can Class Demographics Influence the Design of a Unit Topic?

Student background and interest can play an important role in unit design. What are the funds of knowledge that children bring to the table? In many classrooms, students have different social and ethnic backgrounds. Using those backgrounds to identify topics and the examples used to study those topics can pique the interest of students. Imagine a preschool or K–3 class that has a diverse group of students, some of whom are new to the United States.

Assume the topic is neighborhoods and that the class will study a generalized US neighborhood and two others over five weeks. One of the students is from Mexico and another is from China. By studying a Mexican and a Chinese neighborhood, students gain a global perspective of this type of community. They can learn about the similarities and differences of the three neighborhoods.

Students also learn more about classmates and their original countries. In turn, the students whose home country neighborhoods are studied have their identities and cultures validated. Where they lived is important enough to study in school. In some cases, the students may come from different types of communities. If the school is in an urban area and some students previously lived in a rural or suburban area, that sets up a rich study of three different types of neighborhoods.

In some smaller cities, the neighborhood may not be diverse, since everyone in the community has lived there for generations. Or the community may be bifurcated, with some families from established roots and others who have come to Iowa or Delaware to work in the chicken or beef factories.

Other examples of tapping into student demographics exist. Holidays and food can bring parents or other family members into the class to share aspects of their heritage and culture. Holidays have become a controversial topic in early childhood education, but, in social studies, these celebrations open rich doors of opportunities to learn about other cultures.

In a preschool during the holiday season, a Jewish student asked the teacher about reading a book on Hanukkah. There were no other Jewish students in the class. The teacher embraced the idea and had the student bring in a book. Another teacher of kindergarteners encouraged a class member to share the Advent calendar for Christmas. The same scenario could play out for Ramadan or other holidays. And in one community, a teacher was startled to learn Buddhists do not observe holidays per se. Her kindergarten class included Jewish, Catholic, and Buddhist families.

The point is that student backgrounds are a rich repository of ideas and possibly expertise. Giving students a voice to influence what they study lets the students gain control over their learning and realize that their opinions matter. They scaffold their learning to make sense of the world. This also helps students learn more about their classmates and other people and cultures.

As the holiday example shows, students can bring up ideas that the teacher may not have considered that become important parts of the curriculum. There also are international, national, state, and local holidays that help students learn much about the world, the United States and other nations, and local communities. Earth Day is a good example of a world holiday that can promote learning, such as with a recycling project. July Fourth and Cinco de Mayo are national holidays of political importance.

Using holidays for focal point discussions must come from the demographics of a particular group of children. It is best that they emerge organically rather than through the old-fashioned practice of organizing the school year around such celebrations as Halloween, Christmas, winter, St. Patrick's Day, Easter, Mother's Day and Father's Day, and so on (Derman-Sparks & Edwards, 2020). As is true of any curricular decision, the rationale for studying a holiday must be justified by it meeting important learning objectives.

How Can Standards Be Used to Help Select a Unit Topic?

Because they are required in most public school situations, standards often come into play when selecting a topic of study. There are two approaches. One starts with the standards and proceeds to the design of the unit (or lesson). The other leaves the standards to the end of the design process and then applies them, revising the unit (or lesson) as needed. Content knowledge and experience may influence the use of an approach, as do the policies of the school. For example, second-grade standards in Massachusetts require teaching about ancestors (Massachusetts Department of Elementary and Secondary Education, 2018). Teachers can bring this content to life by sharing personal narratives from their learners.

The state sets up the curricular expectations that are then applied by districts and schools to meet local conditions. Often, districts or schools provide unit topics. In some cases, the curriculum is prescribed so teachers have little unit planning to do. Most states just list standards but some supply more information, including grade-level subjects. Using kindergarten as the example, table 1.2 shows how some states identify grade-level subjects and potential unit topics (California State Board of Education, 2017, p. 31; Illinois State Board of Education, 2016, p. 16; State Education Department, 2017, p. 16; Georgia Department of Education, 2016, p. 1).

TABLE 1.2 **Kindergarten Subjects**

State	Curricular Document	Kindergarten Subject(s)
California	History Social Science Framework	Learning and Working Now and Long Ago
Illinois	Social Science Standards	My Social World
New York	K–8 Social Studies Framework	Self and Others
Georgia	Social Studies Georgia Standards of Excellence	Foundations of America

Note that the subjects are broadly phrased to allow districts leeway to meet their local needs.

In Illinois, "My Social World" is the theme for kindergarten. Based on our discussion so far on unit planning and the standards, what potential unit topics do you see? Could you plan a unit that met several standards? For example, we discussed briefly a unit on neighborhoods. Could the focus be on studying one or more neighborhoods over time, to compare life in the past with life today? Could it be a project on who lives in farming communities? Or maybe, what is that factory down the street making and do our families work there?

Why Unit Length Is Important

In PreK–3, teachers may plan shorter and longer units depending upon the content and the activities. How long a unit is depends upon several considerations. At the beginning of the school year, unit length presents a dilemma. On one hand, it probably will take students longer to become acclimated to the classroom and to learn new things. On the other hand, student attention span may be less after a summer out of school, though the issue may not be as prominent in childcare settings with summer programs. Teachers can plan units of shorter duration on narrowly defined topics. For example, in kindergarten there could be two-week units on rules or maps.

Over time, as students learn the ropes of school, they adjust to school life. They have knowledge, skills, and dispositions to approach units with sustained attention and joy in learning, guided by skillful scaffolding on the part of their teachers. Kindergarteners are supported in a culturally responsive and individually appropriate way (Developmentally Appropriate Practice Position Statement, NAEYC, 2020), as they learn the content required by state standards.

Units can become longer and more general. The community park example was plotted for three to six weeks. In preschool, a community workers unit focusing on the post office for four-year-olds extended over two months (Davey & Elijah, 2015).

How Will Students Demonstrate What They Learned?

Answering the question of how students will show what they learned requires being clear on the learning goals. In grades PreK–3, assessment includes not just academic performance regarding content knowledge and skills. It also encompasses social-emotional learning, everyday behavior, and interaction with other students and the teacher, among other things. An important consideration for preschool would be the professional practice that calls for positive and caring relationships with adults and other children. If assessment is approached with the idea of helping young children improve, it can be a highly effective motivating device.

All subject areas tend to follow a similar strategy involving two categories of assessment. Formative assessment evaluates student performance during the learning experience. It is an everyday assessment. Summative assessment is the culminating evaluation at the close of a unit. It provides students with the opportunity to showcase the results of their learning.

An important aspect of assessment is its purpose. Is the purpose of the assessment to diagnose student learning, offer ideas on how to improve, and provide an opportunity to improve? Is it to provide a final judgment on some aspect of student learning? With more emphasis in today's schools on standards-based assessment rather than grades, the answers to these questions are probably a qualified yes. Standards-based practices focus on the learner's accomplishments, leading to expectations for teacher scaffolding for additional or alternate teaching and learning strategies.

As students move to elementary schools, letter grades are often required, especially if districts have not embraced standards-based performance assessments. To guide formative assessments and to gather evidence for required summative assessments, many teachers use rubrics that clearly delineate expectations for success to assess children. This evidence is shared with families routinely and regularly, not only at summative six- or nine-week intervals. Families gain perspectives and insight to support their children and the teachers who guide them. In addition, students often offer comments for families or guardians.

For formative assessment and documentation for summative assessment, school districts often provide templates and guidelines. When these guides are inappropriate for young children, teachers can often gather evidence to support required reporting on learning standards. In some cases, the school or district will provide assessment templates and guidelines, though teachers generally have some wiggle room to adapt assessments to meet classroom needs.

Conclusion

This chapter introduced social studies examining what it is, why it is important, and how to develop an understanding of social studies for young children. In many ways, academic learning also involves the social-emotional development of the young learner. The goal of social studies is to prepare children to participate as effective citizens. A major part of achieving that goal requires learning how working with others is for the good of all. Inquiry-based learning taps into the natural curiosity of young learners, helping them build essential skills as they learn foundational content.

As you read the chapter, what ideas and points did you find most interesting or most helpful? Thinking back on your own social studies education, would you teach the subject in a similar fashion or would your teaching be different? How and why would it be different?

Activities in the Field

1. Visit a preschool or elementary setting. Observe how social studies is taught and find out where it fits into the curriculum. Ask the teachers how the teaching and learning of social studies contribute to the overall development of the students. Discuss findings with your colleagues.
2. Interview several teachers in various grade levels. Ask about the cultural composition of the students and how that composition influenced how and what they teach. Ask about how they develop culturally relevant pedagogy. Find out how the teachers interact with parents and other family members and how that interaction influences their teaching and learning.
3. Based on your observations and interviews, how is technology used in the PreK–3 classroom? How does its use compare with your own experience throughout your education? How do you see technology being used in PreK–3 social studies teaching and learning?

Activities in the Library

1. Review the last several issues of *Social Studies and the Young Learner* and *Young Children*. What social policy issues are discussed? What are some of the curricular and instructional strategies highlighted in the journal articles? How will you use your findings in planning social studies teaching and learning in your class?
2. In a curriculum library at your college or public library, explore the social studies materials available. How do these materials compare to those available when you were a child? What issues, topics, and strategies are prominent today? Discuss your findings with colleagues.

Study Questions

1. What is social studies, including its goal?
2. What are three major themes of social studies education?
3. What is the general curriculum of social studies in grades PreK–3?
4. What is inquiry and what role does it play in social studies education?
5. What do young children learn in social studies?
6. How does what is learned in social studies connect to the overall development of the PreK–3 student?

Reflect and Reread

1. Why is studying social studies important?
2. How have the actions of the National Council of Social Studies influenced social studies teaching and learning?
3. Why is social studies taught as it is today?

Suggested Readings

Ladson-Billings, G. (1995). Toward a theory of culturally relevant pedagogy. *American Educational Research Journal*, Vol. 32, No. 3 (Autumn, 1995), pp. 465–491.

Souto-Manning, M. (2013). *Multicultural teaching in the early childhood classroom: Approaches, strategies and tools, preschool-2nd grade.* New York: Teachers College Press. Practical application of teaching utilizing a framework of respect—rich vignettes

Swan, K., Lee, J., & Grant, S. G. (2018). *Inquiry design model: Building inquiries in social studies.* Washington, DC; National Council for the Social Studies and C3 Teachers. A primer for developing inquiry-based learning using a C3 Framework model

Websites for Additional Information

C3 teachers. http://www.c3teachers.org/
An organization dedicated to supporting the Inquiry by Design Model of implementing the C3 Framework

National Association for the Education of Young Children. https://www.naeyc.org/
The national association for the promotion and advocacy of education of young children

National Council for the Social Studies. https://www.socialstudies.org/
The national organization for the promotion and advocacy of social studies

Chapter 2

How Are Literacy and Social Studies Inextricably Linked?

Marie Ann Donovan, Ed.D., and Gayle Mindes, Ed.D.

When children learn language, they are not simply engaging in one kind of learning among many; rather, they are learning the foundation of learning itself.

—*Michael Halliday**

TERMS TO KNOW

citizenship	language stores
digital divide	literacy
digital literacy	media literacy
digital native	new literacies
funds of knowledge	social-emotional learning
inquiry	social studies literacy
Inquiry Arc	

Overview

This chapter starts with a broad view of the meaning of **literacy** as the ways humans come to know about themselves and the worlds they inhabit. Young children's earliest, deep life questions are centered around wanting to know "Who am I?" "Who am I in my family?" "My community?" "My school?" "The larger social world?" These questions both form and inform social studies curricula for the young. Young children are natural inquisitors who explore their immediate worlds by using myriad tools in their environment. Children take in the world, consider it, and then produce new personal knowledge about it in symbolic ways. In their social

---

* Halliday, M. A. K. (1993). Towards a language-based theory of learning. *Linguistics and Education, 5*(2), 93–116, p. 94.

roles, children participate as citizens of family, school, and community—their main contexts—in acquiring, using, and sharing their knowledge. This chapter describes how through engaging children systematically and deeply studying these connected life questions and others like them—conducting **inquiry**—their multiple literacies are simultaneously developed and fostered, along with their understanding of the social studies. We also examine how young children's **social-emotional learning** is both a curricular goal and instructional driver of effective social studies programs. The roles and influences of state learning standards, as well as digital media, on how we engage young children in social studies curricula are viewed from the perspective of knowing who our children are and planning with their diversity in mind.

Focus Questions

1. Why is literacy so central to learning?
    * How is literacy defined today?
2. How does inquiry foster young children's literacy?
    * What do social studies literacy practices in preschool look like?
    * What do social studies literacy practices look like across the primary grades?
3. How are learning standards and social learning contexts connected?
    * How do children function as members of formal social groups?
4. What are the social-emotional development connections to social studies literacy?
    * How are citizenship skills developed?
5. How do children personally connect to social studies literacy development?
    * How does the school self evolve?
    * How do childcare experiences influence children's understanding of their world?
    * What else influences and fosters children's inquiry-based social studies learning?
    * How do state learning standards anchor and influence children's inquiry?
    * Where does children's literature fit into the Inquiry Arc?
6. How has the proliferation of media influenced social studies curricula?
    * Who are digital natives?
    * What is the digital divide?
    * Why is media literacy so crucial for all young children?

Why Is Literacy So Central to Learning?

All children come to school with ways of using their literacy to construct meaning from whatever they encounter. In school and at home, they learn to use the language processes of literacy—speaking, listening, reading, writing, and more—to think, organize their thinking, and communicate it. The social conditions within which children become literate at home influence their acquisition and development of school-based literacy, and vice versa. Teachers are responsible for understanding children's various home literacies and incorporating them into teaching and assessing the ways they ask children to be literate in school. They're also responsible for communicating with parents and families how school and home literacies are alike and different. To do all this well, it's important to understand the role of language in learning.

When we contemplate how humans learn, we're struck by the different modes of language in the process over time. At birth, it starts with gurgling, cooing, cries, and gestures. As babies interact with family, they use these modes along with facial expressions to explore and interpret their exchanges. As they develop, toddlers use toys, household items, and other socially available materials to learn language and communicate. Older toddlers and preschoolers express their interests and ideas through questions, simple statements, and gestures. They interrogate their world by constantly asking for *labels*, the words used to name things and people in the environment. When they ask for the label—"What's that?"—they also want to know its purpose (whether or not they directly ask). Through dialogues—conversational exchanges—about these labels and what they signify, as well as by constructing opportunities for children to use these words through immersive play and other relevant experiences (e.g., read-alouds, field trips), kindergarten children acquire thousands of words that form the backbone of their school lives. It's through relying upon these developed vocabularies—their language stores—that young children can connect their prior knowledge and experiences (their schemas) with their new knowledge and experiences as they begin the formal process of becoming literate in grades PreK–3.

Think about what often happens in the classroom: Doesn't it involve children reading, thinking, and communicating somehow? Do you see young children watch closely when you demonstrate how to perform a certain task so they can learn to do it themselves, such as tying their shoes with bunny ears? When you model the process and have young children watch what you are doing and then practice it themselves, talking them through it the whole way, is this a literacy exercise? How about having young children learn to interpret their classmates' facial expressions, body language, or actions so they truly understand the words for emotions and attitudes used in their environment? For example, we often hear, "Look at David's face. What does his face tell you about how he is feeling? What does that make you think?" This reminder often happens when families and teachers intervene in conflicts between children. When you involve children in discussions like these, you're teaching them how to read the world—as well as why. Being able to "read" like this, at its core, is a literacy-based skill set that's essential for thinking about and understanding the social studies. As they progress across grade levels, young children learn the variations in expressing emotions and attitudes across cultures and situations, acquiring additional vocabulary to explain them. In essence, during the early years of school, they start to organize their foundation for understanding themselves and others—through the language of the social studies.

How Is Literacy Defined Today?

If we accept a definition of **literacy** as being able to listen, read, think, and communicate, it is evident these skills are especially pertinent to learning social studies. The term "literacy" is no longer confined to print, however. Whenever we listen, view, and/or read anything, we endeavor to construct meaning from it for ourselves. We communicate our new knowledge in various ways, depending upon its nature and our purpose. For young children, this communication typically occurs vocally, gesturally, and through work products in different media (e.g., drawings, models, role plays, writing).

In the twenty-first century, the term "literacy" is being used in labels that identify specific sets of associated skills and concepts related to language processing and thinking in a particular domain or field. For example, the term **social studies literacy** is now commonly used to capture the breadth of academic vocabulary knowledge in civics, economics, geography, and history. (For older children, the term *disciplinary literacy* is often used.) It also describes one's ability to create and interpret the ways social studies professionals communicate their research perspectives such as through timelines, maps, charts, and graphs. With the rise of digital media and tools available to even the very young, the term **new literacies** developed to express the interconnected concepts and skills needed to process as well as create digital, multimedia, and multimodal (e.g., audio, video) products. As these terms show, there are multiple literacies. Effective social studies curricula and instructional approaches foster these literacies through integrated explorations driven by what children personally want to ponder—inquiry.

How Does Inquiry Foster Young Children's Literacy?

Young children are innately curious, prone to asking questions—lots of them. This natural curiosity is recognized and respected in school by using an inquiry approach in designing instructional units. When we develop inquiry-based learning experiences for young children, we send a clear message—we value children's thinking, their literacy. **Inquiry** is an investigatory process based upon what the learner identifies as most salient and personally relevant in answering a deep question. School-based inquiry projects simulate what historians and other social studies researchers do in their work, thereby authentically developing children's social studies literacy.

Unlike other, more traditional instructional methods where teachers direct and control the information shared and taught, inquiry-based methods situate the children as directors of their learning processes. It's not that teachers sit back and merely observe. Rather, the opposite is the case: teachers spark children's curiosity about a social topic or issue; create an open-ended investigatory environment; and provide the ongoing instruction as well as the tools children need to conduct their explorations. Young children rely upon teachers' guidance in:

- figuring out questions that will sustain an inquiry
- planning their exploratory steps
- choosing and securing the necessary tools for finding relevant sources
- determining the worthiness of those sources
- communicating their findings

Although teachers are actively involved throughout the inquiry process, it's the children who lead themselves through it. The self-directed nature of an inquiry builds children's agency, a key aspect of their overall social-emotional development and a hallmark of developmentally appropriate practice in early childhood (NAEYC, 2020).

Numerous approaches to planning generic inquiry-based units in early childhood are available through basic Internet searching. For social studies instruction aligned with national learning standards adopted by most states, the National Council for the Social Studies' (NCSS) **Inquiry Arc** of the C3 Framework for Social Inquiry (NCSS, 2013) demonstrably weaves social studies literacy and new literacies into an inquiry process that finishes with a natural, final step not always included in other inquiry approaches: acting on the findings somehow. The four dimensions of the NCSS Inquiry Arc are:

1. Developing questions and planning inquiries;
2. Applying disciplinary concepts and tools;
3. Evaluating sources and using evidence; and
4. Communicating conclusions and taking informed action. (NCSS, 2013, p. xxiii)

The impetus for conducting an inquiry is generated by what children wonder about their social world, with the teacher's help. Sometimes this help is in the form of calling or redirecting children's attention to a current event or content of a classmate's self-report during the morning meeting. It also could be by asking children to look together at a poignant picture while you use Visual Thinking Strategies (VTS; see www.vtshome.org) prompts to guide their reaction to it:

What's going on in this picture?
What do you see that makes you say . . . ?
What more can you find? (Visual Thinking Strategies, n.d.)

These simple prompts encourage children's thinking as well as their collaboration in making sense of it. As they talk, they agree and disagree, adding on to each other's ideas. They adjust their focus as they learn from peers what they missed seeing in the image, or if they perceived it differently. These rich discussions provide opportunity for children to build flexibility in thought and criticality, the ability to question what seems apparent yet isn't necessarily so. They learn the language of turn-taking, perspective, and healthy disagreement as they also learn how to ask a deep question and construct an oral argument using evidence from a shared artifact—all skills used by social scientists in the field.

Selecting pictures tied to aspects of your social studies curriculum (e.g., a scene of children helping clean up a littered park) will launch students into asking questions they can personally refine or use to develop another line of investigation through an Inquiry Arc completed individually or with others. The C3—College, Career, and Civic Life—Teachers organization's website (www.c3teachers.org) contains free, downloadable teacher resources (including unit plans for K–12) for learning more about knowing when an inquiry question is a "good" one—compelling or essential—versus one that merely supports a compelling question. (The site's blog also contains ideas for conducting inquiry-based activities of shorter duration or complexity.) The main difference to keep in mind is that a compelling or essential question will sustain interest and exploration over the various stages of the Inquiry Arc process; supporting questions logically flow from it.

Once the inquiry question is finalized, children are ready to locate and review various social studies literacy sources (e.g., pictures, maps, artifacts, print documents, books, videos, and music, etc.) to gather relevant information. As they consider those sources and organize their thoughts, they encounter and use the same vocabulary over and over again, in different contexts. This is the strength of inquiry-based instruction: it builds children's vocabulary breadth and depth, their **language stores**. For children to deeply learn a word and its meanings, they must not only hear and see that word repeated a few times; they also must be taught how that word is a member of a knowledge network (Neuman & Wright, 2014) of related words (e.g., to teach *money*, also teach *earn*, *save*, *spend*, and *budget*). Investigating a compelling question and completing an Inquiry Arc results in a new, deeper vocabulary for all involved—the investigator as well as the audience who enjoy the shared work products. Further, a newer line of reading research suggests that by spending more instructional time immersing children in social studies investigatory learning benefits not only their vocabulary development but also their overall reading comprehension skills (Tyner & Kabourek, 2020).

Once students complete their investigations and are ready to share their findings, they need guidance in determining how to communicate them. This is another opportunity to build children's social studies literacy by teaching them the methods and means used by the field to disseminate research (e.g., graphs, charts, maps, timelines, essays, multimedia presentations, podcasts, speeches). As students match their content with their mode of expression, they also learn other authorship considerations such as anticipating an audience's interests and needs, in addition to synthesizing and identifying key messages to convey. The thinking skills they use to do all this are ones they learn to use while comprehending what they read and hear across the school day, throughout the year. The C3 Framework's Inquiry Arc's distinctive step—using the findings of an inquiry to take action—affords children yet another space and opportunity to authentically connect their personal thinking with their larger social world. Young children thrive when they can concretely apply what they learn. They also remember and want to use what they learned yet again, long after the project's completed.

There are many reasons why inquiry-based teaching is gaining popularity today. Throughout the Inquiry Arc, numerous literacy skills are connected, practiced, and improved. Children come to realize that what and how they think can inform and affect others—once they figure out how to communicate it beyond themselves and their teacher. Having a reason, a real purpose for learning, engages young children in the life of school—and beyond. The ways in which the multiple literacies just described are developed across the early childhood years are many and myriad, as you'll discover in the following sections. You'll also see how the state learning standards for social studies influence components of the Inquiry Arc, especially the work products developed throughout.

What Do Social Studies Literacy Practices in Preschool Look Like?

Frequently, preschool environments are described as being emergent- or project-based in their instructional approaches. In an emergent-based preschool, the social questions examined stem from the daily curiosities that children bring about their world. For example, Megan, a four-year-old, came to school one day after visiting her grandmother in Indiana. While there, her grandmother showed her how to cross-stitch a simple napkin tulip. When she shared this with her friends at school, they wanted to know how she made it. That day, their teacher led the friends and others in a circle-time discussion to learn more together about both the cross-stitching process and the significance of cross-stitched items in Megan's family. In this example, the children learned about cultural traditions related to history. Another day, Harold came with the question, "Why did they change the name of Eskimo Pie?" The children then were led to investigate and discuss bias in product naming as it applies to their world—a beginning for making racial and economic literacy connections.

Preschool teachers facilitate children's literacy skills and social studies knowledge acquisition by creating learning environments focused on twenty-first-century learning goals (Battelle for Kids, 2019). These goals emphasize critical thinking, problem solving, digital literacy, and collaboration. Examining these goals helps us realize just how active, self-exploratory, and discovery-based all learning experiences must be. To effectively engage children in learning twenty-first-century social studies, then, teachers need to establish an environment and classroom culture where children can freely develop and use their critical thinking, communication and cooperation skills, and creativity for authentic purposes—as we saw with Megan and Harold. In this way, children learn to speak, read, write, interpret symbols, and use the tools of the social studies that they then can apply to other aspects of learning.

Young children use a vast array of communication strategies and capacities to interpret social interactions at home and in the community. Their manners of communication and interpretation are highly dependent upon their prior social experiences with family, childcare, and other community settings. Keeping the academic content of the social studies in mind, teachers observe and make anecdotal notes of classroom conversations to determine children's baseline knowledge of civics, economics, geography, and history. They look and listen for opportunities to introduce young children to using maps, charts, and (safe) Internet surfing to find personally relevant information. They plan projects such as interviewing family members to create a family history and publishing it digitally, for families to access, celebrate, and treasure. Teachers know that projects like these must emerge from children's everyday lives; otherwise, they do not make sense to the children. For example, as part of a project on learning about local rivers surrounding the school's attendance area, Ms. Baum asks young children to interview their great-grandparents, other senior relatives, or community experts by asking some simple questions the class generated for this purpose: "Did you live in Kansas City when there were floods?" "What happened to your house?" "How did you get through the disaster?" As children share results of their interviews, Ms. Baum records the answers on chart paper hung around the room. Later, the children will summarize the answers to develop a flood history of Kansas City across the years, creating a timeline to illustrate. The project might lead to another investigation: "Why haven't we had any major floods since 1951?" The questions can then lead to a discovery of dams and examining their economic impact on farms near Tuttle Creek. In this exploration, a contrast chart might be drawn—dams: good for the environment; dams: bad for farmers and lost towns, who lose their existence to the new river trajectory.

As preschool teachers, we know we must approach all youngsters where they are functioning. Thus, to enrich their literacy capacities, we learn about children through conversing with them. We connect home learning by collaborating with their families. Finally, we provide a rich environment for exploration and play, keeping in mind how preschool is their first, large social group learning situation. Of course, in preschool, our environments vary in location—home childcare, center-based childcare, or traditional preschool environments—but all are stimulating. It is here that rules for social behavior become formalized. Children learn to be school citizens as well as how to function as engaged community members. They hone their debating skills, respectful listening to friends, and even how to participate in resolving class issues through voting on possible solutions generated by the group. For example, in Ms. Donohue's four-year-old class, the girls came to a class meeting claiming the boys always got the ball for their sports. Through discussion, the children proposed solutions. They weighed the merits of each and finally agreed upon a rotation system for use of the class ball. As we see, social studies literacy skills and knowledge emerge through real reasons for considering—and using—them. They evolve further by providing ongoing opportunities like the ones described here during the entire school year.

What Do Social Studies Literacy Practices Look Like Across the Primary Grades?

As children continue in public and private schools for their primary years (i.e., kindergarten through grade three), the social studies curriculum becomes more explicit and standardized according to state laws. Textbox 2.1, Illinois' learning standards (Illinois State Board of Education, 2017), and Textbox 2.2, Pennsylvania's standards for Civics and Government (Pennsylvania Department of Education, 2014), provide examples of how content-specific primary-grade learning is expected to be according to their state legislatures and boards of education.

TEXTBOX 2.1

Illinois Learning Standards for Social Science: K–2

1L6CC.1.L.6: Vocabulary Acquisition and Use
Use words and phrases acquired through conversations, reading and being read to, and responding to texts, including using frequently occurring conjunctions to signal simple relationships.

SS.IS.1.K-2: Inquiry Skills
Developing Questions and Planning Inquiries
Constructing Essential Questions:
Create questions to help guide inquiry about a topic with guidance from adults and/or peers.

SS.IS.2.K-2: Determining Helpful Sources:
Explore facts from various sources that can be used to answer the developed questions.

SS.IS.3.K-2: Evaluating Sources and Using Evidence
Gathering and Evaluating Sources:
Gather information from one or two sources with guidance and support from adults and/or peers.

SS.IS.4.K-2: Developing Claims and Using Evidence:
Evaluate a source by distinguishing between fact and opinion.

SS.IS.5.K-2: Communicating Conclusions and Taking Informed Action
Communicating Conclusions:
Ask and answer questions about arguments and explanations.

SS.IS.6.K-2: **Taking Informed Action**

Use listening, consensus building, and voting procedures to decide on and take action in their classroom.

Illinois Social Science Standards (https://www.isbe.net/socialsciences/)

TEXTBOX 2.2

Pennsylvania Academic Standards: Civics and Government, Grade Three

Standard 5.1.3.A: Explain the purposes of rules, laws, and consequences.
Standard 5.1.3.B: Explain rules and laws for the classroom, school, and community.
Standard 5.1.3.C: Define the principles and ideals shaping local government.

- Liberty/Freedom
- Democracy
- Justice
- Equality

Standard 5.1.3.D: Identify key ideas about government found in significant documents.

- Declaration of Independence
- United States Constitution
- Bill of Rights
- Pennsylvania Constitution

Standard 5.1.3.F: Identify state symbols, national symbols, and national holidays.

Social Studies Academic Standards (https://www.education.pa.gov/Teachers%20-%20Administrators/Curriculum/SocialStudies/Pages/default.aspx/)

In each of these examples, we can see the inextricable link between literacy development and social studies knowledge. In kindergarten in Illinois, children are expected to learn basic observational and inquiry skills (e.g., gather information, create questions for an inquiry) that lead to developing a foundational understanding of civics, economics, geography, and history. By third grade in Pennsylvania, children are expected not only to be able to identify and explain core concepts in the social studies but also to conduct their own inquiries (with teacher guidance) into events, people, and places by using primary and historical sources. This upward spiraling of stated cognitive complexity across the grade levels, as well as the ways that children demonstrate their increased knowledge and skills, reflect the young child's burgeoning capacity for learning and doing more with expert teaching and scaffolding. They also reflect how the nature of literacy instructional practices changes with time.

In kindergarten, children's literacies are especially oral and visual in nature—lots of talking, listening, singing, acting out, and drawing of what's being learned. Teacher read-alouds, with children chiming in whenever possible, are followed by rich discussions about texts' content, themes, and connections to lived lives in and out of the classroom. As reading and writing skills become more established in first grade, a shift to including more self-directed reading and writing opportunities plus small-group work is seen. Teachers continue reading aloud, modeling their thinking as readers throughout, while simultaneously asking provocative questions that lead children to form opinions about what's heard that they then justify orally and in writing. By second grade, children are using their reading and writing skills to process and create more complex texts of their own, in small groups and independently, for purposes tied to curricular concepts. They are able to identify cause and effect, as well as formulate arguments that draw from prior knowledge, including what they have learned from other recent texts and experiences. Their evaluative skills start to show, typically when asked to judge a story outcome or the appeal of the content in an informational text. (Second graders can be fairly opinionated, which is a strength when understood by the adults in their lives.) Third graders are increasingly analytic and synthetic in their thinking, benefiting from multiple opportunities across their school day to read and view connected content. They also thrive when engaged in focused discussions that guide them to interpret authors' messages and purposes beyond any stated explanations or relationships—that is, to use inferencing skills and strategies to construct deeper meaning from what they read, view, and hear. They can use evidence from multiple sources (texts and other forms) to support their contentions. They are able to realize and explain how their opinions and knowledge base change through exposure to new ideas—critical skills for completing the Inquiry Arc, especially in its final step: taking informed action. Table 2.1 encapsulates the main listening and reading comprehension skills taught across the primary grades that students develop and refine through engagement in an inquiry process.

TABLE 2.1 Listening and Reading Comprehension Skills Used in Inquiry

Narrative Texts (Stories)	Expository/Informational Texts
• Identify the theme, lesson, or message in a story and analyze its personal relevance • Identify how characters change over time through interactions with others and their environment • Identify setting and how it influences characters' actions and feelings • Follow a plot's events, in order (sequence) and determine how they connect to each other • Determine how an author uses certain word choices and syntax to convey emotions, precise meaning • Identify an author's or narrator's point of view and how it influences plot, character development	• Identify the main ideas and relevant supporting details • Identify characteristics of settings and the types of interactions within them (e.g., human–other animal, human–human) • Analyze text structures and their organizations (e.g., cause–effect, problem–solution, compare–contrast, chronological/sequential, lists) to learn and remember content • Use text features (e.g., glossary, headings, hot links) to deepen knowledge of content and its organization • Use context and content knowledge to understand new vocabulary presented in texts • Identify and evaluate an author's point of view or arguments

While the learning standards influence instruction as well as the content of what we teach, what most influences our social studies teaching is who our children are as members of a culture outside of school.

How Are Learning Standards and Social Learning Contexts Connected?

Standards reflect the particular learning outcomes established over time and agreed upon as being the best practices for creating a literate society. In many important ways, teachers meet these demands for ensuring all children's overall literacy development while concurrently engaging children in developing social studies literacy by:

- using the social experiences and cultural identities children bring from home and community
- building upon their individual and shared knowledge of the world around them

Beginning in preschool and across the early elementary years, our challenge is to meet children where their experiences have led them and bring them into the new ideas and ways of acting stipulated in the learning standards. We start by working to know our students and their understanding of their family and community cultures. We simultaneously articulate for them how the school world has a culture of its own, in large part formed by the interactions among the multiple cultures who are members of that space. We do all this through forming a shared learning community—a social group—that makes obvious room for all.

How Do Children Function as Members of Formal Social Groups?

Children come to school knowing how to interact with others based upon their home and community experiences. The social rules they've been learning since birth may differ from those at school. Therefore, among the many "first steps" we ask children to take is to interpret and learn the new customs of school. This social learning takes some time for children to accomplish. It also requires a teacher's awareness and sensitivity to the many rule-knowledge variations the children bring, and how home social rules co-exist with those of the classroom in subtle ways. Sometimes, it's hard to perceive the nuances of these home social rules, as teacher Ms. Amory recalls from her early experiences:

> Almira, a first grader, I met in Samoa . . . I did not know that raising your eyebrow to an adult was an indication that meant "yes, I understand" so when I asked this little girl if she understood me and received no verbal response, merely the raised eyebrow, I merely repeated my question multiple times, which was frustrating to both of us. I eventually got it . . . and held that little girl in a special spot the rest of the year, feeling as though I had to make it up to her for helping me eventually learn her culture.

Learning the social rules and customs of the classroom is a common PreK–3 social studies theme that eventually segues into learning about laws. Understanding not only what the rules are but why they are important especially relies upon children's capacity to interpret all the ways we express our literacy—gestures, speech, and other social cues (e.g., remaining quiet when someone else is speaking). Children's adoption of the social rules at school is an integral part of their changing self-concept—their social-emotional learning.

What Are the Social-Emotional Development Connections to Social Studies Literacy?

In the early years, we have critical responsibility for building children's foundational social understanding of their immediate world—that of family, community, and school—as well as the world. Central to doing this work is recognizing the importance of **social-emotional learning (SEL)**: the knowledge, skills, and attitudes for functioning interpersonally in school with peers, teachers, and other adults. State boards of education take varying approaches to connecting social-emotional development with other curricula. Textbox 2.3 shows the broad spectrum of goals outlined in Illinois' Goals for Social-Emotional Learning for all public K–12 schools (Illinois State Board of Education, 2004). Within the goals, you see how Illinois directly links social studies literacy goals with overall social-emotional growth. The goals are a separate set of required standards for all teachers to incorporate in all subject areas across their instructional days. In Textbox 2.4, you see a different approach from Massachusetts. In their History and Social Science Framework, Guiding Principle 10 for the Social Sciences, they clearly state the connection between social studies literacy and social-emotional growth as one of the themes embedded across all their social studies standards (Massachusetts Department of Elementary and Secondary Education, 2018, p. 16).

TEXTBOX 2.3

Illinois Goals for Social-Emotional Learning

Goal 1: Develop self-awareness and self-management skills to achieve school and life success.

Goal 2: Use social-awareness and interpersonal skills to establish and maintain positive relationships.

Goal 3: Demonstrate decision-making skills and responsible behaviors in personal, school, and community contexts.

Social/Emotional Learning Standards (https://www.isbe.net/Pages/Social-Emotional-Learning-Standards.aspx/)

TEXTBOX 2.4

Massachusetts Guiding Principle for Social Studies #10

MA Guiding Principle 10: An effective history and social science education develops social and emotional skills. Teachers support the development of these skills by:

* helping students understand how their own unique experiences and ideas influence their perceptions of and feelings about history and current situations (self-awareness);
* encouraging students' own power to take thoughtful action (self-management);
* increasing students' understanding of others' fundamental needs and human and civil rights (social awareness);

- increasing students' capacity to participate in dialogue across differences and to take on the perspectives of others whose experience and position in the world differs from their own (dialogue and perspective-taking);
- encouraging students to collaborate respectfully with diverse peers (relationship skills);
- providing opportunities for students to define and make informed choices when participating in democratic practices (responsible decision-making); and
- creating opportunities for students to work together on projects that aim to promote a public good beyond the classroom, in the school, or in the larger community (civic action)

History and Social Science Framework Grades Pre-kindergarten–12 (Massachusetts Department of Elementary and Secondary Education, 2018, p. 16).

These states are not alone in recognizing the connection between social studies literacy and social-emotional learning. Key to successfully connecting these concepts, skills, and dispositions is the use of inquiry- and project-based learning opportunities. This makes sense: through collaborating over time on projects investigating concepts in civics, economics, geography, and history, young children naturally grow in understanding themselves, their classmates, and the larger world. Given ample time to work together to represent their learning through discussions that build consensus about shared knowledge products such as charts, maps, timelines, and podcasts, children enhance their multiple literacies. Equally important, they become more secure in understanding and viewing themselves as members of a community with responsibilities and roles—and a voice in decision-making.

Besides learning and practicing social studies inquiry, a broad project-based curriculum offers opportunities for the development of social skills, such as ways to make friends and keep them. These important social skills are established while acclimating children to school life, where they will spend many years. Along the way they will gain a sense of social responsibility—first at the classroom level, then school and community. In Textbox 2.5, you see an example of how teachers can organize a unit on the study of the Self designed to help children develop civics/government competencies. Kansas organizes the scope and sequence of the social studies by its four main disciplines—history, civics/government, geography, and economics. Its stated mission for their social studies standards and related competencies is to "prepare students to be informed, thoughtful, engaged citizens as they enrich their communities, state, nation, world, and themselves" (Kansas State Board of Education, 2020, p. 5). The specific civics/government competencies achieved through engagement in this self-inquiry are listed in Textbox 2.5.

TEXTBOX 2.5

Kansas Sample Kindergarten Civics/Government Unit Outline: Self

Civics/Government (CG): In this discipline, students will recognize the existence and importance of rules at home and at school. They will understand the role of authority figures at home and school and why they are needed. Students will recognize appropriate classroom behaviors and identify characteristics of a friend, a helpful classmate, and a leader. They will demonstrate an understanding of self-efficacy, assertiveness, and empathy. They will recognize and demonstrate traits of being a good classroom citizen.

Ideas: rules, leader, authority, conflict, friends, classroom citizenship

Sample compelling questions:
Who [*sic*] do you listen to when making choices?
What are important rules for the classroom that are different at home?
How do good friends and classroom citizens act?"

(Kansas State Board of Education, 2020, p. 28)

These examples across the states highlight how healthy social-emotional development is key to children's ability to function within their immediate society—their ability to be good citizens. These first formal **citizenship** lessons are taught and reinforced through teachers' articulation of expectations and reasons for them, as well as through establishing a classroom environment where children feel comfortable in taking risks in learning these life lessons.

How Are Citizenship Skills Developed?

Each social-emotional learning goal involves children's ability to interpret social cues, language, behaviors, and structures within the class community. Accordingly, our everyday work must be designed with an eye toward increasing their capacity to interpret cultural and social situations, beginning at the classroom level. In this way, we lay the foundation for understanding citizenship—the most important social studies outcome for a democracy. We begin familiarizing children with the concept of citizenship by developing class rules. Imagine the following scenario on a warm September day in kindergarten:

> Ms. Shiloh received the children as they came to the school door with family members, greeting everyone and asking the children to line up in the hall with an arm's length between friends—establishing the beginning of spatial awareness consciousness for school. Then the children walked down the hall to the classroom, zipping their mouths until reaching the room they had visited before the school year began. Each put their lunches and jackets in their cubbies and then moved to a table of their choice, selecting a place where there was a chair. At each table, Ms. Shiloh arranged puzzles, parquetry blocks, picture books, and other manipulatives for them to explore. After recording attendance and other routine bookkeeping tasks, she called the children one-by-one to a circle made with colorful rug square "seats" to show the appropriate distance to sit next to each other.
>
> At the circle, children introduced themselves. She modeled introduction convention by, "Hello, I am Ms. Shiloh. Good morning!" Then, Ms. Shiloh asked the children to think about "rules" for their class. What must they do so they could work together as friends or team members? Most of the children attended childcare centers in the past and quickly shared rules they knew. The few who came straight to kindergarten from home offered a few ideas as well. Finally, the discussion led to determining five clear rules as shown in Textbox 2.6, An Example of Kindergarten Rules.

TEXTBOX 2.6

An Example of Kindergarten Rules

1. Use words to solve problems or ask teachers to help you.
2. Put away materials when you are done.
3. Use walking feet.
4. Take turns talking, wait until the other person is done talking before you start talking.
5. Respect our friends' bodies and property.

Ms. Shiloh captured the rules on a whiteboard chart as the children developed and edited them for consensus and formal class language. For example, "Shut up when someone else is talking," while useful, didn't make the list. Children returned to the tables and the day continued.

Down the hall in Ms. Hayes' first grade, the day begins with Sarah crying hysterically. Getting to the bottom of the problem, Ms. Hayes learns Diane grabbed Sarah's new backpack when they rode the bus to school. Taking the two girls aside, Ms. Hayes asked the girls to remember a class rule from kindergarten: We respect our friends. The girls resolved the issue after a few minutes of conversation and the day moved along. Although in some schools, this episode may have resulted in a disciplinary referral, this school uses the RULER Approach. This is a "systematic approach to SEL developed at the Center for Emotional Intelligence . . . RULER is an acronym for Recognizing, Understanding, Labeling, Expressing and Regulating emotional intelligence" (Brackett, 2019, p. 55). The whole school participates in the training and adoption of the approach to resolve interpersonal problems. Thus, each girl is enabled to air her grievance, discuss the feelings behind the grievance, and agree upon a solution.

In these examples, we see elements of citizenship responsibilities in action. That is, what are the customs for entering shared space at school? What are the agreed-upon laws needed to preserve classroom order? How are disagreements negotiated? What are rules for walking down the hall? So, what are the social studies literacy and social-emotional learning elements in these examples? Ms. Shiloh showed her structured class management, rules for walking in the hall, ways to enter the class and engage productively in learning, and to share in the development of conventions to function as a citizen in the social world of school. The kindergarteners also saw how to codify the rules by seeing them appear on the whiteboard, which will ultimately wind up on a poster for all to see—much like the "NO PARKING" signs of our adult lives.

Ms. Hayes reminds Diane and Sarah of their prior learning and agreement to the rules for solving conflicts arising in the class community, and appropriate social-emotional behavior. The literacy knowledge, skills, and attitudes needed for resolving these types of school issues include:

- capacity to listen, observe, and interpret social structure
- opportunity to see the symbolic interpretation of rules
- opportunity to express thoughts and ideas orally

Rule and community, essential social studies content concepts, were engrained into the management and culture of these classrooms. A significant portion of learning social studies is embedded into these classrooms' daily routines. Literacy plays an important role in learning and communicating, whether in print, picture, or gesture.

In turn, understanding these concepts and practicing them helps children learn how to be good citizens.

Throughout the year, Ms. Shiloh and Ms. Hayes will make explicit the literacy connections to social studies. They will model ways for children to use their literacy concepts, skills, and strategies as well as assess their ongoing development through checklists, rubrics, peer and teacher evaluations, anecdotal notes, among many others. In these ways, children will acquire important cognitive and social-emotional skills appropriate for school and the greater community while also exploring the social studies.

For successful experiences in education generally, as the above examples show, literacy is a fundamental tool allowing access to the world of school and knowledge building. Through the social studies, young children acquire capacities to interpret all aspects of literacy—symbols, gestures, language, culture, and social interaction. Such experiences employ books, graphs, maps, pictures, drawings, and digital media both as sources of knowledge and ways to express increasing accomplishment of social studies literacy skills.

How Do Children Personally Connect to Social Studies Literacy Development?

Children bring their lived lives to school, including ways to navigate social contexts and to understand historical and political forces. For example, what are the conventions for addressing adults who are not family members? Mr., Ms., Mrs., Dr.? Or Aunt, Uncle—by first name, Geraldine, Edwin? What are the rules for child behavior in the presence of adults—silence? Engagement in the conversation? Who asks questions? When? How? Who decides? The capacity to understand experiences like these, and to recognize them as ways to think and act—to be social—are among the **funds of knowledge** (Moll et al., 1992) children bring to their classroom communities. Other aspects of funds of knowledge include children's understanding of their family and community economics—what knowledge related to money do children bring into the classroom? Do families have bank accounts? Do they use food stamps? Did they emigrate from a country where currency was hidden for safety reasons? Still other funds of knowledge children bring to school involve their understanding of family and community circumstances: What foods do they eat? Where do they secure food? Are they permitted to watch television news? What languages do they speak? Did the children participate in Black Lives Matter protests? Do the adults vote? The answers to these questions and more are the knowledge children will apply to their interpretation of the social studies, as well as connect them to academic literacy learning in multiple ways.

Think further about what children carry into school at the beginning of the year based on how they function in their family and outer social world—their experiences in childcare, soccer leagues, t-ball, dance, gymnastics, church, temple, mosque, and so on. When communities are small and homogeneous, the translation of ways to behave and how to interpret social cues across interactions and settings (including school) are relatively easy. In more diverse settings, however, interpreting social cues or ways of behaving is more complicated and requires greater assistance from family, teachers, coaches, and other caring adults to understand and negotiate. Consider the following scenarios:

> In Oklahoma City, kindergarteners come to school from home childcare, Montessori preschools, and church-based childcare centers, among other locations. The funds of knowledge these kindergarteners have varies greatly, as we see in the following.
>
> Laura and Charley come from sharing experiences in home childcare with baby Maria and thirty-month-old Juan. In this setting, the baby and toddler napped while Laura and Charley rested quietly with books and puzzles. They enjoyed home-cooked soups and casseroles for lunch in a bilingual environment.
>
> Arthur came from staying at home with his grandmother, living on Tinker Air Force Base while mom was deployed. Arthur's grandmother routinely read stories, took him shopping and to the playground, and on visits with multigenerational neighbors.
>
> Susanna, Brigid, and John come from a Montessori school where they spent the last two years in the morning session of a half-day preschool program. Their afternoons included t-ball practice, dance classes, and play dates.
>
> Salalai's father is an executive in an oil and gas company. Her family's roots are embedded in the Cherokee Nation. Her family participates regularly in Cherokee Nation Events. Salalai often visits her grandmother, where she learns family traditions and arts, and respects her grandmother's storytelling techniques.

All these five-year-olds come to Ms. Amory's kindergarten with funds of knowledge garnered beyond home—ways of thinking and behaving in home childcare; experiences of living with grandmother while mother is deployed (and maybe experiences in moving from place to place); structured preschool and afternoons of leisure and play. For Ms. Amory, the central questions for planning social-emotional and citizenship learning goals are: How can these children become effective citizens in their classroom and school community? How will each come to understand the social conventions for functioning in kindergarten? What language, gestures, and rules have they developed across their diverse lives that need to be articulated and understood among us? How will they express their ideas, based on their various knowledge banks? Answering these questions through systematically learning about her students and their families will enable Ms. Amory to help them develop their school selves, as well as their social studies literacy.

How Does the School Self-Evolve?

While we may think of personal expressions of knowledge, skills, and attitudes as evidence of literacy, they're also funds of knowledge for the social studies, particularly citizenship. As children learn rules and norms for behavior in groups, their sense of citizenship—being part of a collective somehow—is established. School is a place where children develop another identity—their school self. With time, experience, and teacher guidance, children learn to differentiate between and among their school, family, and neighborhood selves. They shift their behaviors according to the various social conventions of each.

Children from similar backgrounds will share codes for behaving in social groups. They will likely interpret the content of civics, economics, geography, and history from a similar perspective. In such classrooms, we need to be sure to highlight perspectives from the larger world that may be in conflict with theirs. In this way, these children will acquire the lifelong literacy skills they need to critically sift through and analyze the abundance of text, speech, charts, graphs, and media sources in their twenty-first-century lives.

In a class with children from multiple backgrounds, conflict in interpreting and understanding each other's perspectives is inherently possible. For these classes, teachers will be required to ensure protection for divergent positions on topics. The skills of respectful debate and respect for individuals will be built into the articulated requirements for class citizenship. For example, Mr. Perkins, a second-grade teacher, incorporated these straightforward class rules for debates within a topical study related to recycling:

1. Class states the topic, such as: Should we use cardboard lunch trays?
2. Team 1 investigates and presents the position for using cardboard lunch trays.
3. Team 2 investigates and presents the reasons cardboard lunch trays should not be used.
4. Each team listens quietly to the arguments.
5. Everyone uses inside voices.
6. Class discusses the presentations and votes on a position.
7. Class decides whether to forward a resolution about the lunch trays to the school administration.

While the above example is practice, and the stakes for agreement or disagreement may not be high, the rules for civil conversation about a controversy are established and can be used when a more sensitive issue arises.

However, the real world of school today is one where all classes are diverse. The funds of knowledge from prior experiences will spur queries such as "Why don't you eat bacon?" "How come you don't stand up during the Pledge of Allegiance?" "Why does your grandmother live with you?" "How come your dad stays home and your mom goes to an office to work?" "What do you mean you have two moms/dads?" The curiosities of children will drive these questions and many more. As teachers, we help children develop the literacies needed to interpret and respect diverse points of view held by individuals, thereby linking social-emotional learning and social studies literacy.

How Do Childcare Experiences Influence Children's Understanding of Their World?

Now, let's turn to the variances in preschoolers' childcare and educational experiences in homes and centers, which will create **diverse funds of knowledge** upon which they build literacy skills. Consider the following situation.

Lucille, a three-year-old, goes to a childcare home in Detroit, Michigan, with five other children. Lucille's companions are Christine, also five; Shantye, four; Durrell, four; Harold, three; and Melvin, three. The children arrive at more or less the same time between 6:00 and 6:30 am. Their families work as bus drivers, doormen, and housekeepers. They enjoy a hot breakfast followed by free play with the toys Ms. Sharmayne has set out in her living room. While Ms. Sharmayne cleans up the breakfast dishes, the children wander from the living room with their toys to talk with her about them, or about what happened last night at home or on the way to her home. At 8:00 am, Ms. Sharmayne turns to YouTube for "Bob the Train," then the children go back to playing with toys. And so the day goes with snack, lunch, story reading, naps, and free play.

In nearby Palmer Woods, Aretha, a three-year-old, attends half-day preschool at a local church where her teacher, Ms. Jenkins, begins the morning with the fifteen children singing songs, followed by free play and snack. Ms. Luckett, a volunteer mother, helps out by playing with the children and setting out toys and snacks under Ms. Jenkins' supervision. Then, Ms. Jenkins gathers the children to a circle for a story and discussion of an upcoming field trip to the Detroit Children's Museum. As the day ends, Aretha goes home to see baby brother Darren, eat lunch, and nap. After the nap her mother may turn to YouTube for ChuChu TV or to the local Public Broadcasting Station (PBS) channel for "Molly of Denali" and "Elinor Wonders Why."

Throughout the week, Aretha goes to visit her best friend, Serena, who lives a house or so away; attends gymnastics class; and plays games on her Amazon Fire Kids Edition tablet. She often asks Google for answers while her mother is busy with Darren or preparing dinner. Her father comes home from his law office about 6:00 pm, and the family sits down for dinner.

At age five, Lucille and Aretha will enter the same public school for kindergarten. They will share some cultural traditions and extended family experiences. Both Lucille and Aretha will probably go to gatherings at grandparents' homes with all the aunts, uncles, and cousins meeting up over barbeques or potlucks. But the funds of knowledge they bring to the classroom will also show differences based on their experiences with digital media, travel, and enrichment activities such as going to movies, plays, or sporting events. Their kindergarten teacher will recognize and connect these similarities and differences to ensure each learns to the best of her ability. In the process, the Michigan English Language Arts Standards and the connections to the social studies operating under Michigan's Arc of Responsible Citizenship, beginning in kindergarten with "Myself and Others," will be met (Michigan Department of Education, 2019).

To meet these standards given the diversity of the children's funds of knowledge, Ms. Pate, their teacher, will engage them in discussion, debate, charting, map making, reading stories, drawing, and constructing timelines. The children will pose questions, investigate answers in diverse sources—media, books, discussions—and learn to represent their knowledge through the tools of social studies. Families will be invited to visit the class, share pictures and stories, and ask questions of all the children and their teacher.

Ms. Pate also will begin the year with a focus on "Myself as a Baby," then continue with "My Family." In each of these projects or curricular sequences, she will draw on the children's lived experiences with pictures, stories, and sharing of their memories of childcare and family events. The children will be asked to draw pictures of themselves at home and make an outline of their bodies to hang around the room. They may bring in artifacts of daily life at home or in the community to share orally and allow others to touch, ask questions about. Family members will come to class to share histories and family traditions. As a culminating experience, Ms. Pate might ask children to bring favorite recipes to class so they can produce an electronic class cookbook to be featured on the school website and added to the school library's holdings.

Ms. Oswald, another kindergarten teacher, will help her students prepare personal growth picture books at the end of their "Myself as a Baby" project. Throughout the project, children will share photographs of themselves in different settings as babies, toddlers, and kindergarteners. (Children who do not have photographs will be guided in creating illustrations from memory, with teacher and family assistance.) They will document and reflect upon their growth on each page of their picture books. They will include pages showcasing family celebrations, birthdays (none for the Jehovah Witness families), life events such as a family quinceañera or a reunion barbeque. Electronic versions of the picture books will become part of the school library, accessed periodically in class during the year. In their final editing phase, the children will evidence their increased literacy skills gained through preparing their picture books by generating graphic organizers capturing their classmates' similarities and differences. For example, the children might make a tabular chart: "Foods Eaten at Family Celebrations." They also could tally the similar foods and determine which are ones for vegetarians, which are served hot or cold, and so on.

Throughout the first quarter of kindergarten (September–November), all students will be bridging differences in familiarity with print and digital media by being systematically introduced to using school-based tools and other resources—classroom computers and tablets, a SmartBoard™, wireless network (and how to do safe Internet surfing), software and other apps, the classroom print library, manipulatives and markers, etc. Both teachers will carefully explain to children what each tool or resource is, its purpose in their learning, how to use it appropriately (e.g., "We turn pages in a book by gently lifting the corner, as I'm showing you now"), and how to troubleshoot if need be (e.g., "If it doesn't start, check to make sure you clicked twice on the yellow button"). Recognizing that being in kindergarten can be very different from previous experiences in a childcare or home setting since birth, teachers also constantly reinforce the purposes and procedures for daily classroom routines while performing them (e.g., "Let's now take turns coming to the carpet to enjoy our read-aloud—purple table, I see everyone's sitting quietly and looking at me, so I know you're ready to move"). So that children will grow in understanding and using a range of inquiry strategies and tools, teachers will constantly provide concrete choices for them to make (e.g., "Your question might be investigated by looking here on the NatGeo website or at this book about cities. Which do you think would work better? Choose one and use that"). They also are guided in learning to document their sources of information, a set of connected concepts and skills that develops over time beyond kindergarten. By setting the foundation for inquiry at this grade level, showing children not only how but also why asking deep questions is a natural human enterprise, at the end of the year the now six-year-olds are ready to expand their world views even further during their first-grade experience. They understand how to "do school"—and enjoy it.

In other wings of the school, first- through third-grade teachers also find themselves still bridging childcare experiences with their classes. Childcare experiences at these grades run the gamut. Some children stay in the building with teachers for tutoring, enrichment, games, or outside activities after serving snacks. Some children attend after-school Japanese language classes nearby. Some go to soccer practice, dance class, esports programs, or other community activities. Finally, some with a key around their necks will go home to empty houses, with TV or video games for company. All these various experiences influence children's access to the world of school and their learned tools of inquiry. As seen with the kindergarten teachers, these other primary-grade teachers also devote considerable daily instructional time to articulating their grade level's particular inquiry tools and purposes; showing how inquiries are sparked and informed by what children know and do outside of school, not only inside it; and how to become more independent in following an inquiry to its logical conclusion.

What Else Influences and Fosters Children's Inquiry-Based Social Studies Learning?

In its purest form, early childhood-age inquiry learning begins with questions stimulated by children's experiences and those posed by teachers implementing required curricula. In preschool and childcare settings, the inquiry approach is connected to project-based learning. The projects emerge from the careful observation of the children at play and helping them develop questions about what they want to learn. As teachers, we may stimulate children's thinking with "I wonder . . . ?" or (since four-year-olds are famous for asking) "Why?" Posing these types of questions conversationally might evolve as described in the next section. As you read, notice how the inquiry reflects and respects the developmental stage of these children (four- and five-year-olds).

> On their morning walks in the neighborhood, older preschoolers noticed how each day, fewer boats were seen in the harbor. They hypothesized daily about why this was so during their walks. After a few days' observation, their teacher, Ms. Moss, led them in a classroom discussion about their observations. She guided them to center on the question, "What happens to boats that leave Belmont Harbor in October?" They created a supporting question, "Why do they leave the Harbor?" Ms. Moss guided them in organizing their investigation and determining ways to find answers. They decided to invite experts—harbor personnel and boat owners—to visit and talk about what they knew and did. They listened to stories about sailing and informational texts on boats. They viewed short You-Tube videos on harbors and piers. They followed up on the experts' suggestions to visit a boat yard. Throughout the weeks of the project, children represented their findings in photos, pictures, and charts prepared through discussion with Ms. Moss and each other. Their project culminated by sharing their learning with families through drawings, booklets created by the class, and labeled photos of key ideas and facts they discovered. Some children created a mural of the harbor depicting departing boats, headed to the nearby boatyard. Once the children summarized and communicated their findings, they moved on to another topic of interest—though their project artifacts remained part of their classroom's materials for everyone to enjoy.

Projects also emerge from events in the school and community or through learning centers we set up for children to explore. For example, you might set up pictures of adobe houses near the sand table and read stories as well as informational books about early and current life in New Mexico and Colorado. As the children follow their curiosity, you might consider making adobe bricks with them to develop the project further. This way, children are able to make tangible what otherwise might remain fairly abstract. Too, it provides rich opportunities for them to keep using their new knowledge network vocabulary (Neuman & Wright, 2014), as well as acting it out. Recent research (Andrä et al., 2020) in children's vocabulary development is reinforcing what early childhood teachers sensed for years: children need to physically represent the words they learn if they're to remember them accurately for a lifetime. Inquiry presentations and taking action on inquiry findings provide authentic, multiple opportunities for accomplishing all this critical language learning.

You could expand this initial inquiry by making it part of a longer unit specifically on Pueblo families and communities. The children would create new compelling questions that would lead them to explore where and how the Pueblo lived across history, why their houses were made of adobe in the desert environment, etc. They could read books, examine pictures, watch videos, and then use their brickmaking skills by building an adobe house. They also could construct a timeline detailing the evolution of Pueblo life up to the present day. They could chart what they learn about the Pueblo diet of long ago and participate in creating a Venn diagram comparing how the Pueblo gathered and prepared food then and now. In these myriad ways, children develop an understanding of a particular culture and how it changed over time. Through an integrated, ongoing study like this, students evolve as social studies learners. They simultaneously develop the literacy knowledge, skills, and attitudes necessary for school success.

Beginning in public school kindergartens, projects may become more prescribed, relating to local school and state guidelines for the English language arts and social studies. Prescribed units and projects do not need to rely upon textbook-driven learning, however. With the introduction of the Common Core State Standards in 2010, adopted by most states, schools now place greater emphasis on nonfiction or informational text reading of all kinds, from a broader range and type of sources (e.g., blogs, wikis), not only print. The national social studies standards of the C3 Framework (NCSS, 2013), also adopted by most states, require inquiry- and project-based learning experiences that feature student choice. K–3 teachers therefore have the latitude to develop inquiries and projects that promote local, state, and national discussions emerging from children's curiosity about family conversations or even television news. For example, in Washington, by the end of first grade, children are expected to meet the social studies standards shown in Textbox 2.7 (Washington Office of Superintendent of Public Instruction, 2019). Each of these standards has a literacy component—listening to class discussions; reading stories and news; evaluating the truthfulness of the news; thinking beyond the news through raising questions; and recognizing one's own understanding of history, as measured by their lives and their understanding of a long time ago. There also is an emphasis on investigating and learning differing points of view and determining appropriate sources (beyond the news) that best answer compelling questions. All these standards align with the type of meaningful and purposeful work students conduct through inquiries and projects.

TEXTBOX 2.7

Washington State Learning Standards for First Grade Social Studies

SSS1.1.1 Distinguish different points of view on one event.

SSS1.1.2 Use questioning strategies.

SSS1.1.3 Retell the sequence of events that have happened over time.

SSS2.1.1 Explain how questions are used to find out information.

SSS2.1.2 Use texts, audio, visuals, and other evidence to identify the main ideas or key details to study life outside of school.

SSS2.1.3 Explain what a compelling question is and why it is important.

SSS3.1.1 Engage in discussions to learn about different points of view on issues that impact their communities.

SSS4.1.1 Determine the kinds of sources that will be helpful in answering compelling and supporting questions.

C1.1.1 Recognize the key ideal of public or common good within the context of the school community.

C1.1.2 Apply the key idea of the public or common good to uphold rights and responsibilities within the context of the school community.

C1.1.3 Explore and give examples of services a government provides (e.g., teachers, police and fire protection, maintenance of roads, snow removal, etc.).

C2.1.1 Explain the purpose of rules in the school.

C2.1.2 Know the people and the roles that make and carry out rules in the school.

C2.1.3 Describe how rules provide structure for problem solving within the classroom and school.

C3.1.1 Explain why rules are different in different communities.

C3.1.2 Identify different types of relationships and diplomacy tribal nations exercised with European nations, colonies, and the United States.

C4.1.1 Identify that citizenship and civic involvement in the neighborhood and school community are the rights and responsibilities of individuals.

C4.1.2 Explain, give examples, and demonstrate ways to show good citizenship at school.

C4.1.3 Describe the importance of civic participation and identify neighborhood examples.

E1.1.1 Identify differences between natural, human, and capital resources.

E1.1.2 Explain how and why families make choices between wants and needs.

E1.1.3 Evaluate the outcome of choices.

E1.1.4 Explore the different resources that families use to access what they want and need.

E2.1.1 Demonstrate how sharing and bartering are basic economic systems.

E2.1.2 Give examples of how people earn income.

E2.1.3 Describe how consumers spend money or use markets (banks, goods and services).

E2.1.4 Explain why people save money.

E3.1.1 Examine the difference between public and private providers of goods and services.

E3.1.2 Explain the purpose for public and private providers of goods and services.

E4.1.1 Explain that people need to trade for products that are not found in their geographic region.

E4.1.2 Describe why people in one country trade goods and services with people in other countries.

E4.1.3 Describe products that are produced abroad and sold domestically and products that are produced domestically and sold abroad.

G1.1.1 Be able to identify local geographic locations and bodies of water.

G1.1.2 Be able to identify large continental landmasses on a map or globe.

G1.1.3 Be able to identify major bodies of water on a map or globe.

G2.1.1 Explain the way family life is shaped by the environment.

G2.1.2 Discuss why families make decisions to move to new geographic locations.

G2.1.3 Identify human events and human-made features.

G2.1.4 Identify natural events or physical features.

G3.1.1 Explain how movement happens and its impact on self and community.

G3.1.2 Identify the common and unique characteristics of different global environments.

H1.1.1 Create a family timeline to show events in a sequential manner.

H2.1.1 Examine the factors that influence the student's family experiences and choices.

H2.1.2 Explain how one's own family's actions can cause a positive change in the future.

H3.1.1 Identify that there are different family structures and dynamics.

H3.1.2 Explain how actions of people in the past influence us today.

H4.1.1 Define how knowledge of personal history can be used to make current choices.

H4.1.2 Explain how different historical documents and artifacts inform our understanding of historical events.

(Washington Office of Superintendent of Public Instruction, 2019)

Sometimes, a shared text sparks the development of an inquiry or project. Consider a recent article appearing in *Scholastic News 1* magazine with the headline: "Smile like a crocodile." At first glance, this may seem to be a science-based article. Let's look a bit deeper to explore the topic to include the cultural component of smiling: When is it appropriate to smile? What are the smiling conventions for the members of your class? Does everyone smile readily? How can we as a class find out? Your discussion may be part of a project related to science (e.g., animals of many kinds) or health (e.g., related to dental health and access to care). You could use this news magazine piece to initiate a longer project with the children or treat it as a source for minimal discussion. Either way, you could easily include aspects of social studies content (e.g., cultural expressions) into the discussions and individual pondering you lead children in doing.

Your discussion of this article also could build in social-emotional learning by leading children in distinguishing the range of their own smiling behaviors: Sometimes you smile when you are happy. Other times, you smile when you are nervous or in response to an adult because you think that is the right thing to do. Sometimes you smile because something is funny, and you know it is not appropriate to laugh.

Moving beyond kindergarten, the inquiry questions or projects become more complex and potentially more sensitive. In a project unit for first graders reported by Sohyun An (2020), students were guided in learning how non-White children made history in fighting to receive the education they deserved. She shared the stories of three lesser-known BIPOC girls who fought to desegregate their schools in the years before Ruby Bridges (who also was included in the unit). Students read, wrote, discussed, and further investigated the historical settings of each. They learned about why these girls struggled and developed arguments for why their treatment was unjust. They synthesized their broad and deep knowledge gained through this integrated study using graphic organizer charts that became part of the classroom environment, demonstrating and documenting their social studies literacy for all to review and learn from.

In an inquiry reported by Swan, Lee, and Grant (2018), third graders explored the question of "Do people around the world care about children's rights?" To answer this compelling question, they devoted time to developing supporting questions that guided their collaborative research. They then gathered evidence about economics and economic systems, geographic reasoning, and civic participation (Swan et al., 2018, p. 157) to identify the core issues and multiple perspectives on the question. They summarized their findings and represented their learning in digital and print media presentations. A question like this one can remain broad in scope ("around the world" and "all" children's rights) or become narrowed through discussion and consensus building. For example, other third graders pursuing this question might first turn their attention to one core children's right: education. They could further limit their question to the United States. Using the Visual Thinking Strategies (n.d.) approach described earlier, they could be guided through viewing some of twentieth-century social reformer Lewis Hine's images from the Library of Congress' National Child Labor Committee Photograph Collection (https://blogs.loc.gov/teachers/2012/09/analyzing-photographs-child-labor-from-a-childs-perspective/) to see the impetus for the Fair Labor Standards Act of 1938. Using Internet searching, they then could investigate child labor issues in America today, starting with those reported on at the Human Rights Watch site (https://www.hrw.org/united-states). As students form personal perspectives on this compelling question, they also might interview family members who work as farm laborers, or older generations who entered the workforce relatively young. Findings could be summarized, analyzed, and critiqued in essays, a compositional form that third graders focus on refining throughout the year. They could use their essay notes to prepare a news conference that they record as a podcast for the school's website. They could create PowerPoint or other digital presentation formats that summarize their main arguments, using them in a class, grade, or school debate about the age at which one should enter the workforce. (Some students may be engaged in a family business, so this might be of particular interest.)

The direction of any inquiry-based learning will be shaped by the required school curricula, the interests of the children, and often by current events. Using the tools of social studies literacy (e.g., timelines, video scribing, interactive charts and graphs) throughout their projects, children develop their capacity to choose evidence to support theses; arrive at conclusions supported by evidence; and propose or conduct informed action. The advantage to conducting inquiry in the twenty-first century is the wide availability of both digital tools and digitized primary resources, not only textbooks and trade books, for thinking and working like a historian or an economist or a sociologist, wherever your school and home are located.

How Do State Learning Standards Anchor and Influence Children's Inquiry?

Teachers in public school settings typically are required to develop inquiries coordinated with state social studies learning standards. As children move through kindergarten into first, second, and then third grade, the complexity of questions posed and the levels of analysis and synthesis needed to explore, document, and present inquiry findings all increase across the standards. Preschool-level investigations usually start with curiosities close to children's growing awareness of the world around them—"My Family," "My School," "My Community," "Ways to Travel," "Recycling," "Elections," etc. Preschool teachers tend to have more freedom of choice in determining inquiry themes and topics as well as lengths of study. When children enter the primary grades in public schools, state standards and local curriculum requirements shape the inquiry topics and themes, though the children's interests remain among planning factors. The scheduled lengths of inquiries become more standardized, to accommodate other units of required study and instructional periods for physical education, art, music, etc.

Another shift from preschool to the primary grades in many public schools regards the increasing specificity in the content of social studies curriculum. This results in teachers needing to navigate teaching some hard topics in anti-racist ways without always having appropriate materials. For example, many state standards require primary-age children to learn about the origins of national holidays in the United States. Available texts for this age group frequently gloss over or trivialize the harsher parts of our collective history, and/or tell the stories of our holidays' origins from a singular perspective, stereotypically presenting the United States as a cultural monolith. Look at Textbox 2.8, Nebraska Social Studies Learning Standard 3.1.2c (Nebraska State Board of Education, 2019, p. 18). This standard is tricky for early childhood teachers to plan for (Derman-Sparks et al., 2020), as we seek not to focus our grade level's social studies curriculum exclusively around holidays and "special" months (e.g., Women's History). Rather than focusing on the holiday or month as the curriculum driver, we include these holidays when grounding unit content (e.g., the various contributions of the early presidents to our nation's history; the ongoing civil rights struggle). We recognize the importance of teaching children about these holidays and months as part of our overall teaching about cultural diversity and expression. We teach children to think critically about these holidays, to learn what they signify to some as well as to others. This is complex work to do—and very necessary. We actively seek children's books and other media on the unit topics to share, evaluating them carefully to be sure the collection we use includes multiple perspectives for children to consider and grow through.

TEXTBOX 2.8

Nebraska Third Grade Social Studies Standard 3.1.2c

SS 3.1.2.c Communicate the background of national holidays or historical events, their significance, and how they are recognized in the local community. For example: George Washington's Birthday, Abraham Lincoln's Birthday, Presidents Day, Dr. Martin Luther King, Jr. Day, Native American Heritage Day, Constitution Day, Memorial Day, Veterans Day, Thanksgiving Day, Patriots' Day (Recognition of 9/11)

(Nebraska State Board of Education, 2019)

Consider these issues in the context of a national holiday under serious reconsideration in schools seeking to create an anti-bias curriculum: Columbus Day. Yes, it is observed as a national holiday and often required to be taught. Most currently available children's books and materials show Columbus sailing from Spain to the Caribbean but leave out the acts of violence he committed upon arrival. Statues of Columbus are found in city parks that commemorate him for "discovering" America. Few instructional materials available for children highlight the Taino of San Salvador's perspective on Columbus (https://www.loc.gov/exhibits/exploring-t he-early-americas/columbus-and-the-taino.html) or tell the story of how he captured six men and took them back to Spain, thus beginning the long history of slavery by White explorers (https://www.history.com/news/columbus-day-controversy). How, then, does a PreK–3 teacher deal with this holiday in the school calendar? Several decisions are open to us:

1. How much time in the social studies calendar is devoted to the discussion of Columbus?
2. How does a discussion of Columbus connect to current events?
3. What are the perspectives of the families in my community?
4. How do we create or adapt available texts to make sure children learn the whole story?
5. What do we need to do to fill gaps in our own knowledge and feelings about Columbus and the origins of other national holidays and heroes and heroines? Where can we access this information? Whom should we work with to guide our rethinking?

Whether it is Columbus Day, Slavery, Holocaust, Immigration, Child Labor, or another unit topic that needs revamping through an anti-bias lens, we must find and use materials supporting social studies literacy skills at the children's developmental level. In most cases, this means teachers will need to augment adopted textbooks and other materials the school provides. Organizations such as Learning for Justice (formerly Teaching Tolerance; https://www.learningforjustice.org/) and Facing History (https://www.facinghistory.org/) provide guidance and links to where you can find developmentally appropriate media from multiple perspectives to share with children. They also offer periodic webinars and other training opportunities for current and prospective teachers, at low or no cost. The Zinn Education Project (https://www.zinnedproject.org/), although focused on middle- and high-school students, is also a teacher resource for learning how to critique the textbook approach to teaching our nation's history and who is represented in it. Slowly but surely, more culturally relevant resources are emerging to use with younger children, ones that address these issues in enlarging our collective perspectives on who we are as a nation.

Where Does Children's Literature Fit Into the Inquiry Arc?

Social studies literacy skills begin forming while children listen to the stories their family and community tell—children's earliest form of literature. Starting in preschool, we listen closely to the stories children bring from home—as they enter the room; at circle time, where we model how to take turns speaking and listening, and how to respond as an audience; and across the instructional day, as children make sense of what we teach. We tell and read stories, including ones in the form of poetry, to children. We invite guests to share their stories. We use music and other media to tell stories. Throughout, we connect stories to our lives in school and those outside and beyond its doors. We listen for the questions that the stories attempt to answer and talk about whether and how they do so.

One of the most powerful ways to link social studies and literacy development is through children's literature. Picture books can serve as mirrors of our lives and windows into those of others (Sims Bishop, 1990). Selected for depth of theme and content, as well as diverse viewpoints, these books serve as springboards for children's reflection and group thinking (Donovan, 2020). We celebrate personal milestones in children's lives—the birth of brothers or sisters, pet adoptions, a new bicycle—by sharing relevant books. We show compassion and condolences for family loss, fires in the neighborhood, floods in the community while pausing and talking through thematically related books read aloud. We rely upon picture books to provide a model or inspiration for investigating and representing new understanding. We teach children how to make illustrated scrapbooks of field trips, class walks, and other adventures. We ask them to practice writing and drawing like the authors and illustrators they come to know well through reading and rereading their books that resonate with our classroom community.

Preschool literacy activities form a bridge to kindergarten. In September of that year, we might read *The King of Kindergarten* (Barnes & Brantley-Newton, 2019) or *A Kiss Goodbye* (Penn & Gibson, 2011), part of the *Chester the Raccoon* series. As the year continues, we might read aloud from big book collections such as Ellen Labrecque's series on the "Places We Live" and "Workers Who Help Us" to connect to projects and themes in our social studies curricula. We share a balance of stories and informational texts for students to grow in their proficiency and understanding of how to create different forms of literature documenting their burgeoning knowledge (e.g., stories, event descriptions, labeled pictures detailing steps in a process).

Children's literature selections continue to serve a critical purpose across first through third grades. We organize our classroom libraries to include a variety of genres (fiction, nonfiction, poetry), themes, and topics that align with and reinforce social studies curriculum content. We collaborate with the school librarian or media specialist to teach children how to find other literature in the library that supports and expands their interests and questions they develop through inquiry or other means. We continue reading aloud daily from picture and chapter books whose characters, themes, and content reflect who our learners are and what they want to learn next.

During the K–3 years, we facilitate children's learning best when we integrate the curriculum through projects that promote inquiry-based learning. As described above, this kind of learning begins with centering on questions to investigate by using the literacy skills of civics, history, geography, and economics; evaluating the evidence gathered through the use of children's literature and other sources; and communicating the results of learning. The literature teaches both the content and the perspectives children need to consider as they conduct their investigations.

It also contains the possible formats for representing their findings—including digital.

How Has the Proliferation of Media Influenced Social Studies Curricula?

We understand that family and community experiences influence children's funds of knowledge, skills, and attitudes that they bring into the classroom community. Another important influence on their funds of knowledge is their experiences with media, which shape their notions of how to behave as well as their capacity to assimilate and accommodate new knowledge schemas into their thinking. For example, consider the generational changes in the toys of childhood. As young millennial teachers of today, you might bring experiences playing with My Little Pony, Teenage Mutant Ninja Turtles, She-Ra (complete with castle), Speak and Spell, Star Wars, Nintendo's Super Mario Bros., and Sega's Sonic the Hedgehog to your classroom practice. You might have watched *Sesame Street* and *Mr. Rogers*. Besides the concrete objects of the rocket ships, castles, figures, and game consoles, you still might recall or own other tie-ins to the books, movies, cartoons, and games you played (e.g., lunch boxes, T-shirts, bedsheets). You were the first generation to see smaller cell phones, electronic calculators, and computer labs in elementary schools. You were early explorers on the Internet as high schoolers or as undergrads. All these toys and media served to expand your world beyond your immediate family, community, and school. For those of you from Gen Z, your world may have included electronic toys such as the Nintendo 3DS, Webkinz, and Teksta Puppy as well as the more traditional My Little Pony, Pound Puppy, Slinky, and Cabbage Patch Baby. Contrast your own experiences with those of your parents and grandparents, who came to school with toy kitchens, blocks, dolls, board games, coloring books, and no cable television or video streaming services. How was your world experience broader and more connected to a larger world? What knowledge did you bring to school about places far away, especially with access to lower airline fares? Grandparents moving south to Alabama or retiring to Florida, providing you with travel opportunities for holidays where you could experience what you'd learned through your digital media? Your lifelong experiences in mediating the world digitally shaped you in ways unlike the generations before you, a **digital native**.

Who Are Digital Natives?

Children of today and even some teachers have never known a world without Internet, video streaming, cable TV, and computers in all forms—phones, tablets, laptops, desktops, appliance controls, etc. While many contemporary children also experience conventional toys and games enjoyed by past generations, their reliance upon digital devices to negotiate their daily world influences how and what we teach them. These devices are a kind of literacy experience of their own, one that moves beyond conversing, reading, and interpreting language. Knowledge is acquired and evidenced in a unique fashion in the digital world. Consider, for example, communication methods such as emails, texts, emojis, Twitter, and social media sharing platforms. More than ever, young children have varying experiences and facility in using these methods, based on their home experiences. As teachers, then, we need to consider which **digital literacy** skills and concepts to teach children as they use these methods on various devices. Buttons, icons, symbols, even the devices themselves require users to read in order to use them effectively. Think about the babies and toddlers you see in restaurants playing on cellphones, game consoles, and tablets. Such devices offer ways for children to engage quietly with an electronic device while adults enjoy a conversation. Some of these devices do not offer a challenge or real play activity, however. Pushing a button to move a ball from one location to another provides pleasure through visual and auditory stimulation, perhaps, but not cognitive engagement. Nevertheless, this activity provides experience with controlling electronics and developing facility in locating favorite activities on menus—and maybe even knowledge of cause and effect ("If I push this, that will happen").

Our preschoolers and younger elementary-aged children have never known a world without the Internet or digital toys. Many share experiences with "Hey Siri!" or "Alexa!" or "OK Google!" Teacher blogs are full of stories about young children suggesting the class "Ask Siri" when there's a question to investigate or for help in solving a math problem. They play with LeapFrog, Touch and Learn, and spend time exploring on LCD writing tablets, baby phones, and cameras. They are exposed to a wide range of often self-accessed content a click away on YouTube, network television, and streaming services. Each of these devices prepares children to learn in new ways and provides a wider view of the world. These experiences influence how they think as well as how they express themselves, often in the adultlike language they're exposed to online or through movies. Consider this conversation of four-year-old Jim with his mother: "Mom, the wi-fi isn't working!" (pause) "Come on, Mom, the struggle is real!" Or Nancy, a four-year-old, saying in February, "Abraham Lincoln was shot by a guy who didn't like Abraham Lincoln." Or Peter, a four-year-old, noting to his mother, "Santa doesn't need elves anymore." "He doesn't? Why?" "He has machines now. It's all automated."

Think about the funds of knowledge these four-year-olds bring to kindergarten. How would their home digital world experiences influence or determine your social studies curriculum and instruction? Consider your own funds of knowledge, and whether or how they resemble those of your students. Do you know, for example, all the latest toys and games seen at discount stores, online, and at family or neighborhood gatherings? How to play on the same devices as your students? Depending upon your life experiences and access, and that of your students, the variance in these related digital funds of knowledge across your classroom community could be significant, one type of digital divide concerning educators and others in school communities today.

What Is the Digital Divide?

The **digital divide** initially was characterized as the absence of cell phones, tablets, and computers in a home. The term was typically applied to urban and suburban low-income families and people in rural areas who had poor or no access to the Internet, and limited cable options. As more families added these services and devices when their prices (somewhat) decreased and they became more readily available, the landline telephone disappeared. Families grew to depend even more on the computers in their palms—their cell phones—to communicate, access information, take pictures, and play music, games, and videos. Over a relatively short time, phones and other devices became almost a necessity for families. Yet not all can afford them—another aspect of the digital divide affecting how schools plan their supports of young children's learning today.

Viewing content options for families across different devices also is increasing. Perhaps you are among the generation of teachers who have "cut the cable," enjoying shows on YouTube or Hulu instead of television. Many newer options for viewing content require subscriptions, however, which contributes further to yet another aspect of the digital divide. Not all families can subscribe to Netflix, HBOMax, Disney+, and Apple TV+ to keep up with the latest shows and movies. Access to these entertainment experiences influences and shapes children's perspectives on what they learn in school, along with their cultural awareness and **language stores**. How might your students' knowledge of the world beyond community and school vary as a result of their subscriptions?

Many homes in America still do not have computers; others possess only older models or rely wholly on phones for accessing the Internet. Numerous households do not have broadband access and even if they do, must limit their usage rates or be unable to use high-speed Internet on account of their older devices' limited capacity. In some rural areas, the Internet is spotty or expensive because only one service provider exists. Thus, Internet access has become the new digital divide for families on limited income. Our classroom communities may include children with more limited digital experiences than others, thereby creating a social class or experiential divide. This aspect of the digital divide is pivotal, as we saw during the pandemic of 2020. Then, children's everyday educational experiences were mixed and often limited due to Internet access issues, as well as sharing one family computer. There were nationwide reports of families with several children all struggling to learn on the same computer or tablet needed by other family members forced to work at home. Schools differed dramatically in how digitally evolved they were and how adept in teaching curriculum online. For example, one urban private school offered their PreK–3 students periodic access to a tech room complete with a wall-sized screen, 3D printer, robots, tablets, plus subscriptions to paid networks such as Discover, National Geographic, etc. The students typically also had home access to personal tablets and/or a computer, robotic toys, and personal subscription services, in addition to attending daily class sessions with their trained online teachers.

Contrast that private school with a public one in the same city, where the district's budget was strained to provide Chromebooks to all families, many of whom had no experience with any digital equipment beyond a basic cell phone. Some of the teachers avoided attending professional development sessions for learning how to use digital tools and instructional materials. In turn, they struggled to develop online learning opportunities beyond the skill-drill-kill types. Too, many children in that school chose not to "attend" online. This was not unusual during the pandemic. One other large city found, for example, that only 30 percent of PreK–3 children attended online school. This often was because there wasn't any adult or older sibling to help them with the online worksheets and activities required by their teachers.

Now, think about children from these various environments as they return to your classroom post-pandemic. How will the diversity of their funds of knowledge influence how you teach? What social studies literacy gaps in using symbols, navigating digital devices, interpreting charts and maps, and investigatory skills would you anticipate? What media literacy concepts and skills would you need to work on developing in these students first? What long-lasting impact will this twenty-first-century event have on the way children learn and the way we teach, particularly considering emotional trauma suffered by many?

Why Is Media Literacy So Crucial for All Young Children?

As we saw, children's funds of knowledge are influenced by their experiences with and access to print as well as digital materials, beginning with their earliest life experiences. Their **media literacy**, typically defined as their "ability to access, analyze, evaluate, create, and act using all forms of communication" (National Association for Media Literacy Education [NAMLE], n.d.), is an essential skill set for twenty-first-century survival. Successful multimedia use is influenced not only by access but also by the purpose for doing so. The purpose will largely determine how children process the content and steer their ways through it. Is it only for personal viewing and/or reading? Or will it require subsequent interpretation of the knowledge gained somehow? Another factor influencing children's media literacy is the match between their funds of knowledge with the content itself. How much and what type of preparation for engaging with the content do individual children need? What type of follow-up? How will their reported media experiences be discussed and evaluated? Finally, another salient factor influencing children's media literacy is their familiarity with the content's presentation format. Young children need to be taught how to comprehend content on a website versus that in a game or a video, as well as in books. Explicit instruction in using pull-down menus, radial buttons, page advance symbols, etc., is as central to developing their media literacy as is teaching them how to use text features (e.g., table of contents, map legends, illustration captions, glossaries) that appear in both digital and print forms.

For teachers of early childhood social studies, we need to be sure we assist young children in critically analyzing the materials and other knowledge products we share, along with ones they independently research. In a recent RAND Corporation report entitled *Truth Decay: Media Use and Literacy in Schools* (Hamilton et al., 2020), we learn that only 11 percent of elementary teachers studied indicated they placed an emphasis on developing children's *critical* media literacy. Like adults, children are influenced by the media they're exposed to and use. These media influences are heard during classroom conversations and seen in their classroom work products (e.g., Disney princesses drawn into firehouse field trip scenes). We must teach children how to critically analyze materials, to ask who created them and why, as well as engage the children in thinking through who and what else could be included in the sources they find. This perspective-taking develops over time and is difficult at first for younger children to do. One way to help them "step outside themselves" is to ask them to individually draw a map of the classroom. As the children view each other's drawings, they discover bias based on where they are seated or how their favorite room parts influenced what they included versus what they forgot. This exercise becomes a springboard for subsequent discussions about how "who" creates a literacy product will determine what it contains as well as what it looks like. Transferring these critical thinking skills to other materials, teaching and reteaching through asking questions such as, "Have we read/heard this before? What's different? What's the same?" "Why do you think this was written/recorded?" "Where else can we find information about this topic/question/idea?" develops the criticality young children need in the Information Age of the twenty-first century.

The nonprofit organization Common Sense Media provides a wealth of teacher and parent resources for developing your own and children's media literacy criticality (https://www.commonsensemedia.org/). They feature reviews of movies, apps, hardware and software, as well as children's literature and shows. They link you to other organizations whose resources can help in choosing and using multimedia with children of all ages, including ones that feature children's critiques and reviews of media. Consider incorporating them into lessons teaching your students how to do the same themselves. Publish your students' reviews on your classroom or school website. The more confident children become in forming and sharing their critical thinking, the more they naturally engage in using it every day, no matter the medium.

A framework for facilitating media literacy development in young children is shown in Textbox 2.9, Fundamental Actions of Media Literacy in Early Childhood (Herdzina & Lauricella, 2020, p. 8). You'll note how this framework is similar to how this chapter's been engaging you in exploring ways to develop young children's **social studies literacy**—giving and teaching children to access and choose relevant sources for investigating their deep questions; teaching children how to comprehend as well as evaluate those sources; and teaching children how to create their own sources that document and demonstrate their learning. In using multimedia with all young children, we prepare them with the fundamental tools they need for critically analyzing their world and taking civic action—the learning goals of social studies.

TEXTBOX 2.9

Fundamental Actions of Media Literacy in Early Childhood

To gain media literacy skills, young children need to be given support to:

Access: to effectively locate, use, and select media

Engage and Explore: to intentionally use media for purpose and enjoyment

Comprehend: to understand media messages and practices and transfer that knowledge appropriately

Critically Inquire: to question and analyze media messages

Evaluate: to ask, is this media right for me or my task?

Create: to make media with intention

(Herdzina & Lauricella, 2020, p. 8)

Conclusion

Guided by state learning standards, our role as teachers is to develop an inquiry-based curriculum that promotes children's social-emotional development, literacy development, and social studies understanding. We construct our curriculum while keeping the College, Career, and Civic Life (C3) Framework (NCSS, 2013, p. viii) in mind. The C3 Framework is powered by the shared principles about high-quality social studies education shown in Textbox 2.10, Guiding Principles for the College, Career, and Civic Framework (C3).

TEXTBOX 2.10

Guiding Principles for the College, Career, and Civic Framework (C3)

- Social studies prepare the nation's young people for college, careers, and civic life.
- Inquiry is at the heart of social studies.
- Social studies involve interdisciplinary applications and welcomes integration of the arts and humanities.
- Social studies is composed of deep and enduring understandings, concepts, and skills from the disciplines. Social studies emphasize skills and practices as preparation for democratic decision-making.
- Social studies education should have direct and explicit connections to the Common Core State Standards for English Language Arts and Literacy in History/Social Studies.

(https://www.socialstudies.org/standards/c3/).

The C3 Framework aligns with the principles of Developmentally Appropriate Practice (NAEYC, 2020). Among the core ideas contained in the position statement apropos here, as we consider all that's involved in fostering young children's social studies literacy, is the reminder that

> Educators shape children's conceptual development through their use of language . . . From infancy through age 8, proactively building children's conceptual and factual knowledge, including academic vocabulary, is essential because knowledge is the primary driver of comprehension. The more children (and adults) know, the better their listening comprehension and, later, reading comprehension. By building knowledge of the world in early childhood, educators are laying the foundation that is critical for all future learning. All subject matter can be taught in ways that are meaningful and engaging for each child. (NAEYC, 2020, p. 12)

What also connects the C3 Framework with that of the developmentally appropriate principles is the notion that learning is active and connected. It's through thoughtfully building our curriculum in these ways that children actually develop their social studies literacy. We start our curriculum building with who our children are—their funds of knowledge—and their expectations of school. Using the inquiry approach, we scaffold and spiral children through actively self-directing their explorations of world aspects unfamiliar as well as ones they encounter every day. We create environments where they "try on for size" the citizenship principles and ideals they need for their lifetimes. We know by teaching for knowledge as well as skill and dispositional breadth and depth, children will be successful citizens in their communities and beyond.

Literacy acquisition begins through early language, gestures, and interpretation of cues from family. As young children learn to communicate through speaking, reading, and writing, and become more proficient in processing the multimedia of their lives, they demonstrate numerous capacities for receiving information, interpreting it, and doing something with their new knowledge, skills, and attitudes. They learn to apply their multiple literacies. In the case of the social studies, they interpret as well as produce pictures, tables, charts, maps, graphic organizers, and more that reveal the multifaceted connections they make from their investigations. They also demonstrate how they are learning to function appropriately in an increasingly complex social environment—that of our diverse classroom and school communities today.

Thus, there is an inextricable link across the acquisition and development of literacy and the social studies in the PreK–3 world. The extent to which children are given opportunities to add to their funds of knowledge and social-emotional skills repertoires, and to enhance their ability to understand and participate in school and community, will fundamentally influence their lifetime civic participation.

Activities in the Field

1. Visit a PreK classroom and a third-grade classroom. Identify and sketch the literacy tools you see in each room. Discuss with the teacher how these evolve during the year. Prepare a graphic organizer to compare the developmental progression of each situation.
2. During a classroom visit or while watching a video of a classroom interaction, observe the types of questions posed by the teacher versus the children. Reflect on who asks the majority of questions—the adult(s) or the children. Analyze the questions posed. Were they mostly open-ended (required an explanation) or closed (yes/no/only one possible response)? Analyze the language stores the children were able to demonstrate. What opportunities for personal expression with the target vocabulary of the lesson/unit were provided to the children? What would you change in order for the language use to be by the *children* rather than the adult(s)?
3. Engage children from a kindergarten class and a second-grade class in conversation about their experiences with digital media. Ask them about their favorite programs and tools at home. Ask them which activities they enjoy most at school. Prepare to discuss with your colleagues any variations observed in child experiences in each situation.

Activities in the Library

1. In your college library, public library, or a local school with a makers' space, explore the tools for 3-D printing, Cubelet™ robots, Legos™, etc. Make a plan for using these tools to advance social studies literacy for an age group of your choice. Describe how this plan will advance understanding of civics, economics, geography, or history.

2. Review the International Literacy Association Children's Choices Reading List for the last three years (PreK–3 titles only). Then review three years of the National Council for the Social Studies Notable Social Studies Trade Books for Young People (PreK–3). Prepare a bibliography from these lists for one grade level within the PreK–3 range that helps children learn the required content of your state's social studies standards. Identify any gaps and recent trends in publications you observe in these lists.

3. For a particular grade level of your choice (i.e., PreK–3), find a published social studies-designated unit plan on a teacher resource site that is not designed for inquiry. Using the social studies learning standards for your state and a chosen grade level, rework the plan based on an Inquiry Arc. Provide opportunities for children to explore multimedia resources. Develop activities that foster students' new literacies, including their critical media literacy. Include a list of the unit's core vocabulary taught that would expand children's language stores.

Study Questions

1. How are language stores and funds of knowledge connected? What most influences each in young children? How does your classroom practice change them?
2. What do you as a teacher need to know and be able to do to ensure true inquiry occurs across all dimensions of the Inquiry Arc you develop with your students? What are the roles of your own background content knowledge, research skills, and child development knowledge (i.e., your personal funds of knowledge) in planning an Inquiry Arc?
3. Why do we often link social-emotional learning to the social studies? How is development in each facilitated?
4. How will your classroom's available resources influence your development of children's media literacy? Which resources are essential?

Reflect and Reread

As you learned, children's funds of knowledge influence not only what they're ready to learn next but also how. Given the diversity teachers observe in the funds of knowledge children bring to school, it's important for us to be aware of them before selecting curriculum content and planning instruction.

1. What are the ways you already know how to do this for your own teaching practice?
2. What gaps in your instructional repertoire do you realize you have? How will you resolve those gaps?

Suggested Readings

Adair, J. K. (2014). Agency and expanding capabilities in early grade classrooms: What it could mean for young children. *Harvard Educational Review, 84* (2), 217–241.
Colwell, J., Hutchinson, A., & Woodward, L. (2020). *Digitally supported disciplinary literacy for diverse K–5 classrooms.* Teachers College Press.

Duke, N. K. (2012). *Inside information: Developing powerful readers and writers of informational text through project-based instruction.* Scholastic.

Engel, S. (2021) *The intellectual lives of children.* Harvard University Press.

Gonzalez, N., Moll, L., & Amanti, C. (Eds.). (2005). *Funds of knowledge: Theorizing practices in households, communities, and classrooms.* Erlbaum.

Gutierrez, K. D. (2008). Language and literacies as civil rights. In Greene, S. (Ed.), *Literacy as a civil right: Reclaiming social justice in literacy teaching and learning,* 169-184. Peter Lang.

Immordino-Yang, M., Darling-Hammond, L., & Krone, C. (2018). *The brain basis for integrated social, emotional, and academic development: How emotions and social relationships drive learning.* Aspen Institute. https://assets.aspeninstitute.org/content/uploads/2018/09/Aspen_research_FINAL_web.pdf

Lee, N. T. (2020). *Bridging digital divides between schools and communities.* Brookings Institute. https://www.brookings.edu/about-us/

Muhammad, G. (2020). *Cultivating genius: An equity framework for culturally and historically responsive literacy.* Scholastic.

Yarrow, A., & Fane, J. (2019). *The sociology of early childhood: Young children's lives and worlds.* Routledge.

Chapter 3

How Can Social Studies Anchor the Curriculum?

Gayle Mindes, Ed.D.

Education is the cornerstone of liberty.

—Eleanor Roosevelt

TERMS TO KNOW

baseline	emergent curriculum
big ideas	funds of knowledge
C3 Framework	Inquiry Arc
citizenship	International Baccalaureate (IB)
civic action	Next Generation Science Standards
class meetings	(NGSS)
Common Core State Standards	project-based learning
developmentally appropriate practice	understanding by design (UDL)
documentation panel	

Overview

Our discussion of curriculum begins with the idea that young children's curiosity drives their exploration of themselves and their expanding world as they enter the formal structures of childcare and school. Thus, this focus on child-inquisitiveness guides our thinking on ways to harness child wonder for the acquisition of skills and understanding of the social world. Implicit in this view are the principles of developmentally appropriate practices for all learners. We examine the role pre-school curricular models and required local, state, and international standards play in developing the content of the social studies: civics, economics, geography, and history. We consider the central role of inquiry in developing child knowledge. Of particular importance are the links to social-emotional understandings and skills. Connections to other subject areas are made as social studies skills and knowledge emerge for young children. Finally, we connect social-emotional learning goals to the social studies as part of our work in promoting fully realized potential for all young children.

Focus Questions

1. How do young children learn best and what are the implications for curriculum planning?
2. How should we plan for the implementation of a social studies curriculum?
3. How do we handle contemporary academic issues meaningfully for young children?

How Do Young Children Learn Best? Implications for Curriculum Planning

I show how curricular decisions will optimize the understanding of civics, economics, geography, and history for young children. I connect the content of the social studies to social-emotional learning and the special process skills associated with social studies learning. My argument begins with a focus on the meaning of **developmentally appropriate practice** as it applies to curricular development.

The 2020 statement on developmentally appropriate practice (NAEYC, 2020) calls for curriculum implementation for all young children to be inclusive and culturally responsive.

> The curriculum consists of the knowledge, skills, abilities and understandings children are to acquire and the plans for the learning experiences through which those gains will occur . . . helps young children achieve goals that are meaningful because they are culturally and linguistically responsive and developmentally and educationally significant. (https://www.naeyc.org/resources/position-statements/dap/planning -curriculum)

This description of the curriculum suggests a number of important practices to apply to the implementation of social studies curricula. These practices include the big ideas as shown in Textbox 3.1, Curriculum Development Planning Consistent With NAEYC Position Statement on Developmentally Appropriate Practice 2020.

TEXTBOX 3.1

Curriculum Development Planning Consistent With NAEYC Position Statement on Developmentally Appropriate Practice 2020

- play, small group, large group, interest centers, routines
- builds on prior experiences
- mirrors and windows so all children have experience with diverse, inclusive communities
- collaborative learning
- curriculum is written with space for emergent learning
- uses early learning state standards, Head Start, etc.
- goals updated with input from all stakeholders
- published curricula . . . culturally and linguistically responsive
- uses assessment to adjust
- adapts to meet needs of all learners
- experiences integrate children's learning
- depends on funds of knowledge

* depth and sequence considered to expand child learning
* considers emergent curriculum

Where Do We Begin in Preschool Teaching?

Beginning in the preschool years in many childcare and educational situations, one predominant model for developing social studies curriculum includes a belief in **emergent curriculum**; that is, the idea that educational activities in the classroom are based upon children's interests, issues in their families and community, activities in the learning centers, and in outdoor experiences. This approach to learning capitalizes on individual children's **funds of knowledge**, that is, what information and experiences they already have based on family and community living. This focus allows children the opportunity to connect the understandings they bring to school to the ideas, principles, and practices others know. As well, some of the curriculum comes from serendipitous events in children's lives. For example, four-year-old Sammy may come to school one day and say, "My dad says we are going to get a puppy." Classmates chime in with their experiences with dogs, cats, fish, salamanders, and birds. If there is sufficient ongoing interest demonstrated by children, Ms. Fargo, their teacher, may then develop activities for children to explore "Pets in Our Community." She will then help children investigate the topic, provide props in learning centers, bring books from the library, and help the class document their learning. Thus, assessment of learning is built into the emerging project. The documentation will have links to the civic responsibility of pet owners, economic costs of owning pets, history of animals in the lives of families as pets, and the variation of pets, geographically. Not every class will examine all of these issues, but the potential is there for each of these strands.

Such an approach to curriculum depends on Ms. Fargo's basic planned structure of routines, stories, songs, and props regularly introduced for play. The approach requires careful observation of individual children, listening to their conversations, and queries about the world around them. It is an approach used by teachers to explore consequential life issues, such as "My brother has leukemia"; "My mom says we are going to go live with my grandma"; "My oldest brother is going to jail"; "I'm getting a baby brother"; "My sister is quitting school so she can work." Each of these statements by children may prompt an investigation of the statement, documentation of findings, assessment of individual and group understandings, as well as sharing work products. The approach is dependent upon teachers as nimble planners for the ongoing follow-up of issues to be sure the children have appropriate resources and opportunities to gain meaningful social studies knowledge.

Curriculum Models

Besides an emergent approach to curriculum in preschool, many situations call for a model to be used to provide guidance for topics. Often these childcare situations may include teachers new to the field, with limited formal early childhood education—professionals learning on the job—or in situations where teachers are working long days with limited planning time. In these cases, there are many organized approaches to curriculum based on thorough research and knowledge of the ways young children learn. One model used across the country in Head Start classrooms, for example, is the High Scope Preschool Curriculum, which "includes strategies and detailed activities for all curriculum content areas, charts to help you scaffold learning across developmental ranges, and materials to create an engaging learning environment" (https://highscope.org/our-practice/preschool-curriculum/) (see also Epstein & Hohmann, 2020).

A second widely used curricular model, based on years of research and development, is "The Creative Curriculum® for Preschool." This "whole-child approach to education—one where children develop not only math and literacy skills but also social-emotional, physical, and cognitive skills—is developmentally appropriate and better prepares children well beyond their time in a classroom" (https://teachingstra tegies.com/solutions/teach/preschool/). Each of these prepared curricula offers a foundation for teacher use in the classroom. Of course, there will be opportunities for teachers to include and combine emergent ideas, based on their observations of children and unforeseen events.

In addition to these curricular models found in Head Start and other early childhood classrooms, two additional widely used models to guide planning in preschool (and beyond) are the Montessori approach originally developed by Maria Montessori (1912) to serve young children whose families were the laborers in Italy. The model has evolved as a structured approach to curriculum with guided discovery using specially developed blocks, other manipulatives, and routines. It is a fully elaborated approach using teacher observation to plan, develop, and assess overall learning in young children by preparing an environment (American Montessori Society, n.d.) (https://amshq.org/About-Montessori).

The Reggio Emilia Approach espouses a belief in children constructing their own knowledge through relationships and over time. Teachers are advised to respect the 100 languages of children (Edwards et al., 2011). The languages include drawing, building, modeling, sculpturing, discussing, inventing, discovery, and more. Again, teachers are preparers of an early learning environment supporting inquiry and keenly observing child progress to assess children and plan the next steps for the curriculum. Children demonstrate learning with the products of their work and exhibit their accomplishments to families and communities.

In sum, these preschool approaches to curriculum demonstrate the variety of ways teachers and programs practice developmentally appropriate practice. In these approaches, the social studies learning occurs through prepared environments with various materials: teachers' interactions with children and families; the children's interactions with each other. Typical social studies topics include the investigation of self, family, community, making friends, using money, getting around. Because the approaches to curriculum are multidimensional and include child interests and relationships as cornerstones, children will come to kindergarten with social studies knowledge and experiences grounded in their various childcare and education background, reflecting their funds of knowledge. This sets the stage for teachers to build upon the diversity of perspectives to continue to elaborate social studies knowledge and skills.

How Is Curriculum Guided Beginning in Kindergarten?

While some of the preschool models are carried forward into kindergarten and beyond, and other models are found in private academies, for example, Waldorf Schools, an arts-based PreK–12 system (Steiner, 1919) with strong emphasis on child curiosity and inclusiveness, most public schools write and adopt curriculum based on the various perspectives of their publics and legislative requirements from local, state, and federal government. In practice, this means, currently, states requiring demonstration of learning based on standards for subject area learning. Across the country the standards for social studies vary in adherence to the principles outlined in the **C3 Framework** (NCSS, 2013) developed in part as a response to the **Common Core State Standards** (CCSS, 2010). The CCSS Standards focus on English Language Arts (ELA) and Mathematics. Additional standards driving curriculum decisions in the public schools include the **Next Generation Science Standards** (Next Generation Science Standards, 2013). Behind the standards movement for public education is a complex set of variables driven by citizens and educators to provide both accountability and consistency of learning across the states (Mindes, 2016). The standards movement, in part, was an ideal for children to have access to high quality experiences promoting learning wherever they live. While many will argue, rightly, the movement directed toward meaningful engagement of children in learning was hijacked by a mechanistic approach to accountability. It therefore created an assessment environment often focused on minutiae and unrealistic expectations for achievement goals for individuals starting at different points on a learning curve, based on their prior knowledge.

The results of the requirement for use of standards in curriculum planning serve as a primary driver of content and instruction in public education today. However, all of the national guidelines emphasize inquiry-based education—in keeping with the goal of developmentally appropriate practice, which demands focus on the individual child. The difficulties in implementation of the proposed standards are associated with the assessment practices with narrow foci on rote and easily measurable objectives and the absence of real individualization of learning for all learners. Therefore, the guiding standards are not the enemy, but the friend of teachers seeking to develop social studies curricula based on the **Inquiry Arc**, which proposes developing questions and planning inquiries; applying civic, economic, geographical, and historical concepts and tools; evaluating sources; and using evidence and communicating results.

Project-Based Learning

Consequently, the approach for optimum acquisition of social studies skills and knowledge lends emphasis to **project-based learning**. A project-based implementation relies on the inclusion of both teacher-initiated topic investigations as well as child-inquisitiveness. This approach offers may opportunities to connect and enhance literacy acquisition, mathematical thinking, and application of science principles—the ultimate synthesis and application of knowledge. These opportunities connect to social studies investigation of content.

Components of project-based learning "include giving students opportunities to study a challenging problem, engage in sustained inquiry, find answers to authentic questions, help choose the project, reflect on the process, critique and revise the work, and create a public product" (Grossman et al., 2019). One such example of a project began with this conversation among third graders:

"All of these monuments make me think of Jim Crow.
Who is Jim Crow?
He said black and white children could not be friends.
Does he have a monument?
I don't see it, but I think he is here." (Muller, 2018, p. 17)

The conversation began as children visited the South Carolina State House grounds. Children wondered how the people portrayed in statues where chosen. Why were these individuals shown in monuments? The questions led to a ten-week project-based investigation. These activities show the Inquiry Arc in action. Start with a question, investigate, take action.

Another third-grade project began in New York City with the question: "What languages do we see in our community?" (Shatara & Sonu, 2020, pp. 5–9). The project incorporated the following standards:

D2.Geo.2.K-2. "Use maps, graphs, photographs, and other representations to describe places and the relationships and interactions that shape them"; and
D2.Geo.7.K-2. "Explain why and how people, goods, and ideas move from place to place."

Children began their investigation by documenting with photos their observations in their neighborhood containing English, Spanish, Chinese, Arabic, and other languages. They examined maps, read stories, shared family experiences, and examined the question of language suppression. They concluded this investigation with written essays and proposed **civic action**. Thus, a well-planned topic keyed to social studies standards, using the Inquiry Arc.

An additional example of a project with potential for adapting to many ages in the primary grades is one broadly begun with the question of, who eats lunch? Or, where does my food come from? With these broad questions, children can explore the cultural implications of meals, traditional foods, food insecurity, food deserts, farming practices, food packaging, food safety, grocery stores, costs of food, and many more with direct relevance to social studies knowledge and skills. As part of the investigation, children can contribute family traditions and experiences of everyday food and special occasions food preparing a graphic organizer. They can investigate local cuisine at restaurants. How did the cuisine come to our community? How has it changed from the original recipe and presentation? Use maps to show the journey asparagus makes across country to their locale. Check weather patterns for plant growing trends in their communities. See the effect of wind, tornadoes, hurricanes, fire, and floods on crops. Examine the cost of food by following the price of milk at different stores, and in many other ways develop knowledge of the social studies. Each of these topics have strings tying social studies and other subject areas, providing opportunities for children to develop knowledge, skills, and attitudes across many state standards.

International Baccalaureate (IB)

While our discussion focuses mainly on state and local standards guiding curricula, there is growing interest on the part of the public and progressive school districts on the potential for the use of the guiding principles espoused by the **International Baccalaureate (IB)®** program implemented in schools around the world. The IB Mission Statement "aims to develop inquiring, knowledgeable and caring young people who help to create a better and more peaceful world through intercultural understanding and respect" (2014). Many of the principles, ideals, and approaches to curriculum are compatible with those of our shared understanding of developmentally appropriate practice in early childhood, as well as the overarching principles of curricular approaches to the social studies, using an inquiry approach to learning.

The fully elaborated program includes the familiar ideals of curricula for the development of knowledge, concepts, skills, and attitude with an emphasis on children as agents of their own learning and partners in the educational process. In addition, action is regarded as an essential element, akin to our interest in civic engagement. Assessment of students as part of the curricular implementation process is integral. Accordingly, with the preschool models for curriculum, the NCSS C3 Framework, the IB Primary Years Program, developmentally appropriate practice, and project-based learning in mind, we turn our attention to planning.

How Should We Plan for Implementation of a Social Studies Curriculum?

So, when we plan curriculum for our community of learners, we need to be sure our plans are age appropriate, individually appropriate, culturally and linguistically appropriate according to the *NAEYC Position Statement on Developmentally Appropriate Practice: 2020* (NAEYC, 2020). This affirmation means we must think about the children and their funds of knowledge and all of the requirements for practice in early childhood. To do this work we think holistically, keeping in mind individuals and requirements for our respective settings. A useful way to begin is to think about the myriad of elements in planning.

What Is the Planning Baseline?

All planning for learning begins with consideration of the **baseline**, that is, what must be considered for any curricular implementation. The elements to be considered are the room arrangement, the schedule, the routines, the rules and expectations, the personal interactions, (Berry & Mindes, 1993; Mindes & Donovan, 2001) and the documentation of progress—the assessment piece (added in 2020). The components of the baseline are shown in Textbox 3.2, Elements of the Planning Baseline.

TEXTBOX 3.2

Elements of the Planning Baseline

- **Room arrangement** utilizes traffic patterns to match the classroom activities planned. Learning centers are clearly set up and defined by topic, with appropriate space to match the activities. Equipment and materials are accessible and grouped to encourage child management of them.

- **Schedule** reflects a balance of individual, small-group, and large-group activity structure. A well-developed schedule includes large blocks of time during the week to support project-based curricular endeavors.
- **Routines** facilitate efficient accomplishment of everyday tasks and promote a sense of structure and predictability about the days and weeks of school. These include activities such as collecting lunch money, distributing papers, lining up, and reporting attendance.
- **Rules and expectations** need to be clearly delineated so that predictable consequences provide security for classroom citizens. Behavioral guidelines reflect the values of the school community. Involving students in the creation and modification of classroom rules ensures the practice of classroom democracy.
- **Personal interactions** are the ways in which the members of the classroom community interact. These include student-to-student interactions, teacher-student, and teacher–multiple student exchanges. Teachers choose roles of observer, facilitator, leader, stage manager, and participant depending on the goals of the particular lesson.
- **Documentation** of the knowledge, skills, and dispositions learned by children. The ways in which teachers will assess and help children demonstrate their learning and report to families and others as well as to plan next steps in the curricula.

For social studies planning, we must consider the priorities of our centers and schools regarding guidelines for implementation and assessment of the content of social studies learning in keeping with developmentally appropriate practice and relevant program and governmental standards. It is easier for learners if we think about ways to integrate all aspects of the curriculum to assist in their capacity to consolidate knowledge, skills, and attitudes. For social studies with an emphasis on emergent and **project-based learning,** the Inquiry Arc is particularly relevant.

How Do We Apply the Inquiry Design Model?

Swan et al. (2019) articulate the Inquiry Design Model (IDM) for planning, which "uses questions to frame and scaffold inquiry. Compelling questions address key issues and topics found in and across the academic disciplines . . . state and local standards; supporting questions provide the conceptual structure that helps 'children' respond to the compelling question (p. 14)." The IDM starts with a big question, outlines the relevant standard, develops supporting questions. The children conduct an investigation to answer the question, critically analyzing source material and developing conclusions. Finally, civic action is developed as a follow-up.

A recent example of this approach to meeting history content priorities for most states is a study of Colorado settlers' history (Sell et al., 2018). The project focus in this example was on the Hispano people settling in the San Luis Valley of Colorado. The third graders focused their study on the family of Teofilo Trujillo, who became a US citizen in 1848.

The study included a review of the geography of the San Luis Valley and the history of the development of the Valley. The children might have learned to read literary maps, that is, maps with pictures and words to show history available in public libraries and in the Library of Congress (McGuigan, 2018). They explored the Hispano culture through cultural aspects of clothing, homes, foods of the times, documenting with graphic organizers. They used newspaper clippings and interview transcripts to learn the story of the Trujillo family. In concluding their investigation, the children decided the family's history was representative of Colorado history. The taking action portion of the project was an opportunity for children to tell their own history of arriving in Colorado in family reports. This part of the project was done through collaboration with families. Throughout the project, children used primary sources and discussion to conduct this inquiry project (pp. 26–31).

Through projects such as this one linked to children's lived experiences, making history accessible to their development as thinkers, the project employed the six concepts of historical thinking (Seixas & Morton, 2013, in Krahenbuhl, 2019, p. 25) including the following:

- establishing historical significance
- using primary source evidence
- examining continuity and change
- analyzing cause and consequence
- taking historical perspective
- attempting to understand the ethical dimension of history

For young children this provides "Development of a broad chronological framework of significant and enduring events and figures leading to the development of a big-picture understanding of the society in which one resides and introduction to the historical thinking concepts to the discipline of history" (Krahenbuhl, 2019, p. 25).

Such projects, also, are illustrative of history investigation using the Inquiry Arc, providing a potential model for states across the country. Pioneer history has long been a feature of third-grade history curricula. Updated and modernized following the C3 Framework approach, we can make the content naturally connect to the lived lives of children in many contexts. And we can extend the curriculum to include stories and voices that are frequently omitted from texts about topics like pioneer life, including those who were displaced to make room for the pioneers' manifest destiny. For example, following the Trail of Tears of the Cherokee and Creek Peoples who were forced to leave the southeastern United States, walking west in 1836, so White settlers could grow cotton (cf. History Channel, https://www.history.com/topics/native-american-history/trail-of-tears#section_3). Besides using social studies skills and materials, cross-curriculum links to science, math, and literacy are abundantly possible connections.

An example for California Standard 2.4 Economics: people who supply goods and services lead to child understanding of economic literacy (History Social Science Framework for California Public Schools: Kindergarten Through Grade Twelve, 2017, pp. 51–52). To begin the investigation, Mr. Morrison, a second-grade teacher, asks children in his class: What do you eat at home? What are your favorite foods? The children make lists and draw comparisons of the various foods eaten in their classroom. This leads to an examination of product labels for prepared foods. Children might bring photos of product labels or cut them from discarded packages to identify such issues as real ingredients as compared to chemical additives and preservatives. The project can include investigation of advertising of food on television or the Internet. It might also promote an investigation of where families grow their food or shop for groceries—at farmer's markets, big box stores, online, grocery chains, corner grocer, etc.

In addition to beginning the study with one of these threads, Mr. Morrison will bring books to read, newspaper articles, and children may invite family members or others who work in the food industry to provide expert information. The children might follow the journey of strawberries from California to tables in Lincoln, Nebraska, or in other ways see what happens to foods produced in California to feed the nation. The class may include an investigation of worker safety in the food industry, reading recent news accounts and biographies of farm workers, such as *Harvesting Hope: The Story of Cesar Chavez*. The direction of the project will be guided by the state standards, the goals for the total curriculum in second grade, and the interests and experiences of the children. Connections across the curriculum to science and math are easily made. Outcome experiences may lead to documentation of need for more grocery stores in a community, or letters to representatives to protect workers' rights; that is, the outcomes will follow the inquiry.

In Delaware, the Economics Standard Four K–3a requires that "Students will understand that the exchange of goods and services around the world creates economic interdependence between people in different places." So, the focus of project-based investigation may be upon where the food comes from and where the chicken produced in Delaware travels. The questions from children will emerge from their particular experiences. Thus, the investigation becomes accessible to young children to lead to knowledge and skill in social studies related to economic interdependence. And intercurricular ties can be planned.

In Kansas, a second-grade compelling question is "How does the economy determine how you live?" (Kansas Department of Education, 2020). In a state known for producing wheat, as well as one with many feedlots for producing beef, children may have familiarity or curiosity about the economic issues related to these industries. It may be possible to look into the history of wheat and the viruses that affected it until winter wheat was planted. This investigation can tie to science standards reflecting growth cycles of plants as well. Another area of curiosity leading to understanding of economics and other social issues may occur with the debate about grass-fed beef practiced in some areas of Kansas versus the feed lot production practices. Meat packing practices and shipping may also be part of the investigation.

Finally, in many areas of rural America there are food insecurities. For us as teachers, the book *Heartland: A memoir of working hard and being broke in the richest country on earth* by Sarah Smarsh brings the issue into sharp focus. For children experiencing hunger and relying on school breakfast and lunch for more than two-thirds of their food for the day, it is an everyday reality. This insecurity is linked to poor health overall and chronic disease. How do we make this topic accessible to young children? For those living the insecurity, we do not need to bring it to attention, but to assist in seeking local solutions for the families we serve—both short-term and long-term. The project-based learning can link to an Inquiry Arc to social studies standards leading from a question such as "Are we hungry? What can we do?" All of the newspaper, TV, in-person interviews, and media can be accessed in investigating this guiding question, leading to identifying resources and producing action plans. For children living in more fortunate circumstances, we identify ways to bring attention to the disparity in their community, leading to a culminating action.

Presenting the Learning to Our Publics—the Class, Families, and Beyond

As projects conclude and summarization of knowledge and perspectives are gained, children will want to share their accomplishments with classmates, families, and the larger community. Of course, not all projects will require vast distribution, but the principle of investigation leading to conclusions at a point in time and sharing begins in the primary years. As we think of our years in school, the presentations were often oral reports, written compositions, graphic organizers, acted-out plays, musical performances, PowerPoints, and videos. Today's children have even more options for presenting information in digital formats, going well beyond the **documentation panel** of Reggio Emilia (Edwards et al., 2011). Although paper and pencil (or marker or other artistic or graphic material) is still a powerful tool for summarizing knowledge visually in a public presentation. A number of available digital tools are featured by Pledger, 2018, in a video blog movement: "Share Your Learning," which advocates exhibitions posted by children, conferences led by children, and presentations to be evaluated by peers virtually.

Nevertheless, whether with traditional classroom materials or digital ones, documentation of learning supports the best practice of scholarship—communication and opportunity for critique and advancement of knowledge, celebrating accomplishments. Documentation of learning serves as a way to assess child progress, coordinating knowledge statements with checklists, anecdotal notes, and other record-keeping tools used by teachers to track child progress and monitor the curriculum. The idea is to make a living picture of the children's experience with the curriculum. Artwork, stories, recorded conversations, and digital explorations are linked on large charts or bulletin boards displayed throughout the room. A final panel may be shared in a community space so that children, families, and school community see the learning that has occurred. Implicit in the documentation is a record of questions asked and answered.

Supporting Child Curiosity While Meeting Standards

As we see, state standards can serve as guides or stimuli in service of both requirements for curricula implementation and for answering the myriad questions young children bring to our attention based upon their funds of knowledge. So, how does the concept of the baseline make it possible for curriculum development in our yearly plan? We begin with **understanding by design** (McTigue & Wiggins, 2012) to examine the whole year. This approach advocates starting with end goals, moving backward to determine the important steps along the way to culmination of yearly goals. What must we accomplish for ELA, mathematical thinking, scientific understanding, and the social studies—civics, economics, geography, and history? How do we connect these requirements coherently? To do so, we think about where we want to be at the end of the academic year and apportion goals over the quarters or six-week intervals, where we will be reporting progress to stakeholders: children, families, school administration, and community. What are **big ideas** to anchor child investigation? Such ideas go beyond the immediate notion of such topics as "What words begin with Q?" "What is a pie?" to consider ideas of "How do we communicate—then and now?" "Why do we wear different clothes around the country?" Often, these topics are prescribed by states and school districts. In Washington, for example, third graders study First Nations of North America, so the questions are derived from the state standards.

Next, we think about the room arrangement. Is it intentionally designed to support collaborative work among children? Does it provide private space for those needing to concentrate? Have we established routines, so the school lives of children are predictable and organized? Did we devote enough time at the beginning of the academic year to involving children in creating rules and expectations? Have we posted the rules, and do we update them as needed? After all, the establishment of rules is an activity modeling collective action for the common good. When thinking about the schedule, we ask ourselves: Have we met the prescribed minutes for ELA and mathematics? Do we have dedicated blocks of time for project-based learning? Can we connect the projects to all areas of the curriculum? What are the relevant linking standards?

Always in our mind as we think about planning, how will we document progress for children's acquisition of knowledge, skills, and dispositions? What work products will children produce to show their progress? How will we give them meaningful feedback to scaffold their learning? In which ways will we show stakeholders—children, family, school board, state board, etc.—how children are progressing? What tools will we need to document progress, such as observation notes, checklists, rubrics, work products?

And, finally, perhaps the most important investigatory activity for us: How have we created a warm, respectful climate of personal interactions? Are we listening? Watching? On a daily basis, do we know which issues occupy children's minds? Their understanding of the social world? Do we need to weave their curiosities into an ongoing project? Thus, in these ways, we connect the academics of social studies to the lives of the children we serve. Of course, personal interactions promote the critical development of social-emotional skills relevant to the social studies.

How Do We Connect Social-Emotional Learning Goals to Social Studies?

For example, debate linked to the investigation of multiple points of view on a topic is directly linked to the CASEL Social and Emotional Learning, defined as

> the process through which all young people and adults acquire and apply the knowledge, skills, and attitudes to develop healthy identities, manage emotions and achieve personal and collective goals, feel and show empathy for others, establish and maintain supportive relationships, and make responsible and caring decisions. (CASEL, 2020)

The framework for learning (CASEL, 2020) is shown in figure 3.1, Social-Emotional Learning (SEL) Wheel. Debate, a social studies skill, is facilitated when children learn to use words when problem-solving. In this way social studies is linked to social and emotional learning. As such, arguing over problems or issues is shown as a valid way to make points toward resolution agreeable to all parties.

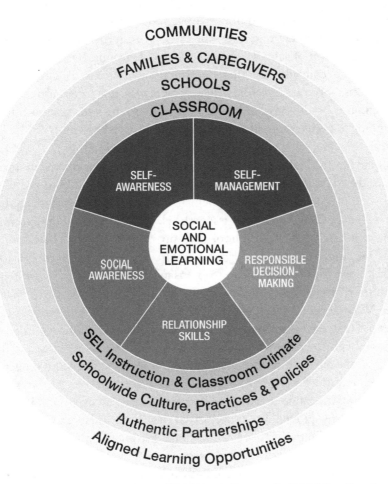

FIGURE 3.1 Social-Emotional Learning (SEL) Wheel. *Source*: © 2020 https://casel.org/what-is
-sel/.

In preschool situations (or certainly in kindergarten), children have learned about sharing even when they do not want to, through teacher practices such as keeping requirements for sharing modest, that is, modeled by teachers, but minimizing infractions when violations are not in direct teacher observation; stressing behaviors rather than moral right or wrong; showing empathy—it's hard to share; comforting the victim of the loss rather than the perpetrator and avoiding punishment to the offender, but explaining the rule (Goodman & Rabinowitz, 2019). Thus, through the development of the rules for sharing and the peaceful resolution of conflict, children begin to engage in the use of the formal language and practice of debate. Debate is an important social studies skill and not learned overnight.

Bailey et al. (2019) suggest a SEL developmental pyramid. Kindergarteners are learning to wait, share, take turns, and to practice following classroom routines. In first grade, young children can learn to listen to teachers and classmates with longer attention spans. Second graders are capable of multistep plans and self-management. It is at third grade that empathy and perspective-taking is more established (p. 55). As we think about the project-based learning at various ages, we must keep in mind the support our young charges will need to practice interactions in the social world of the classroom, learning about **citizenship** as they move along. Keen observation of student actions will assist in fostering behaviors required for successful negotiation of school and other social environments.

One way we can advance these personal interactions in our classrooms is through the use of **class meetings**. The practice is anchored usually sometime at the beginning of the day and is a vehicle to share and discuss information. "We are going to go to the auditorium today for a special assembly," Ms. Donovan announces. "The DePaul Theatre is coming to present *Go Dog! Go!*" The meeting is an opportunity to think about the behavioral expectations for theatergoers.

On another day, the meeting may resolve a class conflict about red markers in February—not everyone has one and they all want to make valentines to share with family and friends. Or a community issue: the electric scooters on the sidewalks near school make it hard to walk to school with my friends. Or to debate the best way to present the results of our kindergarten project on human geography (Jorgenson et al., 2018), or a third-grade project on enslavement—a history topic required in all fifty states (Patterson & Shuttleworth, 2020). What did we learn? Where shall we share? What action do we propose? The answers to these questions, of course, will depend on the developmental and academic skills of the children in our classes.

Thus, through the example projects, we see the capacity to integrate the social studies across the curriculum through the PreK–3 ages. We must no longer see topics connected to grade levels, but to the interests and requirements of our particular classes. Starting with children's funds of knowledge, current events, and curiosities of children, we can engage children in projects at their level and circle the topic through the curriculum as cognitive and social-emotional learning advances, as articulated by Bruner (1966) in *Toward a Theory of Instruction*. This approach requires us to be mindful of the principles of developmentally appropriate practice, including knowledge of child development and the capacity to start where children are, regardless of age, to scaffold their knowledge and elaborate their funds of knowledge of not only the social studies but the ELA, mathematical processes and thinking, and scientific approach to investigation. The outcome of this holistic approach to curriculum is the development of scholars for the ages. Children who will be confident in their capacity to tackle academic and social problems with aplomb.

How Do We Handle Contemporary Academic Issues Meaningfully for Young Children?

As we know, it is in children's first formal early childhood experiences, whether these begin in home childcare, center-based childcare, preschool, or kindergarten, that they learn the conventions of following rules for individual and group behavioral expectations—the citizenship rules for the classroom. Understanding the tenets of classroom citizenship lays the foundation for global citizenship. It is in these first formal group experiences that children learn and practice exercising self-control and develop pro-social skills and social competence. They learn to share materials, work cooperatively, to listen to classmates and teachers, and to resolve peer problems by themselves or with teacher guidance. These classroom behaviors pave the way for young children to understand pooling resources for roads, firefighters; schools teach the basics for understanding the perspectives of others. All of these skills and understandings may be developed by teachers with the Kindness Curriculum developed at the Center for Healthy Minds (https://centerhealthyminds.org/) or the *Good Start, Grow Smart* developed at the Center on the Social and Emotional Foundations for Early Learning (http://csefel.vanderbilt.edu/powerpoints/miniconf1.html) or programs embedded in the *Creative Curriculum*™ and High Scope® Preschool Curriculum, as well as locally developed curricula. Such programs help children to understand themselves and others, as well as how to function in a formal group situation. Thus, the social-emotional skills developed link directly to the social studies subject area of civics.

Beginning in formal school situations, at kindergarten and beyond where children are called upon to work collaboratively, they will need to develop a vocabulary of problem-solving for academic situations as well as in interpersonal class relationships. Such practices teach children the roots of citizenship and civic engagement. In this way teachers "create environments that respect and harness both pluralism and individualism while adopting instructional practices that promote civic agency, critical inquiry, and participatory experiences" (Rebell, 2018, p. 19). Examples of words children say are shown in Textbox 3.3, Children Solving Problems.

TEXTBOX 3.3
Children Solving Problems

* What if I tried it this way? Well, that doesn't work, maybe this way?
* That doesn't make sense.
* I don't understand how you got there. Can you explain it more?
* Well, actually, you are wrong here . . . it should be this way . . .
* How should I start?
* How can we show this?
* We can draw this to show our thinking.
* I think the way to search for this answer is . . .
* I wonder what would happen if . . .
* Is this information really important for our project?
* Is there another way to do this?
* If you have it first, may I have it next?
* What if we take a break?

This vocabulary is critical for children who are working together to begin an investigation using the principles of the Inquiry Arc. The vocabulary might be highlighted by discussion at the beginning of an investigation and then posted for all to see.

But young children do not develop these skills all at once or even in kindergarten. For adults, as well, the very concept of citizenship is fraught with the politicization, pointedly in recent years, of issues related to immigration and those who have historically been included or excluded from citizenship and the full rights thereof. Young children living in today's world experience this politicization in varying ways, depending on where they live and their exposure to social and news media. Thus, the notion of citizen action in the school environment will be influenced as well. For example, young children living in neighborhoods with immigrants may be intimately familiar with neighbors and family members dealing with ICE and the civic action occurring in their communities, such as marches and sanctuary churches.

Meanwhile, children in rural environments may be more familiar with issues regarding the placement of windmills on farms leading to neighbor not speaking to neighbor. And those living in areas facing fire danger will be aware of arguments about forest vs. suburban growth. Families who own small stores will be engaged in issues regarding big box store price cuts on goods and services. Whether families and communities are engaged in civic action—letter writing, running for office, marching, etc.—will vary in communities. Nevertheless, citizenship action, engagement or inaction will be part of the lived experiences children bring to their understanding of what it means to be a citizen and thus must be addressed in our social studies plans.

To guide our thinking as we plan curriculum, the goals advocated by the NCSS for Civics are grounded in beliefs of a democratic notion of our society. These standards, established in 2011, reflect our understandings of the United States society, based on the views of many in leadership positions across the nation at the time. As we know now, the view of those leaders may not reflect behavioral expectations regarding citizenship of everyone, because the issues and beliefs are complicated and diverse. In recent years, the ideal of citizenship is increasingly politicized.

So, however our democratic society should be functioning, as teachers, we must be aware of the issues in communities we serve while striving to prepare young children for effective participation in the society of their futures. Sometimes this work will be uncomfortable based on the lived experiences forming our own knowledge of "appropriate" citizenship behavior. Does it mean only picking up litter? Does it mean letter writing about the proposed dog park bringing more concrete to your urban environment? Does it mean marching in the street? Our own experiences will influence our thinking and plans. However, we are being called upon to be advocates for an improved society with real respect for all our peoples. So, for the moment, let's prepare them for the action articulated by Rep. John Lewis, a giant in the Civil Rights movement, who said in a tweet in 2018,

> Do not get lost in a sea of despair. Be hopeful, be optimistic. Our struggle is not the struggle of a day, a week, a month, or a year, it is the struggle of a lifetime. Never, ever be afraid to make some noise and get in good trouble, necessary trouble.

With the project approach to curriculum development for the social studies, the citizenship skills can be woven into the content-based state and local standards so that children can learn how to demonstrate civic engagement, which occurs "when they maintain, strengthen, and improve communities and societies. Thus, civics, part two of the C3 Framework, is, in part, the study of how people participate in governing society" (Swan, Grant & Lee, 2013, p. 31). Often, children's literature can bring the issues to mind in a way that all learners can access them. For through stories, children can externalize the conversation so that they do not feel pitted against each other in debates and they can be protected with views that may be divergent. Expectations for young children by grade two (Swan, Grant & Lee, 2013) include the capacity to describe roles and responsibilities of authority figures; explanations of why we have rules; why equality, fairness, and respect for authority are important; and the capacity to compare diverse viewpoints. For the social studies curriculum in the early years, our projects are grounded in helping young children to learn respect for each other while conforming to the conventions of school culture and rules.

Conclusion

Setting the stage for the development of respect and classroom citizenship begins with the baseline we establish each year with the children before us. We incorporate and advance their funds of knowledge, collaborate with their families, and identify meaningful social studies actions for the particular communities we serve. Examples of recent projects may begin with such questions as "Why are people marching?" (Ferreras-Stone & Demoiny, 2019). This question was examined to go beyond particular events to describe the many picture books showing the history of political protests through marches, linking the idea to the lived experiences of children.

Contemporary issues may also arise from children's personal experience, along with a need for them to investigate and elaborate on their understanding of big picture issues. The question "Why does my grandmother not want to go to the doctor?" may relate to the loss of health insurance, job loss, or other contemporary issues. The project will evolve with attention to local and state curricular standards and offer many avenues for investigation related not only to civic action but also perhaps to economic understandings.

Projects emerging from our communities and the children we serve may come from issues children are facing on the playground or in their neighborhood, such as bullying, which is often a behavior unknown to teachers and families initially. The project can evolve from an issue to meet the goals of understanding power and authority.

Natural disasters such as floods, hurricanes, fires, etc., often pique child interest and can lead to problem-solving across the curriculum and thoughtful investigation by children, suited to their age, experience, and funds of knowledge. The point is social studies education and particularly civic engagement studied from a project-learning perspective should be an important, living, breathing part of our curriculum for young children.

The key is choosing projects relevant to the community you serve linked to the standards in your state and relating them back to civic engagement skills. In this way, you prepare children for collaborative learning and action-oriented citizenship.

Activities in the Field

1. Plan to visit a preschool program while the class is engaged in a social studies activity. Write a report to describe the philosophy guiding the program. In your report, describe the baseline as it is working. That is, how does the class function with all of the elements of the class structure? Ask the teacher how she implements social studies during the year. Talk to the children about what they are doing. Include the teacher interview and summary of the child conversations in your report.
2. Plan a visit to a primary classroom in a public school. Review the social studies state standards for the grade level you will visit. Write a report to describe the philosophy guiding the program. In your report, describe the baseline as it is working. That is, how does the class function with all of the elements of the

class structure. Ask the teacher how she implements social studies during the year. Talk to the children about what they are doing. Include the teacher interview and summary of the child conversations in your report.

Activities in the Library

1. At the library look at recent issues of *Social Studies and the Young Learner, Young Children*, and *Childhood Education: Innovations*. Make a file of five to ten ideas for social studies learning in a grade level of your choice. Be sure to include complete reference details for each idea, so you can share with classmates and find the details again when you are teaching.
2. Visit a commercial bookstore website. Identify children's books proposed for a topic of your choice. Determine whether these books meet developmentally appropriate practice principles. Then, visit the websites for National Council for Social Studies and National Association for the Education of Young Children. Which additional books for classroom social studies might you find here?

Study Questions

1. When planning a curriculum, what must every teacher consider as a baseline for implementation of goals?
2. Where does understanding by design and big ideas fit in your development of a social studies curriculum?
3. At the preschool level, what roles do curricular models contribute to planning?
4. In the K–3 level, how do state standards influence planning in public schools?
5. How will you use the concepts of funds of knowledge, the Inquiry Arc, and the documentation panel in planning for social studies?
6. How will you use the concepts of emergent curriculum, documentation panel, and project-based learning to guide your practice?
7. What role do class meetings play in the development of the C3 Framework, citizenship, and civic action?

Reflect and Reread

1. Why is the concept of funds of knowledge critical in creating developmentally appropriate practice in early childhood programs?
2. How can you responsibly address contemporary social issues with young children in an appropriate and responsive way?

Suggested Readings

Beneke, S. J., Ostosky, M. M., & Katz, L. G. (2019). *The project approach for all learners: A hands-on guide for inclusive early childhood classrooms*. Baltimore, MD: Brookes Publishing.

Colker, L. J., & Koralek, D. (2019). *Making lemonade: Teaching children to think optimistically*. St. Paul, MN: Red Leaf Press.

Derman-Sparks, L., & Edwards, J. O. (2020). *Antibias education for young children and ourselves*. Washington, D.C.: National Association for the Education of Young Children.

Edwards, C., Gandini, L., & Forman, G. (2011). *The hundred languages of children: The Reggio Emilia approach—advanced reflections*, 3rd edition. Greenwich, CT: Ablex.

Lev, S., Clark, A., & Starkey, E. (2020). *Implementing project based learning in early childhood: Overcoming misconceptions and reaching success.* New York: Routledge.

Responsive Classroom. (2016). *The joyful classroom: Practical ways to Engage Elementary students.* Turner Falls, MA: Center for Responsive Schools, Inc.

Sadker, D. M., & Zittleman, K. R. (2016). Chapter 5 The multicultural history of American education. In *Teachers, schools, and society*, 4th edition. New York: McGraw Hill Education.

Websites for Additional Information

Animoto https://animoto.com/

Capzles https://sites.google.com/site/technoforteachers/capzles

Common Sense Media https://www.commonsensemedia.org/

Fred Rogers Center Digital Media https://www.fredrogerscenter.org/what-we-do/digital-media-learning/

Historypin https://www.historypin.org/en/

Learning for Justice https://www.learningforjustice.org/

Learning.xprize.org https://learning.xprize.org/prizes/global-learning

Learnz http://www.learnz.org.nz/

Prezi https://prezi.com

Sharing Your Learning https://www.shareyourlearning.org/

Technology in Early Childhood https://www.erikson.edu/professional-development/tec-center/

Visual.ly https://visual.ly

Wordle http://www.wordle.net

Chapter 4

Children's Literature for Children's Social Studies

Marie Ann Donovan, Ed.D.

> There are many little ways to enlarge your child's world. Love of books is the best of all.
>
> —*Jacqueline Kennedy*

TERMS TO KNOW

classroom library curation

global literature

interculturalism

mirror books

multicultural literature

sliding glass door books

springboard books

window books

Overview

Our PreK–3 classrooms are busy places of talking, drawing, moving, singing, reading, writing, and listening. (This is the short list.) We design them as spaces where children feel comfortable exploring who and how they are, how they came to be, and where they might go. We anchor our social studies curriculum in fostering children's understanding of what it means to live in a democratic society. This work is complex—for us as teachers, not only the children. Thankfully, to help us do this work we have children's authors and illustrators whose books ask deep life questions embedded in the social studies. These books pull children—and us adults—into worlds we could and couldn't imagine on our own. We read them to see ourselves more clearly, as well as others.

Finding books that both resonate with children and enhance our social studies teaching isn't as straightforward as it may seem, despite how many "recommended" social studies book lists abound in cyberspace. It's because of how relatively individualized our social studies teaching actually is, based upon where we teach, whom we teach, and when. Young children are a fascinating amalgam of curiosity and natural self-absorption. We know that if we aim to teach them about long ago, or how people are interdependent, we must somehow connect these people and concepts to what's familiar, or at least to what's recognizable to them. This is where children's literature comes in: it fills the interstitial gap between what the young child experiences daily with what all young children need to understand and feel, so they can begin self-determining their future. For many professionals, the children's literature they choose—print or digital—forms the backbone of their social studies teaching. This chapter guides you in learning how to make those selections knowledgeably, feeling secure that all your books, including titles set aside exclusively for social studies instruction, enable students to access the world while at school.

Focus Questions

1. How do teachers know which books are appropriate for the social studies curricula?
2. Who publishes children's books relevant to the social studies?
3. Who are the current, leading authors of children's books with relevant social studies themes and researched topics?
4. How do you find quality multicultural and global titles that support the social studies?
5. Which titles are good "starters" for building an early childhood social studies collection?

How Do Teachers Know Which Books Are Appropriate for the Social Studies Curricula?

Incorporating children's books into our social studies teaching requires **curation**—careful, weighted selection. We must know our students individually and our curriculum content fully if we're to find, choose, and match books with children and intended learning goals. Social studies curricula are broad in scope and rich in exploration possibilities. Given that, it's overwhelming to think about starting a social studies book collection—yet we must. Books are vehicles not only for ideas but for the children themselves. We want our students to travel—within and beyond what they already know. Through the social studies, we teach children to envision their tomorrow by examining yesterday and today. Quality children's literature has the power to transport children into other places and times, so they can meet the people who will inform their envisionment of how to live with meaning and purpose.

Over 10,000 different children's books are published annually in North America alone. It's impossible to keep up with them all. Not all books are created equal, however. We require a way to sift through titles not only for quality but relevance. As early childhood teachers, we begin this sifting process by considering our students and their learning needs:

- Which books might serve best as **mirrors** for children, ways of seeing themselves and their experiences represented in published works, so they'll know they're not alone? (Sims Bishop, 1990).
- Which books might serve best as **windows** and **sliding glass doors** for children, ways to see others and situations they don't know or won't ever experience personally, so they can step toward embracing the world beyond themselves? (Sims Bishop, 1990).
- Which books might serve best as **springboards** for our classroom community's ongoing discussions and deliberations, so they'll be sparked to think about matters that *matter*? (Donovan, 2020).

You, the teacher, are the ultimate determiner of which books can serve in these ways—that's the curation aspect of our teaching practices. You know your students and your curriculum. Curation starts with knowing where to turn for critical advice and specific recommendations. There are experts to guide you—professionals and organizations devoted to discovering the highest-quality literature that will resonate with you, your students, and your curriculum. The following tables organize where to locate these experts.

Table 4.1 is a representative list of children's book awards and medals bestowed annually upon high-quality books whose topics and themes are relevant to social studies curricula. The more popular or known awards are not included (e.g., Caldecott, Newbery Medals) because their judging criteria do not exclusively focus on

TABLE 4.1   Young Children's American Book Awards Relevant to Social Studies Curriculum

American Indian Youth Literature Award (Native American culture, history, experience)

Asian/Pacific American Award for Literature (Asian/Pacific Islander American culture, history, experience)

Bank Street Best Children's Books of the Year (nonstereotypical treatment of ethnic and religious differences)

Carter G. Woodson Book Awards (American Library Association and NCSS; respectful depictions of ethnicity, race relations)

Children's Book Council Children's Choice Book Awards (selected by children; students can be sponsored to serve as judges)

Coretta Scott King Book Awards (African American lives and culture, universal human values)

Ezra Jack Keats Awards (positive depictions of multicultural family life, children's strengths, and resilience)

Jane Addams Children's Book Awards (equality, peace, global communities)

Middle East Book Award (Middle East Outreach Council; meaningful contributions to understanding the Middle East)

New York Historical Society Children's History Book Prize

Notable Books for a Global Society (International Literacy Association; promoting understanding and appreciation of the world's cultures, racial and ethnic groups)

Notable Social Studies Trade Books (co-sponsored by the Children's Book Council and NCSS; multicultural experiences, history, interdependence among peoples)

Parents' Choice Awards (honoring children's intelligence, social-emotional and ethical growth)

Pura Belpré Award (Latinx lives, culture, history)

Rise, a Feminist Book Project for Ages 0–18 of the American Library Association (formerly the Molly Bloomer Award)

Robert F. Sibert Informational Book Medal

Schneider Family Book Award (disability experiences)

Skipping Stones Book Awards (multicultural and global books promoting respect and awareness of multiple perspectives)

South Asia Book Awards (South Asia National Outreach Council; positive portrayals of South Asia/Asians living abroad, at home)

Stonewall Book Award (LGBTQIA+ experience, history)

Sydney Taylor Book Awards (Jewish experience, history)

Tomàs Rivera Mexican American Children's Book Award

social studies. Each award listed in the table has a website where you can review the judging criteria, nominated titles, and winning books. Get into the practice of scanning their annual nominee lists for relevant titles worth your consideration. Check with your local public or school librarian to secure review copies of ones that might fit into your master collection. Many states sponsor their own children's book awards and medals (e.g., Connecticut Nutmeg Children's Book Award, Hawaii Nene Award, Illinois Rebecca Caudill Young Readers' Book Award, Texas Bluebonnet Awards), typically judged by students, teachers, and librarians. Their websites explain how you and your students can become involved in their award committees, as a way to extend the social studies inquiry you conduct in your classroom.

Who Publishes Children's Books Relevant to the Social Studies?

A number of large as well as smaller, independent publishers specialize in producing and promoting social studies–related books for young children. Table 4.2 provides a representative sample of these publishers, all of which are commonly distributed to bookstores (online, bricks-and-mortar) as well as public and school libraries. Most publishers and/or their distributors offer free, downloadable teacher's guides, video supports, and lesson or activity plans for their social studies titles. Many also sponsor author or illustrator webinars and appearances at school events, for little or no fee. Sign up for their no-cost e-newsletters, blogs, and catalogues through their websites. Establish a routine of putting your feet up after school and browsing through their latest titles. Reviewing new books is one way to refine how you personally conceptualize the big ideas of the social studies, not only how you teach them to children. Authors and illustrators conduct significant research in preparing their books. Editors in publishing houses do the same. Let their works guide you in learning more about your curriculum.

TABLE 4.2 American Publishers of Young Children's Literature Relevant to Social Studies Curriculum

Abrams/Appleseed	Dial Press	Little Bee Books	Running Press Kids
Albert Whitman	DK	Little Brown	Scholastic
Astra/Boyd Mills & Kane	Eerdmans Books	Macmillan	Simon & Schuster
Barefoot Books	Enchanted Lion	Marshall Cavendish	Sourcebooks
Bloomsbury	Harper Collins	Papercutz (graphic novels)	Toon Books (comics, graphic novels)
Candlewick Press	Henry Holt	Peachtree	
Charlesbridge	Kids Can Press	Penguin/Random House	
Creston Books	Lee & Low Books		

Who Are the Current, Leading Authors of Children's Books With Relevant Social Studies Themes and Thoroughly Researched Topics?

There are many children's authors who are passionate about creating books with social studies themes or topics. Table 4.3 includes authors who recently received

TABLE 4.3 Social Studies–Focused Authors for Young Children

Kwame Alexander	Candace Fleming	Andrea Davis Pinkney and Brian Pinkney	Duncan Tonatiuh
Jennifer Armstrong	Russell Freedman		Padma Venkatraman
Andrea Beaty	Deborah Hopkinson	Doreen Rappaport	Sally M. Walker
Ashley Bryan	Thao Lam	Barb Rosenstock	Alicia D. Williams
Jen Bryant	Patricia McKissack	Suzanne Slade	Jacqueline Woodson
Margarita Engle	Meg Medina	Diane Stanley	
Paul Fleischman	Kadir Nelson		

nominations and awards for their books. You might not recognize all these names. Become acquainted by reading their latest works. Ask your school or local public children's librarian for help in discovering these newer authors and others like them. Maintaining currency in your book collection is key. Perspectives on the social studies change with each generation. Moreover, authors' approaches to how they treat or write about a topic, historical event, or social issue change with time and new research findings. While it's not bad practice to share the classic titles you loved when young, you need to introduce students to the people writing for them today. In doing so, you'll find your students engage more with the texts—and you'll have more springboard books to rely upon in your unit planning.

Publishers are increasingly developing book series targeted to history and other social studies themes. Series appeal to teachers because of their consistent formats and range of related topics or historical figures portrayed. Publishers often discount series sets, which adds to their classroom or library value. Students turn to series much like they do movie franchises: they want to know what's next in a character's story arc, learn more in detail about a time in history, or explore another corner of the world. All the series in table 4.4 were recognized for their accuracy and appropriateness for school—though you'll still need to review individual titles to ensure they align with your community's standards. Advanced readers in the primary grades will be especially attracted to these particular series. Some of the series lend themselves to reading aloud, too. In response to increased sales and award trends, publishing industry executives plan to issue more social studies series for younger children. Presently, most are written for later-elementary and middle-school-age students.

How Do You Find Quality Multicultural and Global Titles That Support the Social Studies?

We are a nation of immigrants, from our founding to our present day. Numerous, various cultural groups live within our borders, some with longer settlement histories than others. The story of our country includes the story of all these groups. **Multicultural children's literature** is a term used to describe, in part, books portraying the experiences of people living in the United States whose stories and cultural perspectives have been marginated or otherwise not routinely and authentically

TABLE 4.4 Social Studies–Focused Book Series for Young Children

Corpse Talk—These "interviews" with famous and significant scientists, women, and monarchs, told in comic/graphic novel form with child humor, appeal to young and old alike. (Penguin Random House/DK)

DK Life Stories—Biographies about famous and fascinating people in history (e.g., DaVinci, Gandhi, Mandela), chock full of illustrations, photographs, timelines, and other nonfiction elements that support unit plan development as well as individual enjoyment by avid and reluctant readers. (Penguin Random House/DK)

Good Night Stories for Rebel Girls—This anthology series, connected to podcasts and chapter books, showcases remarkable achievements of historical and contemporary women (e.g., Cleopatra, Curie, Lovelace, Kahlo, Bader Ginsburg, Rihanna) and how they're positive role models for the next generation. The company's website contains lesson and activity plans for classroom adaptation of the individual stories as well as the chapter books. (Rebel Girls)

History Comics—This nonfiction series in graphic novel format teaches children about periods and events in America's history (e.g., the Roanoke Colony, the introduction of wild mustangs to America, the loss of the Challenger shuttle, the Great Chicago Fire) that deserve but don't receive in-depth exploration and discussion in lower-elementary classrooms. (Macmillan/First Second)

I Survived—These historical-fiction chapter books are narrated by children who navigate historical disasters (e.g., American Revolution, sinking of the Titanic, Pearl Harbor, 9/11, Hurricane Katrina) with resilience and leadership in their communities. The publisher's website offers lesson and unit plans, with student resources and relevant videos. (Scholastic)

Jobs People Do: A Day in the Life of a . . .—Perfect for early readers, this series introduces children to a cross-sector of community roles and responsibilities (e.g., teacher, builder, police officer, firefighter) through photographs featuring diverse people and decodable text explanations. (Penguin Random House/DK)

She Persisted—An "unexpected" series from Chelsea Clinton that naturally grew from her initial, award-winning anthology, *She Persisted: 13 American Women Who Changed the World*. Titles include biographies of Sally Ride, Claudette Colvin, Virginia Apgar, and Harriet Tubman, as well as sports figure compilations. (Penguin Random House)

reflected in mainstream literature (Yokota, 2001). In more recent years, this term's definition is evolving to refer to all people whose linguistic, racial, ethnic, class, sexual orientation, and/or gender identities are not widely depicted in the children's literature published by companies marketing to schools, libraries, and bookstores. **Global children's literature** is books set in and featuring people and how they live in parts of the world outside the United States. These two book types are distinct yet related: titles from both types should be selected to serve as mirrors (Sims Bishop, 1990) for children in your classroom. Teachers also need to select titles from each type that will open windows (Sims Bishop, 1990) for children, so they can learn about people and places they do not know both here in the United States (multicultural) and elsewhere (global). Both types, when crafted authentically and well, should bring children through Sims Bishop's (1990) sliding glass door and into diverse worlds where they meet others who share their humanity.

The dearth of quality and sufficient quantities of **multicultural** and **global literature** presently limits teachers' capacity to find springboard books (Donovan, 2020) for students' personal research and for anchoring social studies units. This is especially unfortunate when you consider educators' twenty-first-century need to foster **interculturalism,** a disposition toward actively working to live *in* diversity, not merely *with* it (Antonsich, 2016). Educators, librarians, booksellers, and publishers are galvanizing around changing this landscape, however. In 2015, Jason Low, one of the owners of the leading American multicultural children's publisher, Lee & Low, unsettled his industry by conducting a study (Lee & Low Books, 2016) of staff diversity in American publishing companies. Low found the overwhelming majority of employees self-identified as White, female, straight, and non-disabled (the main categories of the survey)—proportional to the nature of the content in books issued within ten years of the survey. A subsequent survey in 2019 (Lee & Low Books, 2020) obtained very similar results. Low argues (Lee & Low Books, 2020) that until the publishing industry diversifies its staff and openly commits to publishing works by new, BIPOC authors and illustrators sharing their lived lives, nothing will change: children living in marginated communities will continue not to see themselves authentically represented in the literature adults select for them, in and out of school.

There are signs that "some" change across the industry is happening. Low's revelations about the employees' Whiteness appeared around the same time that organizations pushing to diversify the industry and its titles, such as We Need Diverse Books (United States) and Inclusive Minds (United Kingdom), were gaining hold and influencing the general public about the historic underrepresentation of certain people in children's literature. More booksellers and public as well as school librarians, along with teachers, are pushing for change in the industry, using tools such as the Diverse Book Finder (see table 4.5) to critique their holdings, identify gaps, and hold publishers accountable. While the percentage of books featuring BIPOC characters, topics, and themes continues to trail those with White protagonists (and even characters such as robots, talking rabbits), there is a widespread sense that within the 2020 decade, the landscape will shift and appear more inclusive (Templeton, 2019).

Table 4.5 lists the foremost companies and organizations dedicated to issuing, promoting, and researching multicultural and global children's literature. They all support teachers in learning how to detect quality in these books, and how to use them as mirrors, windows, sliding glass doors, and springboards. They also guide you in looking critically at the books in your current collection to determine which need replacing with titles representing all the children you teach.

Which Titles Are Good "Starters" for Building an Early Childhood Social Studies Collection?

The titles in the lists below were selected to inspire you to start your **library curation** effort. Remember: this is an ongoing process. Don't be afraid to remove a book from your existing collection if it doesn't serve in at least one of the three ways outlined above (i.e., mirrors, windows/sliders, springboards). Add titles that replace ones whose datedness or narrowness won't be relevant to your current students and/or support the weight of meaty discussions and thoughtful responses to what they contain. Ask a school or local public librarian for help in finding books within your budget. Investigate which titles can be purchased in electronic formats

TABLE 4.5 **Multicultural and Global Children's Book Sources**

Companies Supporting the Distribution of Multicultural and Global Literature for Children

Child's Play

This publisher, based in the United Kingdom but with offices and distributors here in the United States, sells not only books but also games, toys, and instructional materials that are either multicultural or global in design and content. Many of its products have won awards for their authenticity, inclusionary content, and developmental appropriateness.

(http://www.childs-play.com/usa/home-page.html)

Curious City: Children's Book Engagement Tools

Curious City is a company founded by a former children's bookseller and publishing industry sales representative, Kirsten Cappy. It's a boon to early childhood educators and parents searching for the latest children's titles and project-based ways to engage children in them. You can search the site by topic or theme (e.g., African American, allyship, early childhood, community service, cross-group friendship, immigrants and refugees, resistance and resilience, social action) or by book title. There are downloadable lesson and project ideas included for the books listed. Cappy also established a nonprofit dedicated to disseminating books about refugees and immigrants as a way for schools and communities to welcome them: I'm Your Neighbor Books—see below.

(https://www.curiouscitydpw.com/about-2/)

Lee & Low Books

Although there are many publishers that feature multicultural books among their offerings, Lee & Low Books was the first established upon the premise that children need access to high-quality titles depicting real-life, everyday people from all cultural groups. In their almost thirty years, this company hasn't wavered in its commitment to exclusively producing multicultural books. In addition to the library and trade books it publishes, more recently Lee & Low developed a guided reading series, along with expanding their titles in Spanish and English, as well as Spanish alone. You'll find numerous, free downloadable lesson and unit plans for their books, along with a resourceful blog for teachers, on their website.

(https://www.leeandlow.com/)

Organizations

Cooperative Children's Book Center (CCBC), University of Wisconsin-Madison

There's no place as comprehensive as the CCBC for learning about children's and young adult literature. Housed in the University's School of Education, the Center's staff are librarians and researchers devoted to critically examining all books published in the United States for infants through high schoolers. Their annual research study of diversity in children's books is the go-to source for measuring publishers' commitment to issuing more multicultural and global books. Their Recommended Book Search tool makes it simple and fast to find the books you need, as well as to read nonpartisan reviews of them to guide your selection process. Their Intellectual Freedom Information Services Division's librarians support educators facing censorship challenges to the books they incorporate into their curricula and libraries, a growing concern as schools adopt a broader range of multicultural and global titles.

(https://ccbc.education.wisc.edu/)

Diverse Book Finder

This ambitious project, started in 2002 by a group of college professors, authors, illustrators, and graduate students to catalog picture books featuring BIPOC characters and themes, continues to grow in depth, sophistication, and utility with time. What makes this project unique is its approach to classifying diverse books: rather than examining the titles merely for "who" is represented (e.g., First/Native Nations, Latinx/Hispanic/Latin American, Black/African/African American), they're also cataloging "how" each racial/cultural group is depicted (e.g., cross-group relationships across difference; folklore; incidental characters; biography; oppression and resilience) plus the message that depiction conveys to the young reader. Their collection is vast but easily searched. Keep in mind that the inclusion of a book does not mean it's recommended. Periodically, the staff do highlight certain titles they think more worthy of teachers' consideration, mostly for their quality. This site is an invaluable resource for all early childhood educators since it focuses exclusively on picture books and constantly leads us to ponder how "diversity" is defined today, given how historically, it's been measured in relationship to Whiteness. Note: you can borrow their books through the WorldCat interlibrary loan program, which is offered through most universities and many public libraries in the United States.

(https://diversebookfinder.org/)

I'm Your Neighbor Books

Kirsten Cappy's nonprofit organization, I'm Your Neighbor Books, provides both in-person and online supports for using books (mostly published in the United States) about the experiences of new immigrants and refugees. The site catalogues books by theme (e.g., adoption, child soldiers, citizenship, detention, generational differences) and immigrant community (e.g., Bengali, Congolese, Ethiopian, Ivorian, Korean, Vietnamese). For a small donation, they'll send you a searchable database of categorized titles along with templates for printing stickers that indicate the titles are part of their researched immigration collection, which you can affix to your own copies of the books they recommend. You also can rent their collection for use in a school or public library, community center, or place of worship as a stand-alone resource for focused programs about immigration that you create. All titles in the collection serve especially well as sliding glass door and springboard books. (https://imyourneighborbooks.org/)

International Board on Books for Young People (IBBY)

A simple way to globalize your children's bookshelf (i.e., those that portray people outside the United States living in their communities) is to include some of IBBY's Hans Christian Andersen Award winners. As with other awards, these books received positive, critical reviews based on their developmental appropriateness and cultural authenticity. IBBY also sponsors the Toronto Public Library's Collection of Books for Young People with Disabilities, another list of global titles to consider in enhancing and extending your global collection. In 2012, IBBY began developing their Silent Books Collection of Wordless Picture Books published in twenty different countries, for use in refugee and displaced persons camps on Lampedusa, an Italian island in the Mediterranean Sea. You can access the list through IBBY's website, along with tips for using them with multilingual children. Most titles are available through school book distributors and Amazon. (https://www.usbby.org/ibby.html)

Tandem: Partners in Early Learning

This San Francisco–based community organization offers underserved families the education and resources they need to prepare their children for kindergarten. Their connected programs are built upon the belief that by working with families' strengths and assets, and teaching them how to foster their young children's literacies, all will thrive. Their Learning at Home resources—Storytime Videos and Activity Guides—include video read-alouds of numerous multicultural and global books by native speakers of diverse languages (e.g., Vietnamese, Tagalog, Spanish, Arabic). (https://www.tandembayarea.org/resources-2/learning-at-home/)

Words of Words (WOW): Center of Global Literacies and Literature, University of Arizona-Tucson

WOW's mission is to establish an international network of like-minded professionals dedicated to understanding, critiquing, and sharing global literature for children and youth. You can read their research journals for no cost on their website, and learn how to adopt global books to your curriculum. Download their free lists of K–12 global literature correlated to Common Core standards. Each title's text complexity measures (in Lexiles and guided reading A–Z) are included, along with resources for using them in classroom and library programs. WOW circulates Language and Culture Book Kits, along with Global Story Boxes, to teachers in the Tucson, Arizona, area. If you're not local, you can download the instructional resources and the kit's/box's book list for free. Each kit or box serves as an integrated curriculum unit. (https://wowlit.org/)

(i.e., ebooks, audiobooks). With newer titles, electronic versions sometimes can be less expensive. After a book reaches its initial hardcover or epub sales goals, some publishers contract their popular titles for inclusion on independent electronic book applications used in schools and homes (e.g., Epic Books). You can readily search for social studies-related titles by age/grade level on them, too—a good timesaver.

The picture book titles below are organized according to the four disciplinary concepts of the social studies—civics and government, economics, geography, and history. Each section is ordered whereby those at the beginning of the list are appropriate to use with younger children (i.e., preschool and kindergarten). Those appearing later are for older children (i.e., grades 1–3) or more advanced readers. Some titles might be read-alouds or used during other teacher-scaffolded experiences, rather than recommended for individual reading. All were chosen to give you a sense of the breadth of the literature now available for invigorating your social studies teaching. If you're wondering whether a title is available in electronic format, check the publisher's website or ask a librarian. Publishers constantly issue new digital versions for their school and library markets. Amazon and other online booksellers might not offer these versions, so they aren't always very accurate catalogues for us who rely upon books for teaching.

All listed titles received positive, researched critiques of their developmental appropriateness and value for children. These books are not part of any published social studies textbook programs, though some textbook publishers might recommend them for use or offer them as supplementary books for their curricula. All titles are available in English. Translations into other languages may be available—check with a librarian, bookseller, or distributor, or search on your own. As you build your collection, demand that publishers issue more titles in languages other than English. When teachers show there's a market, publishers respond.

Books Related to Four Social Studies Disciplines

Civics and Government

Democracy for Dinosaurs: A Guide for Young Citizens (2020) Laurie Krasny Brown, illus. Marc Brown, Little Brown.

As the title suggests, this nonfiction guide uses dinosaurs to model how it looks to live core values necessary to maintain a healthy democratic society—freedom, equality, respect for free speech, truthfulness, and fairness. You might recognize the illustrator of this book—Marc Brown, creator of the *Arthur the Aardvark* book series and PBS television show for children.

Equality's Call: The Story of Voting Rights in America (2020) Deborah Diesen, illus. Magdalena Mora, Beach Lane Books.

The lyrical rhyme scheme ("A right isn't right / Till it's granted to all.") and intriguing, textured illustrations add poignancy to the sad facts explained in this book: across America's history, not all people were guaranteed the right to vote until they fought, sacrificed, and eventually changed the law. Despite its serious topic, readers will appreciate the lessons, not only the message, condensed in this book. Backmatter resources add detail and references for use in developing instructional units anchored by this book.

Sofia Valdez, Future Prez (2019) Andrea Beaty, illus. David Roberts, Abrams.

Sofia takes matters into her own hands when a local landfill becomes a dangerous eyesore. Despite being told by city hall officials and others that her idea to turn the landfill into a park won't work, she plucks up her courage, becomes a community organizer, and gets it done.

A Small History of Disagreement (2020) Claudio Fuentes, illus. Gabriela Lyon, trans. Elisa Amado, Greystone Kids.

Chilean elementary students return to school after holiday break to find construction equipment ready to cut down a beloved, old tree to make room for new STEM classrooms. The school becomes divided over the plan. Protests, fights, and even a student strike break out. As tension builds, a teacher suggests they debate and then vote to settle the disagreement. Readers and listeners alike will be captivated by how the children plan arguments, listen to one another, and eventually collaborate to reach an acceptable solution. This global book is a fine example of how social studies inquiry can be turned into action, written in child-friendly language.

Economics

Money Monsters: The Missing Money (2019) Okeoma Moronu Schreiner, illus. Sandhya Prabhat, FinKidLit.

Kai's imagination gets the best of him after depositing his monetary Chinese New Year's gifts into his parents' bank. Fretting an ATM monster is eating his money, he develops an elaborate, superhero-assisted plan to get it back. When his parents realize his confusion, they patiently explain how banks work (including how he can track his interest). Brightly colored illustrations add detail and necessary emphasis to the explanations. Backmatter resources such as questions and prompts for adults to pose during and after reading are designed to expand children's understanding of how banks are an essential service in all communities.

We Are Water Protectors (2020) Carole Lindstrom, illus. Michaela Goade, Macmillan/Roaring Brook.

This award-winning book will be a solid springboard for discussions about humans' interdependence with natural resources. Through an old tale related by a young Native girl, vibrantly illustrated in jewel tones that dramatize light and dark moods, readers are spurred to think about their responsibility as "stewards of the Earth," weighing the costs of exploiting these resources for profit and short-term economic gain. The author's notes and glossary provide ample background on the Water Protector movement whose members continue protesting the Dakota Access oil pipeline in North Dakota. The publisher's website features free, downloadable economics and geography unit plan ideas and activities for ages three to eight years, including a Water Protector pledge suitable for classroom use as part of an integrated environmental studies unit.

A Different Pond (2017) Bao Phi, illus. Thi Bui, Capstone.

Based on memories from his refugee childhood, author Bao Phi recollects the predawn fishing trips he made with his father to catch the family's main food, returning home in time for his father to leave for work. Scenes of the extended family enjoying the fish and each other, along with poignant exchanges between the father and son about life in Vietnam before emigrating, make this a perfect springboard book for discussing not only sacrifice and scarcity, as well as resourcefulness, but also family and family values.

Rock, Brock, and the Savings Shock (2017) Sheila Bair, illus. Barry Gott, Albert Whitman.

Twin brothers Brock and Rock learn quite different yet equally important lessons about saving when they independently handle their weekly allowances from their grandfather. The appendix tables on how interest is compounded will appeal to second and third graders (and the adults in their lives), whereas the rhyming main storyline will charm even younger listeners, driving home the critical concepts of saving for tomorrow by differentiating today between wants and needs.

Geography

A Gift for Amma: Market Day in India (2020) Meera Sriram, illus. Mariona Cabassa, Barefoot Books.

Set in a street market of southern India, we stroll from stall to stall as a young girl tries to find the perfect gift for her mother (amma) among the colorful array of vendors' offerings—fabrics, spices, kebabs, flowers, and more. The sounds of the market feature as prominently as its sights, drawing students in to join the search and weigh the numerous options. An informative backmatter section explains the wares and how they're used in Indian homes. It also describes other types of street markets around the globe, and how they feature locally grown and crafted products. When shared with other popular books about markets (e.g., Ted Lewin's *Market!*), this title would fit a glaring gap in "market" books for young children: depictions of South Asian communities.

No Place Like Home (2019) Ronojoy Ghosh, Eerdmans Books for Young Readers.

Grumpy, short-tempered polar bear George is on a quest to find the "right" home after living in a city that feels like it's closing in on him. He ventures across topographies in search of where he belongs—jungle, mountaintop, desert, and then (finally) cold ocean water. As he rows he discovers a brilliant, white landscape of ice and snow—the perfect place to settle down and make new friends (e.g., penguins). Knowing you're where you belong brings an inner peace that shows on your face and in your actions.

La Frontéra: My Journey with Papa (2018) Deborah Mills and Alfredo Alva, illus. Claudia Navarro, Barefoot Books.

Based on the emigration experience of coauthor Alfredo Alva in the mid-1980s, this bilingual (Spanish and English) picture book portrays the bravery, courage, and perseverance needed to journey from Mexico, cross the US border (*la frontera*), and settle into a new world and new life while longing for home. It also plainly (and elegantly) shows children the fundamental reasons people take such risks (to find a safer, better life for their families) and how simple it actually is to welcome immigrants (through everyday kindness and care). Backmatter notes can be used in planning emigration/immigration units for ages five to eight years.

Sugar in Milk (2020) Thrity Umrigar, illus. Khoa Le, RP Books/Hachette.

This is more than yet another immigration story with a newly arrived child protagonist. It's a reminder to us all that immigrants contribute much to where they arrive. This message is related through the child's aunt sharing a folktale that dates back to when their ancestors, the Zoroastrians, left Iran and headed to India.

In the tale, the émigrés were denied landing rights at first. The king who tried to turn them away couldn't communicate why they could not stay. He bridged the language gap by showing the refugees a glass of milk, filled to the brim, to explain how their lands were already overcrowded. The Zoroastrians' leader stepped forward and added a spoonful of sugar to the milk, stirring it in without spilling a drop. This concrete demonstration of how immigrants can and do merge into their new homes convinced the king in the tale to grant them admittance. It also helps the girl in a modern-day US city see that she can—and will, with her aunt and uncle's help—find ways to fit in and become an authentic part of her new world.

History

Pride 1 2 3 (2020) Michael Joosten, illus. Wednesday Holmes, Little Simon.

Despite over five states now requiring their elementary schools to include contributions to US history made by LGBTQIA+ people in their curricula, a dearth of books and other materials to support teachers in doing so remains. This concept picture book (counting) for toddlers through kindergarteners can serve as a springboard for introducing the annual Pride Parades held around the country and explaining what they signify. Illustrations show families, friends, and community members of all kinds and compositions. Each number's two-page spread invites you to linger and notice the details in the bustling activity as attendees coalesce to celebrate inclusivity and unity. You'll find this title a good springboard book, one that children will dip into and out of for various personal reasons after you share it.

If You Want a Friend in Washington (2020) Erin McGill. Schwartz and Wade Books.

Learning about the presidents is an essential aspect of young children's American history education. It's sometimes difficult to bring those people alive and show how they're relevant, however, especially to primary-grade children. Numerous picture book biographies help do so, especially ones that include stories about the presidents' childhoods. This book takes a fresh, different approach to the presidents: categorizing them according to their pets, a favorite topic for primary-grade children. Although there aren't too many details about the presidents and their terms in office included, the descriptions and explanations are sufficient to intrigue readers or listeners to want to learn more about these pets' owners.

The Undefeated (2019) Kwame Alexander, illus. Kadir Nelson. Versify.

This multiple-award-winning title by prolific author Kwame Alexander is an illustrated version of a poem he wrote in 2008, soon after his daughter was born and Barack Obama was elected president. In it, Alexander encapsulates Black Americans' experiences from the days of the transatlantic trade through the Civil War, the Civil Rights Era, and up to today's Black Lives Matter movement. Nelson's lush, at times almost pulsating, illustrations bring to life not only the people and their experiences but, more importantly, convey the struggle and the anguish as well as the pride in accomplishing despite the odds.

Todos Iguales/All Equal: Un Corrido de Lemon Grove/A Ballad of Lemon Grove (2019) Christy Hale, Children's Book Press.

Americans familiar with the *Brown v. Board of Education* landmark school desegregation case of 1954 may not be aware of its precedent, the 1931 *Alvarez v. the Board of Trustees of the Lemon Grove School District* case. Told in *corrido* (ballad) form (in Spanish and English) by the plaintiff, twelve-year-old Roberto Alvarez, this book details the district's segregation attempts against Mexican American children and how the affected community rose to fight for their civil rights. While some events in the story are stark and expose the underlying bigotry that spurred the segregation effort, Hale's word choices and illustrations depict them with a sensitivity that doesn't impair accuracy. The backmatter notes elaborate upon the historical setting (agricultural California during the Depression), key figures in the case as it advanced through the courts, and how the community evolved after the decision. It also includes a brief explanation of the *corrido's* unique form and significance in Mexican culture. This book is a reliable springboard for opening up discussions about race, ethnicity, immigrants, equality under the law, and the need to acknowledge each other's humanity.

Activities in the Field

Search for the blog of an early childhood-age teacher who writes about social studies-related books being shared with students. Check at least five recent posts on that blog for the following information: (a) copyright dates of the books listed (you might need to locate them on the publisher's website); (b) range of topics, people, and themes addressed in the books; (c) which titles received awards or other distinctions; (d) whether you deem any books described are multicultural or global. Categorize which books would serve as mirrors for a classroom of children you know. Ask yourself which books would serve as windows or sliding glass doors for them, too. Then reflect on how you might use at least two of the books highlighted as springboards for class discussions and further social studies investigations.

Activities in the Library

Learn more about the awards in table 4.1 by conducting an Internet search to find their selection criteria. Then choose two books (either from the same list or two different ones) for early childhood-age children that were awarded within the last five years. (Your books should be about different topics, themes, or people.) Read them yourself. Then read the awarding organization's rationale for selecting these books for recognition. Keeping a classroom of children you're familiar with in mind, reflect on whether and why you agree or disagree with the committee's decision to distinguish these two particular books. Ask yourself: Would you use them as mirrors, windows, sliding glass doors, or springboards? Why or why not?

Study Questions

1. Accuracy and developmental appropriateness are two key evaluation criteria for teachers to apply in reviewing children's literature for use in social studies instruction. Explain how you will use at least two specific resources referenced in this chapter to guide you in determining whether the books you select for your students meet these two criteria.

2. Explain the text characteristics you will focus upon in determining whether a book is a multicultural title or a global title. Include examples of these characteristics from two books of each type.
3. Describe both the advantages and disadvantages of using trade books, rather than textbooks, for social studies instruction.

Reflect and Reread

There are hundreds of recorded attempts to censor or ban certain children's books from schools and public libraries annually. There also are many unofficially reported attempts to prevent teachers from ordering certain books for their classroom libraries or curricula. As new children's books address more diverse topics, issues, and people's lives, more censorship or banning efforts are inevitable. To prepare yourself for facing this challenge in your career, review the latest entries in the *What If . . . Forum* written by the Center for the Children's Book Intellectual Freedom Information Services Division librarians (see table 4.5). Choose one book challenge situation reported there and read the staff member's response. Then find two books that you think would be open to either type of challenge (i.e., censorship or ban) by a school stakeholder (e.g., community group member or organization, parent). Use the book finders in table 4.5 (e.g., Diverse Book Finder, WOW) or two of the suggested titles in the preceding section to help you. Explain how you would respond to the type of challenges these two books might engender. Use the *What If . . . Forum* to guide you in preparing your response.

Suggested Readings

Kenyon, E. and Christoff, A. (2020). Global citizenship education through global children's literature: An analysis of the NCSS Notable Trade Books. *Journal of Social Studies Research, 44* (4), 397–408.

Martens, P., Martens, R., Doyle, M. H., Loomis, J., Fuhrman, L., Furnari, C., Soper, E., and Stout, R. (2015). Intercultural understandings through global literature. *The Reading Teacher, 68* (8), 609–617.

Muhammad, G. (2020). *Cultivating genius: An equity framework for culturally and historically responsive literacy.* Scholastic.

Pentimonti, J. M., Zucker, T. A., Justice, L. M., and Kaderavek, J. N. (2011). Informational text use in preschool classroom read-alouds. *The Reading Teacher, 63* (8), 656–665.

Venkatraman, P. (2020, June 19). Weeding out racism's invisible roots: Rethinking children's classics. https://www.slj.com/?detailStory=weeding-out-racisms-invisible-roots-rethinking-childrens-classics-libraries-diverse-books

Why Is the Evidence for Equitable and Effective Early Care and Education Programs an Essential Foundation for the Early Childhood Social Studies Teacher?

Iheoma U. Iruka, Ph.D.

I knew that someday, someway, something would break, it was quite a moment to say finally, finally, somebody is listening, and now everyone is listening, and knows the truth.

—Barbara Bowman

TERMS TO KNOW

anti-racist	evidence-based
childcare	Head Start
culturally grounded	workforce
equity	

Overview

This chapter seeks to examine the current state of knowledge about and evidence for early care and education (ECE) through an **equity** lens. It briefly describes the seminal studies, which include mostly Black children, that shape current ECE and the theorists that shaped ECE and those who are made invisible. The chapter also explores potential reasons for the limited or mixed findings regarding ECE and child outcomes. As the workforce is an integral part of ECE programming and systems, educational attainment and compensation are examined, as are disparities based on program type and setting. There is a call to interrogate all aspects of ECE and engage in **culturally grounded, anti-racist** research, program, and policy.

Considering the theory that early childhood impacts children's schooling and life outcomes, there is a need for more rigorous examination, but one that leverages the assets of all children and centers the experiences and scholarship of scholars and communities of color.

Focus Questions

1. What is early care and education and who does it serve?
2. What is the history and who are the scholars in early care and education?
3. What is the evidence for early care and education?
4. What are the reasons for inconsistent effects of ECE on children's outcomes?
5. Who is the ECE workforce?
6. What are the future directions for research, policy, and programs?
7. How can teachers use this information (the three Es)?

What Is Early Care and Education and Who Does It Serve?

Early care and education programs (ECE) are essential in enhancing the cognitive, physical, socio-emotional, and mental health of children with lifelong consequences (NASEM, 2019). High-quality early learning experiences are especially critical for children experiencing poverty or other adverse circumstances (Shonkoff et al., 2012). ECE defines as nonparental care that which occurs outside the home. ECE programs are offered in homes, centers, and schools. According to the US Department of Education's National Household Education Surveys Program on Early Childhood Program Participation: 2019, 59 percent of children between the age of birth to five are in at least one weekly nonparental care arrangement (Cui & Natske, 2020). For children in nonparental care arrangement, almost two-thirds (62 percent) were in center-based care (including Head Start programs, preschools, prekindergartens, and other early childhood programs), 37 percent were in relative care, and 18 percent were in nonrelative care. The number of children in nonparental care increases from 42 percent when children are less than one year old to 74 percent when preschool age (three to five years old). As shown in figure 5.1, there are also differences by child race and ethnicity. The majority of Black and White children are in weekly nonparental care compared to Hispanic and Asian children, who are less likely to be in nonparental care. Black (43 percent) and Hispanic (45 percent) children are also likely to be in relative care, compared to other children (White = 33 percent, Asian or Pacific Islander = 34 percent). In contrast, White (65 percent) and Asian or Pacific Islander (66 percent) are likely to be in center-based care compared to Black (59 percent) and Hispanic (56 percent) children.

There are also differences in nonparental care based on family poverty status (see figure 5.2). Children from households at or above the poverty threshold are likely to be in weekly nonparental care compared to children from households below the poverty threshold. Children from households below the poverty threshold were likely to be in relative care (44 percent) compared to children from at or above the poverty threshold (36 percent). Furthermore, families making $100,000 or more were likely to use at least one weekly nonparental care than families making $20,000 or less (72 percent versus 51 percent).

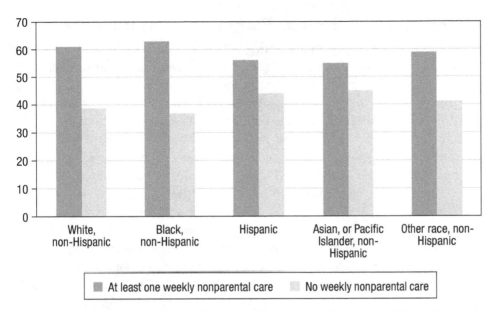

FIGURE 5.1 Percentage of Children from Birth Through Age Five and Not Yet in Kindergarten Participating in Various Weekly Nonparental Care Arrangements, by Child Race and Ethnicity: 2019. *Source*: US Department of Education, National Center for Education Statistics, Early Childhood Program Participation Survey of the 2019 National Household Education Surveys Program (ECPP-NHES, 2019).

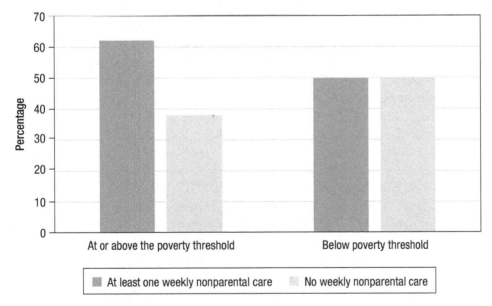

FIGURE 5.2 Percentage of Children from Birth Through Age Five and Not Yet in Kindergarten Participating in Various Weekly Nonparental Care Arrangements, by Family Poverty Status: 2019. Determined by the federal government, the poverty threshold is the income necessary to meet the household's needs, given its size and composition. Income is collected in categories in the survey, rather than as an exact amount, and therefore the poverty measures used in this report are approximations of poverty. Detailed information on the poverty status calculation used in this report is available in Appendix B. *Source*: US Department of Education, National Center for Education Statistics, Early Childhood Program Participation Survey of the 2019 National Household Education Surveys Program (ECPP-NHES, 2019).

History and Scholars of Early Care and Education

Emily Cahan, in her paper, "Past Caring: A History of U.S. Preschool Care and Education for the Poor, 1820–1965," provides a historical review of early care and education, especially the two-tiered system based on a family's economic standing. Low-income families used **childcare** (also called daycare) to work, whereas early childhood education was created for the affluent. Specifically, "the higher quality programs [early childhood education programs] remain those created to enrich or supplement the child's development, and the poorer quality programs tend to be those created to provide custodial care while parents work outside the home" (Cahan, 1989, p. 7). It is also important to note that most of these programs were created to serve White families, with most Black families left out from receiving services and having to figure out childcare when they worked outside the home. Black women have always had the highest labor market participation levels regardless of age, marital status, or presence of children at home compared to other women. In 1880, 35.4 percent of married Black women and 73.3 percent of single Black women were in the labor force, compared to 7.3 percent of married White women and 23.8 percent of single White women (Banks, 2019). According to the US Bureau of Labor Statistics' Current Population Survey, 2018, over 70 percent of Black mothers, regardless of the age of children, are likely to be in the labor force, which is higher than mothers in other groups. For example, according to the US Department of Labor (https://www.dol.gov/agencies/wb/data/mothers-and-families), 71 percent of Black mothers are in the workforce when children are under three, compared to 62 percent of White mothers, 51 percent of Hispanic mothers, and 50 percent of Asian mothers. Early care and education came to national focus when more mothers, primarily White mothers, began to work outside the home during World War II, which continues today.

As part of his war on poverty, President Lyndon Johnson passed a set of policies in 1964, with one of them in the Office of Economic Opportunity (OEO) that provided preschool to help children from economically disadvantaged households develop their full potential. **Head Start** was officially started as a summer program in 1965 with 561,359 children in 11,068 centers located in 1,398 communities. The purpose of Head Start was to meet the needs of the "whole child" by improving their cognitive, social, emotional, and physical health as well as to engage with parents and communities (Zigler & Valentine, 1979). Theorists and early childhood educators believed that early care and education were needed to prepare children from poor households for school and to break the cycle of poverty by intervening with mothers when they were young. "[T]he compensatory education programs of the 1960s and 1970s were established in the hope of ushering in social reform through pedagogical innovation" (Cahan, 1989, p. 33).

Early Childhood Theorists and Scholars

The roots of contemporary early care and education go as far back as the 1500s (Bonnay, 2017). For example, individuals like Martin Luther, who believed that education should be universal, John Locke, who stated that children are a blank slate, to Maria Montessori, who thought that children can learn through trained facilitators (i.e., educators) (see figure 5.3). Others like Friedrich Froebel believed in the importance of play, and Jean Piaget believed that children's development and

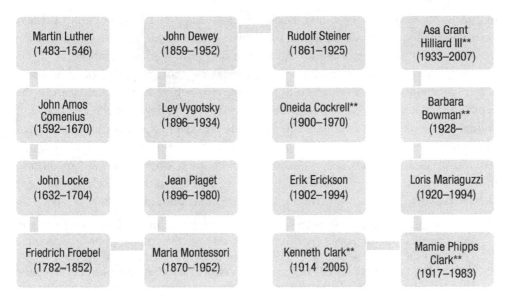

FIGURE 5.3 Timeline of Early Care and Education Theorists and Scholars. *Source*: Iheoma U. Iruka.

learning occurred in stages. Vygotsky believed that children learned through social interactions and needed to be scaffolded, while John Dewey believed that learning should be based on children's interests. You can learn more about these early childhood scholars from Steven Bonnay's Early Childhood Education Blog.

Unfortunately, much of the literature regarding early childhood history makes Black scholars invisible (Broughton, 2020). For example, there is rarely a discussion about Black education scholars like Mary McLeod Bethune, W. E. B. Du Bois, and Booker T. Washington, as well as early childhood scholars like Oneida Cockrell, Kenneth and Mamie Phipps Clark, Asa Grant Hilliard III, and Barbara Bowman, and so many others. Some of these early education scholars are discussed further.

Oneida Cockrell was the founder and director of the Garden Apartments Nursery School and Kindergarten, located in the Rosenwald Apartments in Chicago (Simpson, 2012). The Rosenwald building was built in 1929 by Julius Rosenwald for middle-class Black doctors, lawyers, and professionals. Oneida began her career in early childhood as a volunteer at the Olivet Baptist Church Day Care. This beginning took her to be a teacher, director, educator, author, socialite, and early education and education influencer. She served on the Governing Board of the National Association for the Education of Young Children (NAEYC). Her program, the Garden Apartments Nursery School, which she founded and headed from 1929 to 1969, served as a model program for colleges, universities, and teacher preparation programs. One of the children who went to her program and taught was Barbara Bowman, who also lived in the Rosenwald Apartments.

Barbara Bowman is an early childhood education expert/advocate, professor, and author, who co-founded the Erikson Institute and is a past president of NAEYC (Erikson Institute, n.d.). Her areas of expertise include early care and education. She served as Chicago Public Schools' Chief Early Childhood Education Officer. She has served as a board member for many organizations, including High-Scope Educational Foundation, the Institute for Psychoanalysis, Business People in the Public Interest, the Great Books Foundation, the Chicago Public Library Foundation, and the National Board for Professional Teaching Standards. She is the mother of Valerie Jarrett, a Senior Advisor in the Obama administration.

Asa Grant Hilliard, III, was an educational psychology professor at Georgia State University and San Francisco State University (where he was also dean of the School of Education). Asa Hilliard was a scholar who believed in the excellence of children, especially Black children. He was foundational to the Afrocentric and African-centered schooling curriculum that emphasized the brilliance of Black people's African civilizations and accomplishments even amid oppression and inequities. In his 1995 talk at the Invitational Conference on Defining the Knowledge Base for Urban Teacher Education in Atlanta, GA, Dr. Hilliard noted that

> An African perspective on teacher education must take into account two primary realities: that of the African cultural tradition and that of the political/economic environment within which people of African descent have been situated, especially for the last four centuries. It is the intersection of culture and the political economy that has produced the context for socialization and education, which is our current problem. (Hilliard, 1995, p. 5)

He also stated that "popular theories of learning in educational psychology during the 40s and 50s, part of the era of intensive segregation, did not address the issue of a segregated society and its structured inequalities in education . . . In fact, these theories have yet to do so in any meaningful way. Moreover, today's teaching and learning theories fail to account for the savage inequalities in the service delivery system . . . Yet the political realities determine the structure of education systems in a clear way, e.g., school segregation" (Hilliard, 1995, p. 4–5).

Evidence for Early Care and Education Programs

A multitude of early childhood programs and interventions, federally and state-funded, have been developed since the mid-1960s to address children's needs, particularly those with the highest risk of poor development. Early single-site studies of center-based interventions included the Perry Preschool (Schweinhart, 1985; Weikart et al., 1970) and the Abecedarian Project (Campbell et al., 2001), which showed major effects on cognitive development related to greater academic and employment advancement as young adults, as well as reduction in later criminal activities and teenage pregnancy (Campbell et al., 2002; Schweinhart, 2000; Schweinhart et al., 1993).

The Perry Preschool Project (PPP) was a randomized study carried out from 1962 to 1967 that involved 128 three- and four-year-old Black children living in poverty and assessed to be at high risk of school failure. The preschool was provided each weekday morning in 2.5-hour sessions taught by certified public-school teachers with at least a bachelor's degree. The curriculum emphasized active learning. The children engaged in activities that involved decision-making and problem-solving and were planned, carried out, and reviewed by the children, with support from adults (also called Plan-Do-Review). The teachers also provided a weekly 1.5-hour home visit to each mother and child, designed to involve the mother in implementing the preschool curriculum at home.

Evidence of PPP from developers included (in comparison to the control group):

- higher high school graduation rates, with less time receiving special education services and fewer teen pregnancies at age twenty-seven follow-up
- less likely to serve time in jail or prison, less likely to receive government assistance, and higher median monthly income at the age forty follow-up

Based on work by Nobel Peace Prize Laureate Dr. James Heckman and others, this fifty-year study is often cited as evidence for the lasting, positive impact of ECE and a 7–10 percent return on investment (Schweinhart, 2007).

The Abecedarian Project (ABC) is a center-based intervention that enrolled families in the study between 1972 and 1977 based on a high-risk index. During recruitment, 111 primarily Black infant pairs were matched on high-risk scores then assigned to preschool treatment or control status. Fifty-seven infants were assigned to the experimental group, and fifty-four were assigned to the control group. The study's families were mostly Black, young mothers with less than high school education, unmarried, lived in multigenerational homes, and reported no earned income. The experimental group's service delivery model was a five-year, full-day, year-round center-based program with a comprehensive curriculum (*Learning-Games®*; Sparling & Lewis, 1979) focused on educational games addressing at-risk children's cognition, language, and adaptive behavior. Health-care and family support programs were also emphasized in this program. Activities were individualized for the child's needs, with more conceptual and group-oriented activities as children got older. Families in both the experimental and control groups received supportive social services.

Evidence from ABC developers included (in comparison to the control group at age thirty follow-up):

- more likely to be employed and less likely to receive welfare benefits
- more likely to have graduated from college and completed more years of education
- older than peers when their first child was born

The federal government has also funded many early intervention programs for children placed at risk primarily due to poverty. *Head Start* was established for three and four-year-old children of low-income families in 1965, providing comprehensive developmental services in half-day or full-day programs, with some home-based only programs. A study of randomly selected children attending Head Start for one year or two years showed effect sizes ranging from .05 to .57 for language, academic, and socio-emotional development (see FACES 2000 Technical Report, ACF, 2006).

The *Child-Parent Center Education Program* is a federally funded program implemented in Chicago in 1967 with 1,539 families (93 percent African American). In addition to providing comprehensive services to economically disadvantaged families, the program included preschool and school-age components focusing on the school-age programming, providing continuity from the preschool program. Using a quasi-experimental design matching the intervention group with a control group on age, eligibility for intervention, and family poverty, Reynolds and colleagues (2011) found the following at the age twenty-eight follow-up:

- higher educational attainment, income, socioeconomic status (SES), and health insurance coverage
- lower rates of justice system involvement and substance abuse
- enduring effects were strongest for preschool, especially for males and children of high school dropouts

The *Comprehensive Child Development Program (CCDP)* was a federally funded program that addressed the complex needs of children from low-income households and their families. This five-year program's model was to intervene early; involve the whole family; institute comprehensive child development and social service program; provide service to parents to be adequately involved in their child's development and be self-sufficient and continue service until the child enters kindergarten or first grade. In 1989, twenty-four grantee sites were funded, and 4,410 families were included in the evaluation (2,213 families were randomly assigned to the CCDP intervention, and 2,197 families were randomly assigned to the control group). The majority of the sample was African American and Hispanic, young mothers, less than high school education, and low-income. CCDP study was an attempt to test whether early, "comprehensive" child development services to low-income children and families were effective. No effect of treatment was found in this randomized study, possibly due to poor implementation, poor program quality, reliance on indirect effect, and quite likely due to a weak intervention (case management).

Early Head Start (EHS) was established in 1995 to serve pregnant women and families with infants and toddlers up to age three from low-income households. EHS is a comprehensive program focused on enhancing children's development, as well as strengthening the families. The EHS programs are required to provide comprehensive child development services delivered through home visits, childcare, case management, parenting education and family support, with health care and referrals as needed. Programs choose to be center-based, home-based, or a combination of home- and center-based. For the evaluation component, seventeen sites were selected in which 3,001 infants and their families were randomly assigned into Early Head Start or a control group (1,513 in the program and 1,488 in the control group). Analyses showed that three-year-old program children performed better than control children in cognitive and language development, displayed higher emotional engagement of the parent and sustained attention with play objects, and were lower in aggressive behavior (Love et al., 2005; Raikes et al., 2014). Early Head Start parents, compared to parents in the control group, were more emotionally supportive, provided more language and learning stimulation, read to their children more, and spanked less. The strongest and most numerous impacts were programs that offered a mix of home-visiting and center-based services and that fully implemented the performance standards early. Effect sizes ranged from -0.11 to 0.13, generally low effects.

State-funded preschool and prekindergarten. The seventeenth edition of *The State of Preschool* by the National Institute for Early Education Research (NIEER), a unit of the Graduate School of Education at Rutgers, the State University of New Jersey, is an annual state survey of preschool policies (Friedman-Krauss et al., 2020). The report includes information for every state on child enrollment, resources (including staffing and funding), and quality standards.

It also provides information on where children are served, operating schedules, and other program features relevant to planning children's education. Data from this report shows that states have added more than 930,000 seats, primarily for four-year-old children, with forty-four states and the District of Columbia funding preschool programs. While enrollment for three-year-old children has increased by 6 percent since 2002, the enrollment for four-year-old children has increased by 20 percent. In 2019, 34 percent of four-year-old children were enrolled in state-funded preschool compared to 14 percent in 2002, and it increased to 6 percent for three-year-old children in 2019 compared to 3 percent in 2002 (see figure 5.4). The average spending per child (in 2019 dollars) has decreased from $5,779 in 2002 to $5,374 in 2019. It is important to note that much of NIEER's report is focused on PreK, and their report is not the only metric of what is needed for a high-quality state PreK program.

In their paper about the current PreK landscape, Chaudry and Datta (2017) noted the following: children from low-income households were likely to be in public PreK programs; children from higher-income households were likely to be in private PreK program; overall public PreK enrollment was representative of racial and ethnic groups, but Black and Latinx children were likely to be in Head Start programs; Latinx children were less likely to be in a center-based preschool program (45 percent) than White (58 percent), Black (58 percent), and Asian (54 percent) children; and there were differences based on geographic location, with 47 percent of preschools in rural communities receiving Head Start or public pre-kindergarten funding compared to 36 percent for urban areas, and 39 percent in the suburbs.

In their consensus statement on the current state of scientific knowledge on pre-kindergarten effects, Phillips and colleagues (2017) find the following:

- Children who are from low-income households and have adverse experiences gain more from PreK than their more advantaged peers.
- Dual Language Learners (DLLs) show more increased academic skills, especially in language, than their monolingual peers.
- Programs that promote high-quality interactions like serve and return are more likely to promote better child outcomes.

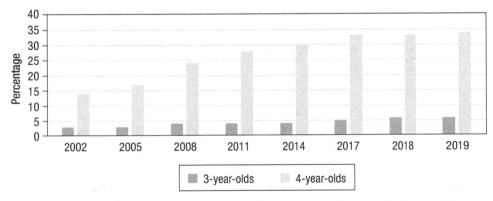

FIGURE 5.4 Percent of US Population Enrolled in State-Funded Preschool. *Source*: Friedman-Krauss, A. H., Barnett, W. S., Garver, K. A., Hodges, K. A., Weinsenfeld, G. G., & Gardiner, B. A. (2000). *The State of Preschool 2019: State Preschool Yearbook*. New Brunswick, NJ: The State University of New Jersey, National Institute for Early Education Research.

- Programs that use curricula that build foundational skills along with professional development and coaching that support teachers' ability to create an organized and enriching learning environment.
- An alignment exists between the PreK experience and early elementary schools that provide "individualization and differentiation in instructional content and strategies" (p. 24).

Furthermore, Phillips and colleagues (2017) find children who attend PreK do better at kindergarten entry than children who do not attend PreK. This has been found with other analyses of other state-funded PreK programs with weighted effect sizes ranging from 0.28 for language, 0.44 for math, to 1.10 for literacy at kindergarten entry (Barnett et al., 2018). However, there is evidence of positive as well as null and negative impact of PreK program participation. That is, the evidence is mixed about the long-term impact of PreK participation with children who did not attend PreK catching up to children who attended PreK, or better yet, the score of these groups of children converging (Yoshikawa et al., 2013).

Quality Rating and Improvement Systems (QRISs) are initiatives implemented to systematically evaluate and improve the quality of early education settings through a uniform approach based on state or local standards. QRIS standards and criteria focus on: licensing, staff qualifications, early childhood education environment, family partnership, administration and management, and accreditation. Though not seen consistently or comprehensively addressed in all QRIS programs, accreditation, curriculum, ratio and group size, community involvement, provisions for special needs, and cultural and linguistic diversity are sometimes included in QRIS standards. Programs are given points or placed at a specific level on a scale based on the criteria they meet within the QRIS (e.g., from 1 to 5, with 5 being the highest level of quality). A program's points or level can then be used to help tailor professional development supports and activities to achieve an even higher level of quality and provide higher reimbursement rates. The number of states with a QRIS and the proportion of ECE programs participating in voluntary QRIS has increased in recent years to almost forty states based on the Child Care and Early Education Research Connections (n.d.). QRIS validation studies are conducted to examine whether this rating and measurement system differentiates meaningful ECE program quality levels and is associated with measures of quality and children's growth in their learning and development.

Tout and colleagues (2017) conducted a synthesis of findings from ten validation studies examining quality ratings of ECE programs participating in state QRIS. They found the following:

- QRIS ratings reflect differences in environments, interactions, and activities in ECE programs at different rating levels.
- QRIS ratings are positively associated, albeit small, with measures of observed quality, especially for center-based programs.
- There is an inconsistent link between QRIS ratings and children's development.

The authors note some of the next steps for future validation studies. These include a closer examination of the quality measures for home-based programs; the inclusion of children with special needs, infants and toddlers, and children who speak languages other than English and Spanish; going beyond traditional metrics of school readiness to ones that capture experiences like school engagement; and examining ratings and other areas of ECE programming such as turnover and compensation. There is a need to examine the extent to which the QRIS is capturing all providers or those mandated to participate, such as those who are subsidy-receiving providers, reviewing whether the standards are meaningful and represent the way quality exists in a diversity of programs, and exploring whether the ratings are a metric of the advantage of a program or true quality.

Reasons for Inconsistent ECE Effects on Children's Outcomes

There are many reasons for the variations found for ECE effects on children's short- and long-term outcomes. Some of the reasons are due to the type of setting, age of entry or intervention receipt, duration of intervention, quality of program/intervention, and risk factors experienced by children and their families. We briefly discuss these issues.

Type of program. Research has documented differences in findings as related to delivery mode. Evidence supporting center-based care ranges from strong to weak. The Abecedarian Project, a randomized center-based intervention with a health component and social service referrals for children placed at high risk of school failure, found a large positive impact of this intense intervention for children's cognitive development that remained a significant, albeit smaller, predictor of later academic achievement and adjustment as young adults (Campbell et al., 2002). Much weaker associations between center-based Head Start care beginning at three years, and children's language and social outcomes were detected in the Head Start Impact Study (US DHHS, 2005). Although not a randomized study, the Head Start FACES study noted, similar to Abecedarian, that children had significant cognitive growth from fall to spring.

Compared to other children from low-income households, Head Start children had significantly, albeit modestly, higher vocabulary skills as measured with the PPVT-R at the end of the program. Other observational studies have shown center-based care, particularly PreK programs in the National Center for Early Development and Learning Study were predictive of children's outcomes (Howes et al., 2008). The NICHD Study of Early Child Care and Youth Development documented positive associations between center-based care and children's cognitive and academic outcomes at entry to kindergarten in a study of over 1,000 children in ten sites (NICHD ECCRN, 2002).

The majority of evidence linking ECE to children's outcomes is primarily from center- and school-based programs. Some studies have shown a link between home-based programs and children's learning and development outcomes. For example, Forry et al. (2013), using data from a multistate study of a professional development intervention, found that home-based providers' child-centered beliefs (e.g., progressive beliefs that children should have autonomy and be allowed to express their ideas) and their perceptions of job demands were related to children's school readiness, emotional health (e.g., initiative, self-control, and attachment), and internalizing and externalizing problem behaviors. Similarly, Iruka and Forry (2018) also found that children in home-based programs that were high quality and engaged frequently in enriching literacy and numeracy activities (e.g., learning names of letters, learning the conventions of print, using manipulatives, using a measuring instrument, learning about shapes and patterns) were likely to have stronger reading and math skills compared to children in home-based programs that were low quality and engaged in fewer enriching activities.

The better learning outcomes for center- versus home-based programs are likely due to higher teacher education and more professional development and coaching (Bradley & Vandell, 2007). However, the larger group size in center-based programs may negatively impact teachers' responsiveness to children's needs (Gordon et al., 2013). Thus, there is a need for a more rigorous examination of the differential impact based on program type and accounting for differences in teacher education and training and socio-demographics of children and families.

Timing of intervention or program. Many publicly funded programs (e.g., Head Start and public prekindergartens) focus on preschoolers, while fewer (e.g., Early Head Start and many home-visiting programs) focus on infants and toddlers. There is good reason to believe that it may be better for children from disadvantaged circumstances to receive a comprehensive education targeting their cognitive, language, and socio-emotional development beginning in infancy. For such programs, including the Abecedarian Project, the Comprehensive Child Development Program, and Early Head Start, there have been mixed results of starting early. The Abecedarian Project provided full-time center care beginning at four months of age and found a strong effect on young children's cognitive development.

In contrast, Early Head Start combined home-visiting and, in some cases, childcare services beginning in infancy. This study found small effects on language and socio-emotional development. The Comprehensive Child Development Program combined case management and home visiting beginning in the child's first year and found no effect of the intervention on children's cognitive, language, and behavioral outcomes.

Other programs have provided services only to preschoolers. Head Start and public prekindergarten programs offer center-based care to children who are three to five years of age. Evaluations of these programs that assess fall to spring gains, such as the Head Start Family and Children Experiences Survey and the National Center on Early Development and Learning (NCEDL) PreK study, report modest to moderate effects on child outcomes. NCEDL conducted studies of the state-funded PreK programs in eleven states to understand variations among PreK programs and, in turn, how these variations relate to child outcomes at the end of PreK and in kindergarten (Early et al., 2005). The differential effects of timing on children's development may be due to the programs' various characteristics, including the age of the children when the intervention began, standards of the program, and the competencies of and support for the **workforce**. It may be that particular groups of children benefit from programs beginning at infancy, while others may benefit from programs later on in life. For instance, Caughy et al. (1994) and Burchinal et al. (2006) found a stronger effect of childcare beginning in the first three years for the children from the most impoverished and disadvantaged communities and weaker or opposite effects for children from middle-class homes. Investigating the effect of whether interventions that begin early or later in the child's life are more beneficial for particular groups of children will help develop programs and selection of children into particular programs.

Educare, an enhanced Early Head Start (EHS) / Head Start (HS) program, provides high-quality full-day, year-round ECE comprehensive services for low-income families through blended funding mechanisms. Educare starts at birth until children are age five. More information about Educare can be found in Yazejian et al. (2013). In a randomized study of 239 children less than nineteen months, Yazejian and colleagues (2017) found significant differences after one year favoring treatment-group children on auditory and expressive language skills, parent-reported problem behaviors, and positive parent-child interactions. Effect sizes were in the modest to medium range. Based on data from Perry and especially ABC, Heckman and Karapakula (2019) concluded that starting earlier, at birth, produces greater gains with 13 percent for every dollar invested in children who could otherwise not attend a high-quality program.

Duration of intervention. The duration of the well-known childhood programs varies, with some interventions lasting for three years (e.g., Early Head Start) and one intervention lasting five years (the Abecedarian Project). It seems intuitive that a longer program should have greater effects, but it is unclear whether the duration is an important facet to existing programs' effectiveness. It may be that children from disadvantaged homes with multiple familial risk factors may benefit from longer interventions, as found with the Abecedarian Project, but this has not been consistently found, such as in Head Start (Arteaga et al., 2014; Yoshikawa et al., 2016). One randomized longitudinal study focused on 141 children from two public Montessori magnet schools from ages three to six showed that over time the Montessori children fared better on measures of academic achievement, social understanding, and mastery orientation, and they also reported relatively more liking of scholastic tasks (Lilliard et al., 2017). In addition to elevating overall performance on these measures, Montessori preschools also equalized outcomes among subgroups (i.e., children of color and children from low-income households) that typically have unequal outcomes.

Quality of childcare. The quality of childcare is an important facet of early childhood programs. Research has shown that out-of-home environments play an important role in children's cognitive, language, and socio-emotional functioning, as well as serving as an antipoverty strategy (Heckman & Karapakula, 2019; Iruka, 2020). In their consensus statement, Phillips and colleagues (2017) find that children's early learning trajectories depend on the quality of their learning experiences before, during, and after their PreK experiences. Furthermore, children from disadvantaged homes and experiencing adverse circumstances are more likely to benefit the most from teachers who stimulate interactions that support learning and are emotionally supportive. Unfortunately, many children in out-of-home care are likely to be in low-quality care (Yoshikawa et al., 2013). Using data from the US Department of Education, National Center for Education Statistics, Early Childhood Longitudinal Study, Birth Cohort, Barnett and colleagues (2013) found that the quality of a national sample of preschool programs serving four-year-olds was vastly low to moderate quality (see figure 5.5). Thirty-five percent of all children enrolled in centers were in high-quality care as measured by the Early Childhood Environment Rating Scale.

In contrast, nine percent of home-based programs as measured by the Family Day Care Rating Scale were rated high. When these data were examined across

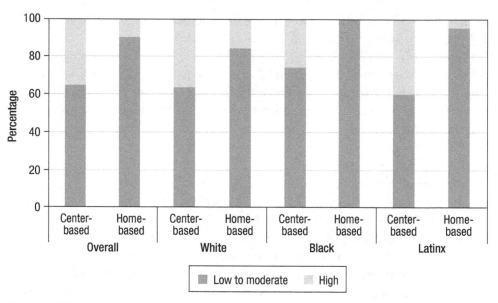

FIGURE 5.5 Percentage Distribution of Quality Rating of Child Care Arrangements of Four-Year-Old Children, by Type of Arrangement and Race/Ethnicity: 2005–2006. *Source*: Barnett, W. S., Carolan, M., & Johns, D. (2013). *Equity and excellence: African-American children's access to quality preschool.* New Brunswick, NJ: The State University of New Jersey, National Institute for Early Education Research, Center on Enhancing Early Learning Outcomes.

racial and ethnic groups, 36 percent and 40 percent of White and Latinx children, respectively, in center-based programs were in high-quality programs compared to 25 percent of Black children. Fifteen percent of White children in the home-based program were in high-quality programs compared to 4 percent and 0 percent of Latinx and Black children, respectively.

Prioritization of access. Adverse childhood experiences (ACEs) are traumatic experiences and events, ranging from abuse and neglect to living with an adult with a mental illness that can have negative, lasting effects on health and well-being in childhood and later in life. The terminology of ACEs is based on the seminal study by Felitti and colleagues (1998). Felitti and colleagues developed a questionnaire with seven categories of ACEs: psychological, physical, or sexual abuse; violence against mother; or living with household members who were substance abusers, mentally ill or suicidal, or ever imprisoned. They found that more than half of respondents reported at least one, and one-fourth reported two categories of childhood exposures. There was also a graded relationship between ACEs exposure and adult health risk behaviors (e.g., alcoholism, drug abuse, smoking, depression, and suicide attempt) and diseases, including heart disease, cancer, chronic lung disease, skeletal fractures, and liver disease. Based on data from the 2016 National Survey of Children's Health (NSCH), Sacks and Murphy (2018) found that: economic hardship and divorce or separation of a parent or guardian are the most common ACEs reported nationally, and in all states; 45 percent of children in the US have experienced at least one ACE; 10 percent of children have experienced three or more ACEs, which places them at high risk of poor outcomes; and the prevalence of ACEs is lowest among Asian children and highest among Black children. Evidence indicates that children experiencing adverse circumstances during early childhood are most likely to benefit from high-quality early care and education experiences (Shonkoff & Phillips, 2000). Most federal and state ECE programs prioritize children experiencing adversities, especially children from low-income households, children with special needs, children from households speaking a language other than English, and children experiencing certain other adversities (e.g., housing insecurity, abuse, and neglect). Children experiencing these social and familial risks, especially when experiencing more than one, are likely to show more cognitive, academic, and socio-emotional challenges than children with no familial or social risks (Masten & Coatworth, 1995; Rutter, 1979; Sameroff et al., 1987). For example, Burchinal et al. (2000) found that young children with multiple risk factors had lower cognitive and language development and acquired language skills at a slower pace.

Who Is the ECE Workforce?

The ECE workforce is necessary for the programming and services for children and families. However, the workforce is diverse in its job requirements, professional development opportunities, workplace support, and compensation and benefits. Early elementary teachers (kindergarten to grade 3) compared to preschool teachers (birth through age five) have clear job requirements, professional development opportunities, workplace supports for planning time, and livable compensation and benefits (Phillips et al., 2016). The lack of a unified system in ECE is the primary reason for the lack of uniformity as it concerns educational expectations, roles, and commensurate wages and benefits. According to the Early Childhood Workforce Index, about two million adults, mostly women, are paid to care for and educate approximately 10 million children, birth to age five (Whitebook et al., 2018). For example, state licensing's minimum qualification requirements based on role vary (see figure 5.6). Forty-one states have no minimum standards for home-based assistants, and twenty-four don't have minimum standards for home-based educators. Nineteen states don't have minimum standards for center teachers, with nine states requiring a minimum of a high school diploma and none requiring a BA degree.

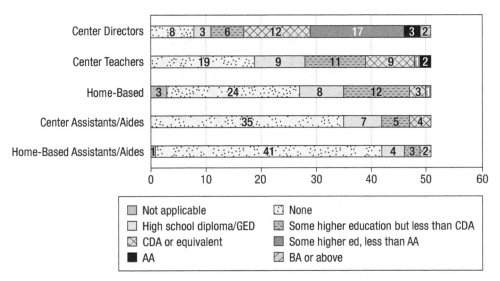

FIGURE 5.6 Minimum Qualification Requirements in State Licensing by ECE Role. *Source*: Whitebook, M., McLean, C., Austin, L. J. E., & Edwards, B. (2018). *Early Childhood Workforce Index*. Berkeley, CA: University of California, Berkeley, Center for the Study of Child Care Employment.

While the many states did not have minimum educational requirements for educators, 80 percent of center-based teaching staff have some college or higher, including 35 percent that have a BA degree or higher; about 50 percent of home-based teaching staff have some college or higher, including 15 percent that have a BA degree or higher (Phillips et al., 2016; Whitebook et al., 2016).

Some additional demographics of ECE teaching staff from the 2018 Early Childhood Workforce Index (Whitebook et al., 2018) follow:

- 27 percent of center-based teaching staff speak a language other than English (information not available for home-based providers).
- About 18 percent and 11 percent of home- and center-based educators, respectively, are born outside the US.
- About 40 percent of the workforce are non-White across centers and homes.
- 52 percent of Black educators are caring for and teaching infants and toddlers compared to 42 percent of Latinx and 40 percent of White educators.
- 75 percent of center-based educators earn less than $15 per hour, with 84 percent of Black early educators earning less than $15 per hour.

TABLE 5.1   **Mean Hourly Wages by Occupation, 2017**

Child Care Worker Employees, All Settings	Self-Employed Home Care Providers	Preschool Teachers, All Settings	Preschool Teachers in School-Based Settings	Kindergarten Teachers	Elementary Teachers
$10.72	$10.35	$13.94	$26.88	$31.29	$32.98

Source: Whitebook, M., McLean, C., Austin, L. J. E., & Edwards, B. (2018). *Early Childhood Workforce Index.* Berkeley, CA: University of California, Berkeley, Center for the Study of Child Care Employment.

Compared to kindergarten teachers, who earn about $31 per hour, ECE educators who work in community-based organizations earn about $11 per hour (see table 5.1). ECE educators who work in community-based organizations make approximately $22,880 annually compared to over $44,000 annual salary (at ten-month contract) for kindergarten teachers. Furthermore, teachers who primarily work with infants and toddlers make less than those in PreK regardless of their educational degree. For example, infant/toddler educators with a BA degree or higher earn an average of $13.83 compared to the average hourly wage of $17.86 for PreK educators with a BA degree or higher (Whitebook et al., 2018). These compensation disparities are often cited as the reason for the high turnover in ECE (range of 8 to 27 percent), which has implications for classroom quality and children's learning and development (Phillips et al., 2016).

In 2015, the Institute of Medicine (IOM) and National Research Council (NRC) released their report, *Transforming the Workforce for Children Birth Through Age 8: A Unifying Foundation*. The committee for this report was charged to "conduct a study and prepare a consensus report on how the science of children's health, learning, and development from birth through age eight can be employed to inform how we prepare a workforce to seamlessly support children's health, development, learning, and school success from birth through age eight, including standards and expectations, instructional practices, preparation, and professional development, and family engagement across diverse contexts (e.g., rural/urban) and populations (e.g., special education, immigrant, dual language learners, sub-threshold children)." In addition to noting that children are born ready to learn, and ECE educators need high-quality supports, they propose twelve recommendations. The recommendations from the report include:

1) Strengthen competency-based qualification requirements for all care and education professionals working with children from birth through age eight.
2) Develop and implement comprehensive pathways and multiyear timelines at the individual, institutional, and policy levels for transitioning to a minimum bachelor's degree qualification requirement, with specialized knowledge and competencies, for all lead educators working with children from birth through age eight.
3) Strengthen practice-based qualification requirements, including a supervised induction period, for all lead educators working with children from birth through age eight.
4) Build an interdisciplinary foundation in higher education for child development.
5) Develop and enhance programs in higher education for care and education professionals.
6) Support the consistent quality and coherence of professional learning supports during ongoing practice for professionals working with children from birth through age eight.
7) Develop a new paradigm for evaluating and assessing professional practice for those who work with children from birth through age eight.
8) Ensure that policies and standards that shape the professional learning of care and education leaders encompass the foundational knowledge and competencies needed to support high-quality practices for child development and early learning in their organizations.
9) Improve consistency and continuity for children from birth through age eight by strengthening collaboration and communication among professionals and systems within the care and education sector and closely related sectors, especially health and social services.
10) Support workforce development with coherent funding, oversight, and policies.
11) Collaboratively develop and periodically update coherent guidance across roles and settings for care and education professionals working with children from birth through age eight.
12) Support comprehensive state- and local-level efforts to transform the professional workforce for children from birth through age eight.

This NRC and IOM workforce report led to the Unifying Framework for the Early Childhood Education Profession, also called Power to the Profession, by a task force of fifteen leading national organizations. The collaborative organizations included many national organizations, such as the National Association for the Education of Young Children (NAEYC), American Federation of Teachers, Child Care Aware, National Association for Family Child Care, Zero to Three, National Head Start Association, Council for Professional Recognition, and many others (NAEYC, 2020). This unified body recommended four major expectations.

1) **A clearly defined profession, with distinct roles and responsibilities.** There will be three distinct and meaningful designations—Early Childhood Educator I, II, and

III. Each designation has an associated scope of practice, expected level of professional preparation, and expected mastery of the newly revised and agreed-upon Professional Standards and Competencies for Early Childhood Educators.

2) **Aligned professional preparation, pathways, and licensure.** There is a focus on three primary professional preparation pathways—early childhood education professional certificate/credential programs, associate degree programs, and bachelor's degree/initial master's degree programs. These programs will prepare participating ECEs for professional licensure, which individuals can obtain by earning a credential from an accredited or recognized professional preparation program, demonstrating evidence of field experiences, and passing an assessment of competencies. Assessments must have multiple measures, be affordable, and not reinforce cultural, gender, racial, or linguistic biases.

3) **Professional compensation.** Compensation for early childhood educators with comparable qualifications, experience, and job responsibilities will be at least comparable to public school salaries and comparable across all settings; include an adequate benefits package; not be differentiated based on ages of children served; and increase commensurate with increased preparation and competency.

4) **Supportive infrastructure and shared accountability.** The *Unifying Framework* lays out the expectations, responsibilities, structures, and supports for each part of the system that advances the profession, including preparation programs, employers/owners, professional organizations and governance bodies, and state and federal governments and agencies.

The importance of implementing the Unifying Framework is clear, as shown in table 5.2, Coronavirus and the ECE workforce.

TABLE 5.2 Coronavirus and the ECE Workforce

The coronavirus, or COVID-19, showed the inequities in the ECE workforce before and during the pandemic. Using one state's data (Virginia Department of Education), there were large differences between ECE educators working in childcare or community-based organizations and those working in schools before the pandemic (Bassok et al., 2020). For example, about half of teachers in childcare centers held a high school degree or less. In contrast, nearly all school-based lead teachers held a bachelor's degree or more. While almost 40 percent of childcare teachers had annual household incomes under $25,000, just 1 percent of school-based ECE teachers fell into this category. Nearly half of childcare center teachers were people of color: 25 percent were Black and 12 percent Latinx, with another 10 percent identifying as another race or ethnicity.

In contrast, only 14 percent of school-based teachers were people of color. According to this report, 38 percent of the childcare workforce reported their earnings decreased, and 34 percent were no longer employed, while 7 percent of school-based teachers saw decreased earnings, and 3 percent were no longer employed. Childcare teachers faced financial insecurity: 12 percent had bills past due (versus 4 percent for school-based teachers), 33 percent worried money would run out (15 percent for school-based teachers), and 35 percent did not have enough money to meet their medical needs (11 percent for school-based teachers). Analysis by NAEYC and Center for American Progress estimates that if childcare providers do not receive adequate support, approximately half of US childcare capacity is at risk of disappearing (Jessen-Howard & Workman, 2020). This amounts to 4,473,601 licensed childcare slots with 2.6 children per slot. The loss of childcare is particularly dire for parents with infants and toddlers who need to be in nonparental care (Keating & Schaffner, 2020).

What Are the Future Directions for Research, Policy, and Program?

Deeper inquiry of racism and systemic inequities in early childhood. The early care and education programs of today are based on the evidence from a few seminal studies, namely Abecedarian, Perry, Child–Parent Center Education Program, and Head Start. The vast majority of children in these studies were Black children from low-income families, though arguably much of the science has focused on the poverty aspect of these early interventions and less on the children's race. This invisibility of the race of children and their families, especially during the time of civil unrest, must be fully interrogated, especially when many Black families were and still are dealing with legal exclusion from equal education, wealth generation, and employment; as well as facing segregation, environmental toxins, police brutality, and many other legally sanctioned inequities and atrocities (Jargowsky, 2015). A 2019 report from Urban Institute shows that early childhood education nationwide is more segregated than kindergarten and first grade, even while enrolling a similar number of students. Early childhood programs are twice as likely to be nearly 100 percent Black or Hispanic, and they are less likely to be somewhat integrated. The main issue with segregation is the high probability that children are also being segregated economically, with limited resources and supports and low-quality early learning experiences, especially in light of their less-than-optimal ecosystem due to vestiges of racism and inequities. Unfortunately, racism is not denoted as one of the ACEs indicators, even with its documented impact on children's health and overall well-being (Trent et al., 2019). Thus, there is a need to develop a theoretical model showing how ECE mitigates racism and inequities, ensuring equitable access, experiences, and outcomes.

Culturally grounded anti-racist system-building and programming. The theoretical frameworks guiding the majority of ECE programs have primarily centered White and Eurocentric lenses, approaches, and thinking, ignoring and making invisible the scholarship and theories of people of color. It is critical that the theories and framing of these scholars of color, especially Black scholars, are leveraged in all aspects of ECE transformation. Incorporating scholars of color will ensure that ethnic minority children and their families' needs are addressed, and their assets and sociocultural strengths are reflected throughout all aspects of the ECE system, from the workforce and program standards, assessments, and quality tools to the outcomes. For example, evidence indicates a lack of a relationship between current program quality tools and child outcomes, calling for a deeper inquiry about what matters for children (Burchinal, 2018). It is critical for the field to inquire: From whose lens are experiences and outcomes being judged? Who is the normative standard for what is considered good teaching, high quality, and positive outcomes?

Conduct culturally grounded, anti-racist ECE research-practice-policy pipeline. Much of the seminal ECE research has been done by and through the lens of primarily White researchers, scholars, and policymakers. Much of this research often frames children from poor households and children of color as always less than without interrogating the systemic patterns of inequities and oppression.

Furthermore, there is a lack of interrogation about assessing assets that children of color and children from marginalized communities bring, such as biculturalism, coping with racism, and flexible language use. Most national and major studies often use assessments and tools that position children, families, and educators of color as always performing less than White children, families, and educators regardless of economic background. Many of the seminal studies have operated in a color-blind fashion without regard for the context of racism and systemic inequities. Similarly, most researchers have conducted research with primarily all-White leadership without ensuring representation of the communities they are researching. Moreover, these research findings are often implemented by and institutionalized by primarily White individuals without discussing implications on poor or minority communities and programs.

Studies of PreK to grade 3 and beyond. While seminal studies, such as Abecedarian and Perry, find meaningful long-term effects for early childhood education, current studies have been mixed, and show minimal effects at best. Furthermore, much of the findings from the seminal ECE studies have focused on deficiencies or low expectation outcomes such as high school graduate, criminal justice engagement, and age and number of pregnancies. There is a need for more rigorous and contemporary studies examining the long-term effects of preschool education on children's health, well-being, learning, and life outcomes. Evidence indicates a convergence, but some studies suggest a potential sleeper effect (e.g., van Huizen & Plantenga, 2018).

The US Department of Education's Early Learning Network, comprised of five sites, is conducting a five-year study to examine the importance of PreK in children's schooling and malleable factors that support children's learning trajectory over time. Specifically, each site is asked to conduct three studies, with a special focus on children from disadvantaged households:

1) Study #1: A descriptive study of school transitions. A descriptive study of state or local policies and practices that are designed to support children as they move from preschool into the early elementary school grades and between grades in elementary school.
2) Study #2: Classroom factors associated with school readiness. A classroom observation study to identify factors that are associated with children's school readiness skills and achievement, including curriculum, instructional practices, classroom climate, and teacher, student, and peer interactions.
3) Study #3: A longitudinal study of achievement. A study that will follow a cohort of students' academic progress over time and identify factors impacting their achievement, including, but not limited to, attendance in preschool and types of preschool programs; parental involvement; continuity in learning goals and expectations; and instruction.

While observational, these studies will hopefully provide some information about mechanisms that impact children's learning trajectory from PreK through grade 3 and policies and contexts that support (or hinder) optimal experiences and outcomes. More information can be found at this site: https://earlylearningnetwork .unl.edu.

How Can Teachers Use This Information (the Three Es)?

This chapter is a beginning and brief introduction to early care and education. It is not an exhaustive literature review of all of the programs and services that make up ECE for children birth through age eight. In fact, much of this chapter does not focus on elementary schools. Thus, it would be important that teachers read this chapter as a starter or as part of a larger reading list prior to developing their curricula. Beyond creating your curriculum, including alignment with standards, scope and sequence, assessment, and lessons associated with this chapter, it is important that teachers have a clear anti-racist and equity lens. This means that we must continue to inquire and read to understand the intention of why a program or service was established and constructed a particular way, and how it fits into the life course of a child and their family. For example, it is important that educators understand the origination of Head Start and how it has served as an important basis for ECE today and whether it is still meeting the needs of a twenty-first-century society and improving the lives of children, families, and communities as intended. Part of having an anti-racism and equity lens is to ensure that we are decolonizing history and looking at whose lens is being used to construct and maintain institutions and whose is ignored. At the same time, we are trying to ensure that the materials are being shared with students in an equitable way, meaning each person is able to access it without obstacles such as ones based on language or special needs.

As you prepare to use this book and this chapter, specifically in your course, I urge you to keep the three Es of education, exploration, and expectation in steps often used to create a curriculum (i.e., standards, scope and sequence, assessment, lessons or activities, differentiation, review, and then continuous improvement). Note that the *three Es* go beyond the scope of this chapter on ECE, but offer some general guiding principles.

Education. When I say "education," I am not advising you to go get another degree or certification, but rather that we need to re-interrogate all that we know about a given topic, including early childhood. Early childhood as a strategy to support children's development and learning in the most sensitive period of life is undisputable. However, there is a need to interrogate the science, practice, and policy and whether it is steeped in the lens, experience, and culture of all people or just the dominant culture. Before engaging in early childhood through an equity lens, it is important that as educators we gain knowledge and language about what racism and White privilege are and how they show up in ECE as well as children's and families' lives. We have to understand how ECE operates from policy to program to community to child, including the historical underpinnings. It is important to understand that racism is not just about not saying the "N-word," but it is about the US system construction that privileges Whiteness at the expense of non-White people. You can begin to ask yourself, how does ECE privilege Whiteness or being White in comparison to Blackness and other non-White culture? Could it show up in the theories, the standards, the workforce competencies and compensation, the research, the research participants, or the program standards? These are the sort of questions you should begin to ask and find out as you prepare your curriculum for this book and then more specifically the lessons tied to this chapter. These are also the kind of questions you can ask your students to examine in more depth and question whether some of the same patterns exist in other institutions and sectors. The more you educate yourself about the goal and role of ECE in children's learning and development, and the more you learn about the racism inherent in the US system and then how it is operationalized in the ECE sector, the more you can begin to engage in decolonizing all aspects of your teaching (Robertson, 2003). This decolonization process may also have you interrogating parts of your curriculum including standards, assessments, and whether the standards are written to ensure that all or some benefit.

Exploration. The second E is "exploration." It is critically important that as part of creating your curriculum you explore your own personal life with an anti-racist and racial equity lens, including the privilege you have had in your life and your profession as an educator. This may be the moment when you begin to feel guilty and sad about what you did not know and how much you walked around life with blinders on, assuming that everyone can pull themselves up by their boot-straps—without realizing that some people had boots and straps that were laced and others did not even have boots and had to walk through hot coals. Part of what educators can do with their students as they read this chapter in particular is to explore and examine the world around them together. For example, *what books are in your classroom and in students' homes? What books did your students read growing up? Do they remember books with characters that had different skin tones, names, language, or even explored non-majority families? Are the textbooks and ancillary materials being used in the classroom mostly from a majority lens, or are there readings written by Black, Indigenous, Latinx, and other people of color?* You and the students can think back on your childhood and examine, *who were your playmates? What was the cultural background of your dentist, pediatrician, etc.? What message does that send to a young child, and how does that influence how they see the world? Are you and your students exposed to people of color who are teachers, school leaders, school counselors, among other things?* A book I wrote with colleagues and released in April 2020 called *Don't Look Away: Embracing Anti-bias Classrooms*, while geared towards early childhood educators and leaders, is as we see it instructive in helping people to explore how their background, training, and lens may bias their thinking about how they see those around them. It may also impact what educators seek to emphasize, de-emphasize or ignore, or even revise (e.g., Africans came to America to work rather than being enslaved, or Native Americans chose to move rather than their lands being taken from them). In one of the activities called "Lemonheads and Whoppers—Is Your Everyday Life Racially and Ethnically Diverse?" we ask educators who the last person to come over for dinner was, who the family doctor is, who their closest friend is, who their favorite actor/actress is, and other questions. These same questions can be asked of you and your students. The responses tell you about your students' and your level of interaction with people of different races and ethnicities. This is an opportunity to explore how you can change the diversity of your experiences and subsequently the diversity and inclusivity of your teaching toolkit. That is, *what do you bring to the teaching discourse that ensures that every student feels connected?* How can you use this chapter to explore who is often made invisible in texts and the history of the US, and how can this be corrected?

Equipment. Through education and exploration, the hope is that educators and their students will be equipped and feel a responsibility for creating an anti-racist and anti-bias learning environment. It is critical that educators don't get trapped into doing nothing because they fear their students are too young or not ready, or that they themselves may get into trouble for interrogating the textbooks. The first five years are critical in children's brain development and lay the foundation for children's emotional development, language, empathy, reasoning, memory, etc. We also know that as early as nine months old children begin to follow faces that resemble their primary caregiver. Even as young as age three, research has shown that White youngsters show a preference for Whites over Blacks, demonstrate prejudiced attitudes and discriminatory behavior toward racial minorities, and see Blacks as less human than Whites. There is no room for educators to allow their students to form and maintain racist ideals and White privilege sentiments. As people who will be held in high regard by many students, it is important that educators take on their role of sociopolitical influence to challenge the current literature and knowledge. You can use this chapter as an example of what is often missing in the text and history; to interrogate and question assumptions that we have about early childhood, research, and programming. Part of your equipment to address equity is this chapter, but as you begin to create your curriculum, keep the *three Es* of education, exploration, and equipment in mind (note that these are high-level examples):

* Examine your school district standards with a lens on how your lessons are inclusive.
* Create a scope and sequence that can be personalized to students' strengths rather than one ideal (and make revisions throughout the year).
* Assessments are critical to helping shape instruction, so ensure that's the purpose of the assessment rather than it being a punitive measure that is gauging traditional intelligence; that is, examine who is actually learning the lessons you seek to give.
* Examine whether there is an opportunity to co-create lessons and activities with the students to bring in their lens, expertise, and lived experiences. This would provide the best avenue to differentiate instruction while also strengthening your relationship with your students.
* Finally, remember to review your entire curriculum, lessons, and activities with an equity-centered lens. Making revisions throughout the year or after the school year based on feedback and your reflection can only make the lessons more impactful for students.

In conclusion, I want to remind all educators that talking about race, racism, and White privilege is not easy. There is no one perfect way to have this conversation. It takes educators along with their peers and school leaders to observe, listen, and re-educate themselves, exploring who they are, want to be, and want their school culture to be, and using the tools they already have as an educator to engage in age-appropriate discussions. This is a journey that will lead to mistakes, confusion, and guilt, but it is a journey that is empowering, motivational, and energizing, and most importantly, educational for all students and their educators.

Postscript

Gayle Mindes, Ed.D.

After reading this important chapter on our history and practice in early childhood education, documenting systemic inequality in our country, think about the implications. Use these pedagogical tools to reflect upon where you are in the picture for the future. Did you live some of these experiences as a child, an adult, or a teacher candidate? Were you aware of the extent of institutionalized racism in our society? So, upon reading this chapter, how will your practice change and what must you do to advocate for the profession, for the children and families you serve? In the following sections, consider the terms and questions, activities, and additional readings to help you go where you wish to be on behalf of children and families and our profession.

Activities in the Field

1. Plan a visit to an infant care center in the neighborhood of your choice. Speak with the director about the salary and working conditions in the center. Ask the director about the credentials of the workforce there. Compare your findings to those described here. Make a graphic organizer to share with your colleagues to summarize your findings in comparison to those described in this chapter.
2. Plan a visit to an elementary school in your neighborhood. Draw a picture of the classroom structure showing the materials in the general room arrangement. You may wish to use one of the room organizer templates found online. Does the room contain the kinds of materials that you would expect to see for exploration and investigation by young children? Are there materials for the social studies? Stop in the school office and ask for the salary schedule for teachers with various degrees. Compare your visit findings to those described here. Plan to share these findings with your colleagues.

Activities in the Library

1. Visit a children's library in your city or town. Look at the books there for young children from preschool to age eight. What is your impression of the selection? Will children of the community see themselves in these materials? What else does the library have for the young children in this community? Be prepared to discuss your findings with your classmates.
2. In the library catalog look for the authors who were leaders in advocacy for young children and their families. What does the inventory in your library show you about the voices featured? Do the journals and magazines reflect the composition of the community? Be prepared to share your findings with your colleagues.

Study Questions

1. Who does early care and education serve?
2. Who are the missing voices in the history of early care and education? Why is this omission of these voices important in our lives today?

3. How do systemic racism and a one-size-fits-all view affect all of society? What are the implications for you as a teacher for improving your own practice and facilitating the learning of young children?
4. Where should research and practice be headed in the near future?

Suggested Readings

Banks, J. A. (2020). *Diversity, transformative knowledge, and civic education: Selected essays*. New York: Routledge.
Delpit, L. (2019). *Teaching when the world is on fire*. New York: The New Press.
Zigler, E., & Styco, S. J. (2010). *The hidden history of Head Start*. New York: Oxford.

Websites for Additional Information

Annie E. Casey Foundation https://www.aecf.org/
Anti-Bias Leaders in Early Childhood Education: A Guide to Change https://www.antibias leadersece.com/
Child Trends https://www.childtrends.org/
Equity Research Action Coalition UNC Frank Graham Child Development Institute https://fpg.unc.edu/projects/equity-research-action-coalition
Head Start Early Childhood Learning & Knowledge Center https://eclkc.ohs.acf.hhs.gov/about-us/article/head-start-timeline
National Black Child Development Institute https://www.nbcdi.org
National Institute for Early Education Research https://nieer.org
National Women's History Museum
    https://www.womenshistory.org/education-resources/biographies/ida-b-wells-barnett
    https://www.womenshistory.org/education-resources/biographies/mary-mcleod-bethune

Chapter 6

Meeting the Needs of Young Emergent Bilinguals

Xiaoning Chen, Ph.D.

One language sets you in a corridor for life. Two languages open every door along the way.

—*Frank Smith*

TERMS TO KNOW

anti-racist pedagogy	funds of knowledge
culturally responsive teaching	linguistically responsive teaching
culture	social justice
emergent bilinguals	translanguaging

Overview

Emergent bilinguals refers to learners who are in the process of developing proficiency in more than one language. Young emergent bilinguals are a diverse group of children with varied needs. Due to their diverse backgrounds, these children bring unique **funds of knowledge** (González et al., 2005) to enrich the school community.

For many children, PreK–3 is the time when they have their first formal schooling experience. As a result, emergent bilingual children may encounter many challenges. The major challenges are: (1) learning a new language, (2) adapting to the school community, and (3) constructing and negotiating identities. In the process, these children explore answers to the questions: "Who am I?" "How do I fit in the communities of home, school, and society?" "What does it mean to be a citizen in the global world?"

In responding to these challenges, this chapter explores early childhood teachers' professional responsibilities and developmentally appropriate practices for working with emergent bilinguals. The goal is to empower these children to make connections to their home language and culture, explore their multiple identities in the intersecting sociocultural communities, and make informed decisions about school and schooling.

Focus Questions

1. Who are young emergent bilinguals?
2. How must early childhood teachers serve young emergent bilinguals?
3. What are developmentally appropriate practices for young emergent bilinguals?

Who Are Young Emergent Bilinguals?

Our educational landscape has become increasingly diverse with children from various cultural and linguistic backgrounds. In light of the diversity in classrooms, we start the chapter by asking the important question of "Who are they?" This question helps us explore further the diverse profiles of these children.

Children aged birth to five who were foreign-born or have at least one immigrant parent have grown from 13.5 percent in 1990 to 24.7 percent in 2018 in the United States (Migration Policy Institute, 2018). In other words, about one in every four children come from immigrant families nationwide. There are some variations at the state level. From 2006 to 2017, the traditional immigration states such as Texas and California experienced a smaller increase in comparison to new destinations such as North Carolina and Nebraska (Children of Immigrants, 2019).

The public-school data indicate that the percentage of students who are identified as English language learners (ELLs) is higher in lower grades than of those in upper grades (NCES, 2019). In fall 2016, for instance, 16.2 percent of kindergarteners were ELL students. It drops to 8.5 percent for sixth graders and 6.9 percent for eighth graders.

Nonetheless, the data on children (birth to five years old) from diverse cultural and language backgrounds are inconclusive. Not all children are enrolled in early childhood care and education programs. In addition, the NCES data report shows family immigration status and provides statistics on school-aged children who are identified as ELLs. The number does not include all children who speak a home language other than English.

Culturally and linguistically diverse children from birth to eight are considered the most diverse age group in the United States. They have a number of characteristics:

- The majority are native-born US citizens.
- They have varied ethnic, socioeconomic, and linguistic backgrounds.
- They are more likely to have parents who have no or limited English proficiency and education background.
- They are frequently challenged to find access to high-quality preschools and health care services (Child Trends Databank, 2019; Migration Policy Institute, 2018; Pew Research Center, 2018).

About Terminology

Various terms are used to refer to learners from culturally and linguistically diverse backgrounds. The commonly used term "ELLs" is the one that highlights the linguistic needs of these children. Formal screening and assessment are required to officially identify students as ELLs and to receive language assistance service.

However, this term fails to acknowledge the funds of knowledge these children bring into the classroom. Their rich linguistic and cultural resources are assets instead of deficits. Teachers should incorporate these funds of knowledge into the curriculum to enhance teaching and learning.

Many children from diverse cultural and linguistic backgrounds are in the process of not only learning English but also developing proficiency in another language(s). So we use the term **emergent bilinguals** (sometimes emergent multilinguals) in this chapter. We use the word "emergent" because PreK–3 children are in the critical process of developing proficiency in one or more languages. We use the term "bilinguals" to feature these children's linguistic resources and the cultural assets they bring to the learning context.

Challenges Young Emergent Bilinguals Face

In An Na's (2001) novel *A Step from Heaven*, the main character is a girl named Young Ju. She immigrated with her family from Korea to the United States at the age of four. The following excerpt shows what goes through Young Ju's mind on her first day at school:

> The lady with the cloud hair is my teacher? But she is a giant person like in the long-ago stories Halmoni [Grandmother] used to tell me so I would be a good girl. My teacher looks like the old witch who ate bad children for dinner.
>
> Apa [Dad] taps my head and says loud, Young. The witch teacher says, "Ho ha do, Yung."
>
> I pull on Apa's shirt and say, Apa. My name is not Young. It is Young Ju. You forgot the Ju part.
>
> Shhh, Young Ju, Apa says, in school you are only Young. Mi Gook [American] people will have too much trouble saying all the syllables. It is better to keep it simple for them. (pp. 50–51)

The above scenario reveals a number of challenges young emergent bilinguals often face in their first encounter at school. Three intersecting challenges are: (1) learning a new language; (2) adjusting to a new school community; and (3) constructing and negotiating identities. All these challenges connect to understanding the social aspects of how a community works, an important topic in social studies education.

Learning a New Language

English is the language children need to fully participate in civic life in the United States. It is important to become proficient in English. Teachers need strategies to support emergent bilingual children in learning English. At the same time, we do not want to frame English as the only legitimate language. Our goal is to set a trajectory for children to become bilingual and biliterate citizens in the global world.

For many emergent bilingual children, English is a new language that sounds different from the familiar tongue at home. They may feel lost when they can't understand the school language. This is illustrated in Young Ju's example above when the teacher attempts to greet her by saying "How are you, Young?" What Young Ju hears is a string of nonsense syllables of "Ho ha do, Yung."

It is also mentally exhausting to listen to a new language and decode the meaning for an extended period of time. Teachers should pay attention to signs of exhaustion. Some children may passively withdraw from engaging in activities. They might appear to be unattentive or bored, or may simply fall asleep. Others might actively protest by being antsy, doing off-task activities, or acting up. When teachers observe these signs, it is possible that children need a mental break.

Emergent bilingual children may also have difficulty communicating their basic needs and wants if they have limited exposure to the school language. They may feel confused and frustrated if no one understands their language. It is ideal to have a bilingual staff member or a peer in the room who can interpret or translate the key information using the child's home language.

If there is no one in the room to help break the language barrier, the teacher can consult with the family on ways to effectively communicate with the child. For example, the teacher can create a schedule using visuals or a list of the most commonly used key words and phrases in the child's home language and English. Technological tools such as Google Translate can be used to support communication as well.

Similar to first language development, there are a total of five stages of second language acquisition (Krashen & Terrell, 1983). These stages are:

- preproduction
- early production
- speech emergence
- intermediate fluency
- advanced fluency

We highlight the first stage here because while children are yet to produce the new language—English—during this stage, they make progress socially, linguistically, and cognitively. The preproduction stage is also called the stage of a silent period. The silent period may last a few hours, but in other cases it can take several months or even a year.

During this stage, children take the time to observe, listen, and process the new language. They can demonstrate understanding by using nonverbal ways such as nodding or pointing to objects. To collect evidence of learning, the teacher can create hands-on activities and encourage responses in multiple modalities. Sample modalities include drawing, body language, and using manipulatives.

We have discussed challenges faced by emergent bilingual children who have limited exposure to English before they start schooling. How about emergent bilingual children who have a certain level of proficiency in English? What challenges do they experience at school?

Learning a language is a complex social process. Different variables such as age, personality, gender, social class, and race play important roles in the process. Further, there is a strong linkage between language and **culture**. Language is the medium of culture (Vygotsky, 1978). Our language uses are shaped by culture and reflect the thinking and understanding of the outside world.

Heath's (1983) study reveals that children's discourse patterns and cultural practices vary significantly among racial groups with different socioeconomic statuses. Children from English-speaking, middle-class communities are more likely to experience consistent practices at home and school. As a result, these children are more school-oriented and familiar with academic discourses. In contrast, emergent bilingual children often experience different discourse patterns and cultural practices between home and school. Consequently, these children are frequently placed in a disadvantageous position in acquiring foundational skills for academic learning (Fillmore, 2000).

Besides the challenge of learning the school discourse, emergent bilingual children are at risk of losing their home language (Fillmore, 2000). A possible factor that expedites home language loss is that emergent bilingual children are under peer and social pressure to assimilate into the mainstream culture. The differences (e.g., primary language, name, or physical appearance) are regarded as undesirable factors that prevent them from fitting in.

Sometimes family is a factor that contributes to the loss. When families have limited education and job opportunities, they believe English is the language leading to prosperity. As a result, they discourage young children from acquiring fluency in their home language. In fact, children with a strong home language can transfer the linguistic concepts and knowledge to enhance the learning of a new language (Cummins, 2011; Thomas & Collier, 2002).

Home language loss begins to occur as early as the age of three when children start early childhood care and education programs. Moreover, if children have limited contact with the home language in the linguistic community, their ability to communicate in their primary language may diminish in just two to three years (Cummins, 1994).

Home language loss can be a serious family and social issue. Family is an important unit of society that has a series of social functions. They include: carrying on family rituals and cultural values, coping with emotional turmoil, and nurturing responsible and productive future citizens. All these functions, however, are realized through meaningful communication, words that family members are comfortable with and feel competent in using.

Adjusting to a New School Community

School is usually the first formal social community children encounter beyond the home. The school community is a micro-culture with specific practices, rules, and expectations. How can teachers support emergent bilingual children learning about culture and making the transition from home to school?

It is common for children to experience anxiety as they leave the comfort of home and go to a formal setting of school. For emergent bilingual children, the level of anxiety is higher. An example of the heightened affective filter is shown in the scenario with Young Ju. She views the teacher as a giant "witch" who will eat children who behave inappropriately.

Young Ju's perception of the teacher comes from stories her grandmother told her. The stories families choose to share with their children usually reflect the cultural beliefs and values important to the home culture. So what is culture? How does understanding of home cultures inform teaching and learning at school?

A deeper understanding of culture must go beyond traditions and holidays. Cultural domains include the *what*, *how*, and *why* (Lynch & Hanson, 2011). The *what* is the most tangible domain as it refers to cultural artifacts such as traditional clothing, food, games, music, art, tools, and language. The *how* domain is the way people interact and communicate with each other. The *why* is cultural perspectives, values, and beliefs that provide the rationale for the *what* and *how*.

Culture has a significant impact on child-rearing beliefs and practices (Cummins, 2000). As a result, the way emergent bilinguals are socialized may be quite different from that of the mainstream school culture. Social studies education is pivotal as children learn how to become members of the school community. They need to know where things are in the room, what the daily routine is, and who they ask for help. They need to learn what the rules and expectations are and how they work. The initial understanding of rules is a precursor for learning about laws and legislation later in life. It is a critical part of civic education that concerns the successful functioning of a society.

The rules and expectations that community members follow support the *how* and *why* domains of culture. For example, how do I address the teacher and peers? What should I say if I sneeze? When can I use the bathroom? How do I participate in group discussion? How do I take turns? Why am I expected to maintain eye contact when talking to the teacher? These are referred to as the "hidden curriculum" (Jackson, 1968) because they are often not formally communicated.

While every child experiences the hidden curriculum to some extent, the special challenges for emergent bilinguals are twofold. For one, the cultural practices and discourse patterns used at home are often at odds with those at school. For another, many emergent bilingual children need to learn the new rules and a new language at the same time.

Learning about school rules and expectations is challenging. At the same time, it offers the teacher and children opportunities to engage in inquiry about families and culture, both of which are at the core of social studies education at PreK–3. Below we share an example of how to engage newcomer emergent bilinguals like Young Ju to learn more about families and home and school cultures.

The teacher, Ms. López, encouraged the children to brainstorm what they wanted to know about rules. The class settled on the inquiry question: Why do we have rules? Ms. López invited children to have a conversation with their families about: (1) What are three rules at home? (2) Who made those rules? and (3) How do the rules influence the way we talk and behave? As they reported back, Ms. López recorded the children's responses on the board. Those who were at the early language proficiency stages were encouraged to share with the class by drawing or acting things out. The whole group identified similar and different rules at home. They then answered the inquiry question by discussing how these rules set boundaries and expectations on their behaviors. The next day, Ms. López engaged the children to create their own classroom rules.

It takes thoughtful planning and scaffolding to help children understand the nuances of culture. Learning to adapt language and behaviors in a culturally acceptable manner in the communities of school and home sets a strong foundation for civic education. It helps children develop an understanding of how to take responsibility and exercise their rights in the global community.

Constructing and Negotiating Identities

Identities are socially constructed and multifaceted. Children define who they are based on their relationship with others. Examples of children's identities include "younger brother/bigger sister," "son/daughter," "boy/girl," "Latina/o," and "kindergartner." These identities indicate children's affiliation and positioning with social, gender, and ethnic groups, among others.

Name is an important part of a child's social identities. In Young Ju's case, her father shortened her name from "Young Ju" to "Young." The teacher mispronounced it as "Yung." The child was given a new identity of "Yung" at school, which could significantly change the pronunciation and meaning of her name. A culturally sensitive teacher would ask the family what the child's name was and learn how to correctly pronounce it. It is also helpful to confirm with the child what s/he would like to be called at school.

Many culturally diverse families adopt Anglo names for their children because their ethnic names are difficult for teachers and peers to pronounce. But with the support from families and technology, saying a child's name correctly is no longer a challenge. There are many online resources (e.g., https://www.pronouncenames.com/) available to help us pronounce names from different parts of the world. It is a small gesture from the teacher's end but goes a long way in supporting the development of a child's social identities.

To help children learn more about each other's culture and families, a project the teacher can engage the class to do is "All About Names." The teacher can share children's books such as *The Name Jar* by Yangsook Choi (2002) as a hook for the inquiry. Children are encouraged to do research about how they got their names, what their names mean, and how they write their names in their home language, if possible. Cultural practices of how the names are presented can also be included in the discussion. For example, in Asian cultures including China, Korea, and Japan, the last name is written before the first name. The convention in the United States is the opposite. This activity not only helps children develop a deeper understanding of culture but also supports community building.

Another aspect of negotiating identities has to do with different, sometimes conflicting beliefs and values at home and in school. For instance, families from Hispanic backgrounds may expect their children to listen quietly and ask no questions when an authority figure talks. This is to show respect in a traditionally hierarchical culture. However, in school, they are expected to ask questions and engage in discussions.

All children from diverse cultural backgrounds experience similar situations to some extent. But for emergent bilinguals, the issue is more significant because they often do not have the language to communicate their challenges effectively. They need help from teachers to articulate and address their unique needs.

Instead of making children choose between the school or the home self, our goal is to enhance children's intercultural competence. Intercultural competence refers to a set of skills to communicate and work effectively with people from other cultures (Leung et al., 2014). These skills include how to adapt thinking and behaviors to function effectively across cultures. Teachers can create meaningful class activities to support children's intercultural competence. For example, the teacher can set up a drama center in the room with prompts describing situations children encounter at home and in school. Children role-play scenarios using culturally appropriate languages and behaviors based on the context of the center.

It is critical for teachers to embrace funds of knowledge from families to develop understanding about children. By doing so, teachers support emergent bilingual children to seek answers to who they are, who they want to be, and how they connect to the communities of home, school, and society.

How Must Early Childhood Teachers Serve Young Emergent Bilinguals?

In light of the challenges that young emergent bilingual children encounter, this section makes the point that, to fulfill their professional responsibilities, early childhood teachers must be advocates for emergent bilinguals.

The NAEYC (2011) Code of Ethical Conduct outlines key obligations and responsibilities of early childhood teachers. The most important commitment related to emergent bilinguals and families is to serve as advocates for equity and social justice. We break down the discussion based on teachers' professional relationships with children, families, and community/society.

Advocates for Emergent Bilingual Children

Children as young as three years old begin to develop knowledge about racial groups (Ramsey, 2004). Husband (2010) found that first graders possessed a significant level of knowledge about race and racism through their personal or family experiences. It is not too early to implement an anti-racist pedagogy with a focus on social justice. The **anti-racist pedagogy** moves teaching and learning beyond superficial notions about culture and race. Teachers make an effort to highlight the perspectives of marginalized groups and invite children to critically examine issues with power structures.

Anti-racist pedagogy also calls for teachers to critically examine instruction and assessment to identify potential linguistic and cultural biases. An example of a cultural bias was to ask children to bring cereal boxes from home to build a fort. The assumption was that cereal is a staple breakfast item in all families. Some children failed to complete this task because they did not understand what a cereal box was, nor did they have any at home. Such biases may put some children without relevant background knowledge in a disadvantageous position.

Teachers use assessment data to make critical placement decisions that may have long-term impacts on children. So, we need to make sure to use a variety of assessment tools with minimal biases. Teachers should also seek input from different stakeholders, including families, when evaluating children's academic progress.

Further, teachers should strive to provide learning experiences that help children achieve their full potential. Our goal is for children to become bilingual and biliterate citizens who can make informed actions. We show children the value of bilingual thinking, speaking, and writing. We do this with charts posted in the languages of our class, with digital media in the languages, and with children's books written in the languages of our class. We invite families to our class to share customs and stories. We also collaborate with families to maintain and support children's development in their home language.

Advocates for Families of Emergent Bilinguals

While working with emergent bilingual children, it is a must for teachers to develop a trustful relationship with families. Teachers should view families as the experts of their children in the context of home and culture. Through the partnership between school and home, we gain insights on how to best support these children to thrive academically and socially. We also help families enhance their understanding of their children.

In some cases, families may not feel comfortable going to an official setting such as school. It may be related to their immigration status, English language proficiency, or their own educational experiences, among others. Another case would be that the families do not have the time or transportation to get to school.

To build the relationship, teachers should be sensitive about families' needs and address their concerns. For example, teachers can make sure that families receive communication in their preferred language. That they have accessible means to reach the teacher and ask questions. Also, the family may feel more relaxed when we change the meeting location from school to home or a frequently visited place in the community.

Emergent bilingual children and their families, with limited English proficiency and access to resources in the community, may not be able to make their voices heard. They rely on teachers' support to navigate the system. We provide guidance on how to meet specific linguistic, financial, or social-emotional needs of families by connecting them to available services and resources.

Another important responsibility is to support the education of families, especially with those from diverse linguistic and cultural backgrounds. The National Center for Education Statistics (2018) shows that the percentage of three-to-five-year-old enrollment in preschool programs corresponds positively to parents' educational background. When children do not have access to high-quality early childhood care and education experiences, they may face challenges in achieving school readiness upon starting formal schooling at the age of five. It is critical to provide educational opportunities to diverse families so they are empowered to support their children outside of school and make informed decisions about their future.

Given the needs of diverse families, schools can provide information sessions on a regular basis on topics such as:

- How do families support primary language and literacy development at home?
- What activities can families engage their children in to promote social-emotional learning?
- What roles do families play in building an inclusive community?

Session organizers need to work with families to identify a convenient location, time, transportation, childcare, and language translation service.

Advocates in Community and Society

Collectively, teachers have the social responsibility to advocate for children's rights. Teachers play an active role in ensuring policies are in place to protect children's well-being. At the school level, emergent bilinguals may face bullying or discrimination because of their unique cultural practices. For instance, the teacher noticed that Saima was sitting at a corner all by herself during lunchtime. After talking to her, the teacher learned that Saima was teased because of the lunch she brought from home. Other children said that the food looked weird and had a strong smell. The teacher used the incident as a teachable moment to discuss how food and dietary preferences vary among people. Everyone enjoys different kinds of food. To create a safe school environment for all children, teachers should reinforce a policy of zero-tolerance to bullying. All members of the community are invited to participate in continuing education and courageous conversations on culturally and racially sensitive topics.

At the societal level, emergent bilingual children face unique challenges. For example, children whose parents are undocumented are at risk of being separated from their families under the anti-immigrant political climate. On the first day of school in 2019, the US Immigration and Customs Enforcement (ICE) raided seven food processing plants in Mississippi. Close to 700 undocumented immigrants were detained. Many of them were parents of young emergent bilinguals. These children, having nowhere to go at the end of the school day, were scared and stressed. This example shows how teachers should work with community activists and local officials to advocate for the best interests of children and immigrant rights. Emergent bilingual children and their families are assured that no matter what their immigration status, what language they speak, and what their religious beliefs are, schools provide a safe shelter from discrimination and persecution.

What Are Developmentally Appropriate Practices for Young Emergent Bilinguals?

Building upon the professional responsibilities of early childhood teachers, we discuss three developmentally appropriate practices revolving around the social studies themes of families, culture, and communities. Classroom scenarios are provided to elaborate on what it looks like when we apply these practices in working with emergent bilinguals.

Creating an Optimal Learning Environment

An optimal learning environment is essential for emergent bilingual children. What does such an environment look like? The physical environment should look inviting and create a sense of belonging for young children. It is important to post welcoming signs in different languages. Also, the environment should include visual images, cultural artifacts, and children's books that represent diversity in the community. Children enjoy seeing representations of diverse families and familiar places such as neighborhoods, parks, local markets, and possibly their homeland.

An optimal learning environment also considers the social aspect of the environment. Children are more likely to be successful in learning a new language in a positive learning environment with a low level of anxiety (Krashen, 1982). The most critical disposition that teachers should demonstrate is ways to embrace and celebrate diversity. Besides names and greetings, teachers should develop a deeper understanding of the linguistic system in children's home language. There are alphabetic (e.g., Spanish), syllabic (e.g., Japanese), and logographic languages (e.g.,

Chinese). The phoneme (sound), grapheme (letter or symbol), and syntax (grammar) can vary greatly from one to the other. Some linguistic features can positively influence the learning of the new language. For instance, the English word *family* is almost identical to the word *familia* in Spanish. They are called cognates. Teachers can develop targeted instruction based on their understanding of children's home language systems.

Most importantly, optimal learning conditions mean that different cultures and languages are treated with respect and equal status. Children view the school not as a place where everything is different from or contradictory to what they have learned at home. Rather it is an extension of their growing social world, and they see themselves represented positively in the curriculum and by teaching staff and peers.

Getting to Know Young Learners Through a Whole-Child Approach

Second Language Acquisition (SLA) theories show that both group variables and individual traits play significant roles in language learning (Guerrero, 2004; Fillmore, 2014). Group variables include socioeconomic status, primary culture and language, and immigration status. Examples of individual traits are age, personality, learning style, and previous education. Due to the different variables among emergent bilingual children, teachers should get to know their learners as a whole child. A whole child approach is to consider all the factors, both inside and outside school, to inform policies, practices, and relationships that ensure each child's engagement and success (Association for Supervision and Curriculum Development, n.d.).

Knowledge about children comes from an understanding of the context of family, community, and culture (NAEYC, 2011). Vital information may include the family's immigrant experience and educational background, language(s) used at home, cultural beliefs, their children's early education experiences, personality, and learning style. Knowing the child is the most foundational principle for effective teaching of emergent bilinguals (Short et al., 2018).

Classroom practices teachers can use to know the learners focus on exploring the social world of children. This is one of the key themes of social studies education for young children. For instance, the class can work on a digital storytelling project that uses family photos and narratives to answer the question: "Who am I?" The digital form is beneficial to emergent bilinguals because narration can be rehearsed ahead of time. Use of home languages is welcomed.

Working with emergent bilingual children from a whole-child approach provides teachers opportunities to discover more about cultural practices and perspectives diverse families have. One example is that the teacher noticed that only one parent came to Jayden's parent–teacher conference at a time. Also, the mother and father did not have the same last name. This might give the impression that the parents were divorced or not involved. The teacher planned a home visit to learn more about the family. During the home visit, the teacher observed that both parents were present in the house and they interacted with each other like a happy family.

In a more in-depth interview, the teacher learned some key information about the family and their culture. One was that a woman does not change her last name after getting married in their culture. Also, it was not common for the family to hire an outsider (e.g., a babysitter) to take care of their children. As a result, one parent had to stay at home taking care of the children while the other attended school activities. As a result of the home visit, two school practices were adjusted. One was to change the practice of addressing the parents as "Mr. and Mrs. [Family Last Name]" to "Mr. [Father's Last Name] and Mrs. [Mother's Last Name]" in school communication. The other change was to offer a more flexible schedule that allows both parents to participate in school events.

The above example shows how to adopt a whole-child approach to resolve potential cultural dissonances between home and school. In the example, the teacher positions diverse families as experts about their culture and children. By doing so, teachers learn how children are socialized at home through a cultural lens. They also gain insights into the values and beliefs that are important to children and their families. Working with families and communities through the whole child approach, teachers are able to successfully meet the varying linguistic, cultural, social-emotional, and cognitive needs.

Developing and Delivering Culturally and Linguistically Responsive Instruction

Building on a solid understanding of who young emergent bilingual learners are, teachers can effectively implement culturally and linguistically responsive teaching (CLRT). CLRT combines two related thrusts of research, namely, **culturally responsive teaching** (CRT) and **linguistically responsive teaching** (LRT), into one framework.

CRT refers to pedagogical practices to help children achieve academic success and cultural competence (Ladson-Billings, 1995). These pedagogical practices include drawing on children's diverse cultural backgrounds and lived experiences in order to achieve equitable educational outcomes and promote **social justice** (Hernandez et al., 2013; Ladson-Billings, 1995). Culturally responsive teachers make efforts to plan and implement curricula and strategies that leverage emergent bilingual children's funds of knowledge.

The following scenario provides an example of how to implement CRT in a second-grade classroom. The teacher, Mr. Miller, built on emergent bilingual children's cultural background to create an engaging social studies unit.

Veterans Day was around the corner. Traditionally, teachers use the time to discuss the patriotism US citizens show by serving in the military. The school was planning to hold an assembly to honor veterans. Students were encouraged to interview family members who had served the country and share their personal stories and pictures. Ray was a student whose parents were first-generation immigrants from China. Eager to be part of the honored families, Ray had a conversation with his mother after school:

Ray: Mom, do we have a veteran in our family?
Mom: Yes, your grandpa on your father's side served in the military. He fought in the Vietnam War.
Ray: Great! Shall we bring a picture of him to the school for Veterans Day?

Mom: Well, are you aware that your grandpa was a Chinese citizen? At that time, he served the Chinese military and fought against the US.
Ray (sounding a bit confused and disappointed): Oh?!

After a moment of silence, Ray moved onto a new topic. Yet he had some unanswered questions lingering in his mind: "Who are veterans and who are not? Why? Who am I? Which side would I be on if there was a conflict between USA and China?" Later that day, Ray's mother reached out to Mr. Miller and shared the conversation they had at home.

As a culturally responsive teacher, Mr. Miller moved a step further to expand the focus of Veterans Day from the US perspective. He started an inquiry-based unit in the class by posing the compelling questions: "Who is a veteran? Why are veterans honored?" Using pictures of veterans and the personal stories students gathered from home, Mr. Miller engaged children in a number of activities to expand their perspectives. They first compared how the veterans look alike or different. They then sorted the veterans into different categories according to time in history, war(s) they fought, and countries they served. A world map and a student-created timeline were visuals to support comprehension. Next, they described characteristics of the veterans. Finally, students created a class book with personal accounts from the veterans' perspectives.

Through these activities, children were able to see the veterans as well-rounded people who might be both brave and scared. Moreover, they were able to draw the conclusion: No matter which side they were on in a war, veterans dedicated themselves to serve the country they loved. That was the reason veterans are and should be honored.

The unit on veterans serves as an example of how a culturally sensitive teacher integrated emergent bilinguals' cultural backgrounds and experiences to learn about a US holiday. Instead of excluding some voices (e.g., Ray's grandfather being a veteran in China) and creating a dichotomy of right or wrong, teachers are able to help children build understanding about family and communities in a nuanced and contextualized way. This also empowers children to negotiate multiple, sometimes, seemingly conflicting identities of who they are.

The second component of CLRT is linguistically responsive teaching (LRT). The goal of LRT is to develop teachers' essential orientations, knowledge, and skills for working with culturally and linguistically diverse children (Lucas & Villegas, 2010). LRT practices focus on identifying and activating all linguistic and non-linguistic resources to provide comprehensible content.

A related concept to LRT is **translanguaging** (García & Wei, 2014). Contrary to the notion that bilinguals have two distinctly separate languages, they draw from one linguistic repertoire. A translanguaging space blurs the boundary between languages. It creates a space where children are provided with opportunities to use multiple linguistic resources they have to communicate with others. A translanguaging space fosters interlinguistic comparisons and metalinguistic understandings (Alamillo et al., 2017). Velasco and Fialais (2016) noted that the simultaneous biliterate practice in a dual language kindergarten class greatly enhanced "the students' interlinguistic abilities specific to print, phonology and meaning across languages" (p. 1).

The following scenario provides an example of how teachers can strategically create a translanguaging space for the community to learn about each other's language, family, and geography.

I visited a preschool (four to five years old) room where Ms. Helen student-taught. Ms. Helen informed me that the class recently welcomed Reiko, a new girl from Japan. I was curious to see how Reiko was doing. When I entered the room, the children were at the transition time, finishing their work at tables. Paper, markers, and crayons were scattered around. I saw an Asian-looking girl, sitting quietly by herself at the table. I sat down by her side, attempting to start a conversation with her. "Hello," I spoke softly with a smile, "What's your name?" The child smiled back at me, yet not responding to my question.

I quickly realized that Reiko didn't respond because she might not understand my question in English. So what should I do? First, I tried to activate my linguistic resources in her home language—Japanese. Although I only remembered a few words from the college years, I managed to greet her and introduce myself. Realizing that I spoke her home language, she beamed with a big grin, eager to talk more with me in Japanese. Yet I had no idea what she was saying. What should I do next?

I reverted to the use of visuals to continue the communication. I started out drawing a map of Japan, hoping to find out which part of Japan she came from. Then I drew a picture of my family (the stick figures on the right-hand side of figure 6.1). She picked up the idea quickly, drawing a picture of her brother and her and a Japanese national flag indicating her nationality (figure 6.1 on the left). She also wrote her brother's name in the Japanese alphabet (Hiragana) on the top of the page.

Ms. Helen joined us as I continued to learn about Reiko through drawing on the other side of the paper. In figure 6.2, Ms. Helen drew her house and her pet dog on the left. She wrote the word "DOG" with an arrow pointing to the dog. Following suit, Reiko drew her house and dog on the right. Ms. Helen wrote the word "DOG" again with an underline.

Reiko wrote her mother's name in Japanese Hiragana on the top of the page. On the lower right hand of the page, Ms. Helen and I wrote our names in English. Reiko wrote her name in both Japanese Hiragana and English. She even wrote all

FIGURE 6.1 Me and My Family (Part I). *Source*: Xiaoning Chen.

FIGURE 6.2   Me and My Family (Part II). *Source*: Xiaoning Chen.

the numeric numbers she knew. At the bottom of the page, I wrote down the Chinese characters "日本人" (means "Japanese people") as this was a cognate between Chinese and Japanese Kanji.

Through the use of several strategies, Ms. Helen and I got to know the child's name, her family, and her home country in a short timeframe. Moreover, the scenario illustrates how a teacher allows multiple languages and literacies to be acknowledged and celebrated in the classroom. The LRT practices have helped Reiko to negotiate her identities. She was originally positioned as a newcomer who didn't speak English. By embracing her home language and celebrating the translanguaging practices, we acknowledged and confirmed Reiko's identity as a resourceful communicator who had an accelerated level of literacy.

As shown in both scenarios discussed above, the CLRT framework highlights teachers' practices in leveraging emergent bilingual children's cultural and linguistic resources as assets while building proficiency in language and content. Such pedagogical practices are critical to the core areas of child development and learning, individual child characteristics, and social and cultural contexts.

Conclusion

Emergent bilingual children have unique characteristics and needs. They face challenges of learning a new language, adjusting to a new school community, and negotiating multiple identities between home and school. As teachers of young children, we can advocate for equity and social justice. Using the social studies themes of families, culture, and communities, our practice is developmentally appropriate for young emergent bilinguals.

Since PreK–3 marks the beginning journey of a child's first formal educational experience, it plays a critical role in shaping future citizens and the prospects for our society. Thus, with practices for young emergent bilinguals described here, we contribute to the goal of social studies education to develop college and career-ready citizens who have global perspectives and make informed decisions in civic life (C-3 Framework, NCSS, 2019).

Activities in the Field

1. Engage in an ethnographic study of the community you teach or the one you are interested in teaching. Study the history and people of the community. Look at how ethnic and racial composition, languages spoken, socioeconomic status, and family structures have been changing over time. Identify cultural centers and social resources available to support culturally and linguistically diverse families and their children.
2. Conduct a home visit with a culturally and linguistically diverse family with young children. Make sure translation service is available if no common language is shared between you and the family. Observe how the family members talk and interact with each other. Ask questions about the family's experiences in the community. Reflect on how such information contributes to the understanding of learners as a whole child.

Activities in the Library

1. Consult with a librarian to create an annotated bibliography of multicultural children's books in the library. Categorize these books based on themes, genres, cultures represented, and languages (monolingual versus bilingual). Reflect on which books positively connect to the experience of emergent bilingual children in the community.
2. Take an inventory of what resources and services are provided for young children in the library. Reflect on which ones are accessible to all families in the community and which ones are not. Bring suggestions and rationale to the library staff to promote social justice.

Study Questions

1. How do you define culture? Which aspects are most important to you and why?
2. Reflect on a time when you were puzzled by an emergent bilingual child's behavior or language use. What did you do? What else could be done in order to make sense of what was going on?
3. How can an early childhood educator create a positive learning environment to support emergent bilingual children's language and social studies learning?
4. What is hidden curriculum? Identify practices that are part of the hidden curriculum in your classroom. How do you plan to address them with newcomer children?
5. What are effective developmentally appropriate practices that leverage emergent bilingual children and their families' funds of knowledge to create positive learning experiences at school?
6. What are the responsibilities of early childhood educators in their relationships with emergent bilingual children and their families?

Reflect and Reread

1. Why is the term "emergent bilingual children" more inclusive than others? How does the term shed a positive light on young children's cultural and linguistic assets?
2. What are unique characteristics of emergent bilingual children? What challenges do they face? What are the implications for early childhood educators?
3. What does culturally and linguistically responsive teaching mean to you? How do you implement this framework in your daily work with young emergent bilinguals?

Suggested Readings

Brouillette, L. (2012). Supporting the language development of Limited English Proficient students through arts integration in the primary grades. *Arts Education Policy Review, 113*(2), 68–74. doi: 10.1080/10632913.2012.656494

Cummins, J. (2016). Multilingual education: pedagogy, power, and identity. In A. Kalan (Ed.), *Who is afraid of multilingual education?* (pp. 62–85). Multilingual Matters.

Greenfader, C. M., Brouillette, L., & Farkas, G. (2015). Effect of a performing arts program on the oral language skills of young English learners. *Reading Research Quarterly, 50*(2), 185–203. doi:10.1002/rrq.90

Peregoy, S. F., & Boyle, O. F. (2016). *Reading, writing and learning in ESL: A resource book for teaching K-12 English learners* (7th ed.). Pearson.

Ralabate, P. K., & Nelson, L. L. (2017). *Culturally responsive design for English learners: The UDL approach.* CAST Professional Publishing.

TESOL International Association Writing Team. (2018). *The 6 principles for exemplary teaching of English learners.* TESOL Press.

Selected Children's Literature

Choi, Y. (2003). *The name jar.* Tronto, Ontario, Canada: Dragonfly Books.

Fields, T. (2007). *Burro's tortillas.* (S. Rogers Illus.). Mount Pleasant, SC: Sylvan Dell Publishing.

Levine, E. (1995). *I hate English.* (S. Björkman Illus.). New York: Scholastic.

Morris, A. (2000). *Families.* New York: HarperCollins.

O'Brien, A. S. (2018). *I'm new here.* Watertown, MA: Charlesbridge.

Penfold, A. (2019). *All are welcome.* New York: Bloomsbury Children's Books.

Recorvits, H. (2014). *My name is Yoon.* (G. Swiatkowska Illus.). New York: Square Fish.

Woodson, J. (2018). *The day you begin.* (R. Lopez Illus.). New York: Nancy Paulsen Books.

Websites for Additional Information

Colorín Colorado: A bilingual site for educators and families of English Language Learners: https://www.colorincolorado.org/

Teacher Toolkit: English Language Learners (ELLs): https://www.teachingchannel.org/blog/2014/11/04/english-language-learners-resources/

The Teaching Channel: https://www.teachingchannel.com/

TESOL: Teachers of English to Speakers of Other Languages International Organization: https://www.tesol.org/

US Department of Education-Office of English Language Acquisition (OELA): https://www2.ed.gov/about/offices/list/oela/index.html

WIDA early years: https://wida.wisc.edu/memberships/early-years

Chapter 7

How Are We Including and Supporting All Children, Helping All Children Thrive?

Michelle Parker-Katz, Ph.D.,
and Amanda Passmore, Ph.D.

For there is always light. If only we're brave enough to see it. If only we're brave enough to be it.

—*Amanda Gorman*

Overview

In this chapter we focus on the first and fourth domains of the C3 Framework: that is, *developing questions and planning inquiries*, and *communicating conclusions and taking informed action*. We do this by presenting a vignette about Ms. Leslie teaching social studies to a class of five-year-old children and thinking with her about being responsive to all her children. We look at her planning and how planning is informed in part by her questioning as well as her planning inquiries. Likewise, she draws on her interpretations of varied sorts of data to enact her teaching choices. Thus, she is taking informed action in her teaching practices.

The chapter's aim is twofold. One aim is consistent with the disciplines of social studies. That is, we focus on democratic principles of inclusion for all children, diverse in their strengths and challenges, along with holistically addressing multiple aspects of a young child, including social-emotional learning, as well as academics. A related second aim is to make the case that social studies teachers' exploration of two foundational ideas (ecological frameworks and Universal Design for Learning) helps them establish core values in their practices. Together, these ideas will help teachers create practices so they can help all students thrive. We focus on three major interventions related to the centrality of home–school relationships: family connectedness through eco-mapping, child self-monitoring, social stories, and student–teacher signal systems. What is critical to teachers changing and enhancing their practices to implement instructional interventions and assess them, however, is a personal systematic study of their practices. By conducting teacher action research, teachers support their ongoing development, which in turn enhances children's learning. This recursive cycle is paramount to effective practice. Teaching social studies especially invites techniques to facilitate teacher inquiries focused on supporting a wide array of children in terms of their strengths and challenges as they develop their identities.

Focus Questions

1. How do we address all children's potential, recognizing all children have assets and challenges?
2. What foundational ideas could help teachers like Ms. Leslie make decisions about their next instructional steps?
3. How do family connections link with ecological conceptions?
4. How do teachers move from theory to practice?
5. How does the development of core professional values draw on theory and link it to practice to help teachers?
6. How do teachers implement planned strategies to help all students thrive?
7. How can sustained, systematic teacher action research inquiry help teachers support all children in learning social studies?
8. How can a teacher begin conducting teacher action research?

How Do We Address All Children's Potential, Recognizing All Children Have Assets and Challenges?

To explore this question, we follow a teacher named Ms. Leslie. She is a kindergarten teacher in a public school with a widely diverse student population. Using an "inclusion model," the school personnel work collaboratively to educate all children in mixed heterogeneous classes where children from diverse language groups, cultures, and abilities interact as they learn together. The school has multiple personnel with expertise to provide services to help all children thrive. Special educators and teachers with English as second language expertise, for example, work with Ms. Leslie and other teachers to provide specialized supports through resources, consultations during planning, and at times collaborative teaching in the same classroom. These support structures are a school-wide project involving Ms. Leslie and all her colleagues preschool through second grade. She also emphasizes that this school often provides the first time young children can gain insight from others outside their immediate families. So, the interactions of children, teachers, and staff, along with the use of multiple materials and strategies, can together provide great assistance for all children's school success.

Ms. Leslie is closely studying one of her students, Lola. Lola shows many great strengths in learning. She is curious and gets excited about new ideas. She likes to role-play, talk with others about things, and at times use art to show what she is thinking. Often, she likes to work in small groups, either during directed learning or during "learning center time," where Ms. Leslie carefully plans self-guided or peer learning opportunities. Yet at times, Lola seems to explode with an angry statement, or grab some object from another student, or even throw something. Here is one example. Lola had been so happy during the small-group discussion about friendships. It was a learning experience within a four-to-six-week unit, which Ms. Leslie planned with great care, focusing on ideas in both the fifth and sixth thematic strands of the National Council for the Social Studies; that is, experiences focusing on the "study of interactions among individuals, groups, and instructions," along with "study of how people create, interact with, and change structures of power." These standards integrate the Common Core State Standard CCSS.ELA-Literacy RL.K.10: "Actively engage in group reading activities with purpose and understanding."

During the fifteen-minute directed teaching session, Lola had contributed in terrific ways, showing her well-developed five-year-old social skills, along with academic focus and positive interactions among friends. She had nodded her head vigorously in agreement when her pal Juan said friends can play many things together. "Like when we played outside yesterday!" she exclaimed. Ms. Leslie decided to interject that she liked how Lola, Juan, and Aisha took turns deciding who was "it" and would try to tag other friends. Xander joined the group a few minutes late, and the other kids welcomed him. Ms. Leslie elaborated on Xander's entry, deciding this was a good "teachable moment." "Sometimes people join the group or leave it," she said. "When we are friends, that's okay. Can you think of times when people leave or join your group here inside our classroom, too?" Along with others, Lola recounted a story. She told about last week when she'd left a morning meeting. She said she had "needed some time away." Wow, thought Ms. Leslie. She is talking about our new "calming corners" strategy! Ms. Leslie was helping Lola learn to acknowledge when she was getting upset and furthermore to attach an appropriate action of walking away before her anger flared. She knew this practice was helping Lola learn self-regulation and self-determination; that is, Lola was learning to do a self-check to see what she wanted and needed.

Yet just as Ms. Leslie sat wondering about what parts of the "calming corners strategy" might be working, she heard Lola scream and start throwing crayons during the follow-up activity. Wow, she thought. What triggered that behavior? The planned follow-up activity for the children could be done alone or with others. Children were to show a time they were with friends by drawing, recording a story, or using clay to show what it looked like. Doing this activity required much higher-order thinking involving synthesizing ideas and creating. Oh my, Ms. Leslie thought. Did this task frustrate Lola? Or was she tired? She'd come to school today with fewer smiles and chatter than usual; was something bothering her? But what should she do now, while Lola was clearly in some rage?

What Foundational Ideas Could Help Teachers Like Ms. Leslie Make Decisions About Their Next Instructional Steps?

Ms. Leslie had crafted three interconnected "interventions" to support Lola's academic learning along with her social-emotional learning (SEL). These interventions were (1) using social stories, (2) developing a signal system to remind Lola about possible good choices she could choose and implement, and (3) sustained ongoing partnership with Lola's grandmother, who was raising Lola and her siblings. Before we explore these interventions, let's look first at how Ms. Leslie intentionally devised her plan. By integrating the learning outcomes she wanted for Lola's learning and success, Ms. Leslie made choices and monitored how those affected Lola. Through this targeted approach, Ms. Leslie was laying in place ideas that are in fact similar for children as seen in the C3 Framework stated earlier; that is, *developing questions and planning inquiries*, and *communicating conclusions and taking informed action*. While planning for her children, in other words, Ms. Leslie was simultaneously setting up a teacher action research inquiry, which is a way a teacher explores and revises practices while in the midst of teaching.

Ms. Leslie draws on two major foundational ideas to set her professional values and make decisions for action. One is using *ecological frameworks* for addressing how her children's learning in school overlaps with multiple factors both in and out of school. She also draws on Universal Design for Learning as a way to plan her curriculum in multiple ways that can link to related social studies instruction.

First, we explore how an ecological lens can help Ms. Leslie support young children's learning within inclusive environments—in part because we can focus on the pivotal nature of how people interact through varied networks and structures. As conceived by Bronfenbrenner (1992), the framework focuses on how varied aspects of the contexts within which a child grows have determinant consequences. Yet concurrently, as individual children develop, they also influence those contextual structures, consequences, and effects. Children reside in and move through

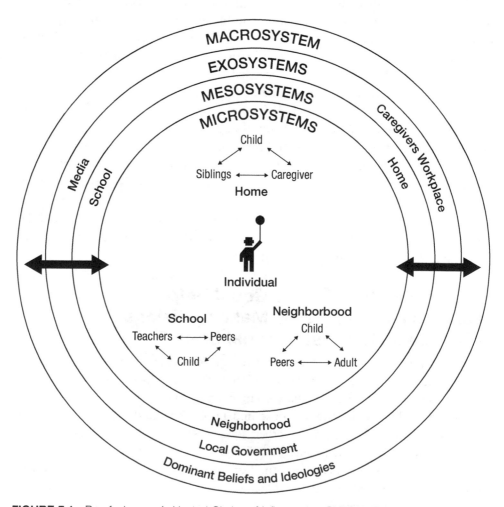

FIGURE 7.1 Bronfenbrenner's Nested Circles of Influence on Children. *Source*: Michelle Parker-Katz and Amanda Passmore.

multiple environments that have multiple structures and systems. Neal and Neal (2013) suggest further that the image of contexts nested within each other, long acknowledged as key to Bronfenbrenner's early work, may be viewed more like a network of interacting parts rather than solid pieces that rest inside each other inertly. This network is shown in figure 7.1, Bronfenbrenner's Nested Circles of Influence on Children.

Seeing our children and ourselves as teachers as parts of interlinked networks is very aligned with effective social studies teaching. Epstein (2014) points to two components of social studies in early childhood. One is social systems of norms and processes affecting human relationships in our day-to-day lives, understanding different people's roles in making communities work, experiencing differences in how people think and act, and seeing how different families and communities share cultural patterns, customs, and beliefs. Another component is learning social concepts such as history and economics. Early childhood learning prepares children through their participation in role-play, studying sequences of time, and understanding goods and services, for instance. Teachers' observations and focused collection of information as they watch children can help them see patterns of learning these social skills.

How Do Family Connections Link With Ecological Conceptions?

In teaching social studies, we concurrently address multiple networks and systems that support human beings. In teaching young children, we especially recognize in a particular child's growth the centrality of the family structures and those possible extended networks. Teachers focus and draw on the funds of knowledge children gain and construct from their families and see and hear ways they build on existing knowledge in their emerging personas. Moll and Gonzalez (1994) emphasize this idea as they explain the "funds of knowledge" approach, writing that the funds are

> those historically accumulated and culturally developed bodies of knowledge and skills essential for household or individual functioning and well-being. As households interact within circles of kinship and friendship, children are "participant-observers" of the exchange of goods, services, and symbolic capital which are part of each household's functioning. (p. 443)

Families draw on diverse, rich amalgams of social understandings. In fact, when children begin their schooling it is often their first interaction with a community outside their family. For this reason, as Epstein (2014) argues, children need instruction and practice in civic engagement among a community other than their family. Therein also, social studies teaching and learning for young children can play a big role. Using pretend play, for instance, children can imagine and act out how to react to peers or several other adults who are school personnel. They can play out how to exchange goods and services, ask for things, or express confusion or dismay in the community outside family and home.

We recognize multiple family factors are part of the dynamics of a young child's learning. Furthermore, these dynamics, along with the interests and dreams of the child themselves, and the family for the child, can operate conjointly with a child's school experiences. Person-centered approaches like these are used in and out of education for planning, therapies, and research methodologies. The concept refers to a set of beliefs giving way to a set of experiences to plan intentional supports for identity development over time (Corcetti & Meeus, 2015).

Drawing on Bronfenbrenner's notions of interconnectivity, Hartman (1978) developed for social workers a graphic way to represent webs of associations the children with whom they worked had. The visual showed supports that were both informal (friendships, family bonds) and formal (early childcare providers, health-related practices). This idea is now referred to as a tool called eco-mapping. The visual emerges from and depicts the assets a family has, including values, beliefs, and resources. The purpose of an eco-map is to identify supports and resources such as friendships, leisure activities, groups with whom the child and family interact, health-care providers that are part of a child's life. Also, the eco-map can depict any gaps in help, as well as any stressors for the family. Ultimately, the eco-map can be used to see the relationships that exist, what might be cultivated, and how multiple players and resources can be brought together to help children thrive in their families and at school. Interconnected bridges to support these outcomes can be planned, studied, and adjusted as needed. Researchers in the National Early Childhood Transition Center (see https://ectacenter.org/topics/transition/transctrs.asp) and other scholars have provided excellent descriptions of the ideas and related templates to carry out the planning (e.g., see Dunst, Sukkar, & Kirby, 2016; Jung, 2010; McWilliam, 2010; Underwood et al., 2018).

Universal Design for Learning

A second conception Ms. Leslie draws on to devise curriculum and related instruction in her social studies teaching is Universal Design for Learning (UDL). When we look through a UDL lens, we focus on removing barriers. Instead of looking at a *person* as having limitations, we look at possible ways to change the *environment* to support success (Rose et al., 2006). Emerging from work in the field of architecture, the idea of "universal" refers to making spaces accessible to all persons. When the universal design principles moved into education, the focus on accessibility became coupled with the inclusion of all learners without segregation based on their particular abilities (Al-Azawei et al., 2016).

The Center for Applied Special Technology (CAST) has become a kind of one-stop-shop for learning about UDL. CAST defines UDL in part for what it is not: it is not an inflexible one-size-fits-all curriculum model. Scholars at CAST argue that the idea of one size fits all actually creates barriers impeding learners' successes. Because people have varied capacities, we must have variation in goals for individuals and use varied methods, resources, and assessment practices to create learning environments where all can do well.

UDL principles are linked to brain research, and the framework is comprised of three interlocking principles corresponding to brain networks activated during a learning experience. With each principle, UDL scholars provide guidelines for teachers to enact a curriculum that draws on children's strengths and enables making adaptations to the environment. We use our *recognition networks* to consider *what* we learn; that is, to focus on ways we represent information. We use our *strategic networks* to focus on *how* we learn; that is, to focus on our interests and preferences and ways to stimulate them. We use our *affective networks* to look at ways to build excitement and connection to learning. (See http://udlguidelines.cast .org for thorough practical guidelines.) In fact, Hayenga and Corpus (2010) suggest a connection between person-centered approaches to intrinsic and extrinsic motivators in middle school children. A person-centered approach of exploring the child's life experiences and identity development can provide a useful association between UDL and brain networks. The concept is illustrated in figure 7.2, Universal Design for Learning Social Studies.

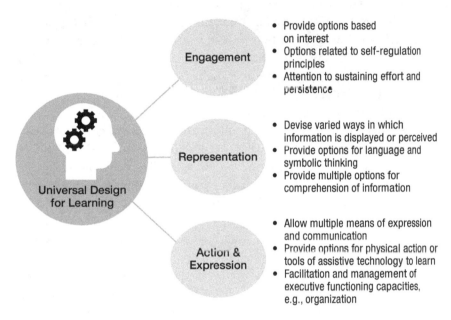

FIGURE 7.2 Universal Design for Learning Social Studies. *Source*: Michelle Parker-Katz and Amanda Passmore.

How Do Teachers Move From Theory to Practice?

Let's look back to Ms. Leslie's current dilemma of how to respond to Lola. Ms. Leslie knew that answering questions we teachers pose to ourselves is essential to enacting our practice while enhancing it. We never know for certain why a child might act as they do, and how our actions as teachers might affect our children's success in the moment and for extending their learning into long-term generalization to other situations. So, we observe. We wonder. Ms. Leslie's questions emerge from what she actually observed (for example, fewer smiles than usual the morning of the incident we discussed) to speculation about reasons why Lola acted as she did (for example, was Lola frustrated with the goals and/or learning experiences?) to thoughts about what immediate actions she could take (for example, remind Lola of the strategy they'd been working on when she gets upset). Since Lortie (1975) first wrote about what he called the immediacy and presentism of teachers' work, many others have talked about the conundrum of the reality: often teachers need to act quickly, yet at the same time, act thoughtfully.

How Does the Development of Core Professional Values Draw on Theory and Link It to Practice to Help Teachers?

Inclusive classroom environments. As Ms. Leslie continues to build her teaching practice even after her seven years in practice, she felt surer of two professional values: both revolving around integration, intersection, and interconnection. First, she believes strongly that children should *learn in inclusive classroom environments* in which the diversity of children's backgrounds and strengths is integrated into the assessment, planning, and learning opportunities children have. In recent years, the field of education has demonstrated confidence in the inclusion of diverse learners as a benefit to learning outcomes for children with and without disabilities and including those not assessed yet but perhaps showing the potential of having a disability (Guralnick & Bruder, 2016). In a joint position by the National Association for the Education of Young Children (NAEYC) and Council for Exceptional Children's (CEC) sub-division Division of Early Childhood (DEC), both these leading national groups recognized that high-quality inclusion services promote access, participation, and supports for children with and without disabilities (DEC/NAEYC, 2009). Moreover, such a vision is not limited to one context. The inclusion of diverse learners takes place in a variety of organizational and community settings (e.g., childcare, community centers, public schools, after-school programs, community recreation clubs).

Rather than segregating children with disabilities, teachers can create successful learning environments incorporating a range of supports and services to provide access to the general curriculum for all children. The 2020 NAEYC Position Statement on Developmentally Appropriate Practice espouses the "core consideration" of "the understanding that all development and learning occur within specific social, cultural, linguistic, and historical contexts" (p. 6). This statement affirms the imperative for teaching all children no matter their abilities socially and/or academically. Using age-appropriate standards and teaching approaches is not only doable but is also equitable. Ford et al. (2017) and Florian (2019), among others, point to the barriers that might be present for marginalized and disenfranchised populations owing to race, language, and cultural intolerances. To deny these children access to possibility could further breed inequity.

Moreover, findings associated with successful adult outcomes for persons both with and without disabilities support early access to inclusive opportunities (Harvey, 2002; Test et al., 2009). These findings are important evidence as Ms. Leslie and others shape early childhood teaching practices. One of many study findings showing important outcomes from inclusion practice is West et al. (2018), for instance. This study identified factors of strong expectations by families and strong self-advocacy skills as two sets of interconnected and important outcomes. Thus, our practice of collaboration with families to affirm their beliefs in their children, and teaching children to advocate for themselves, will have a lifelong impact as they continue to shape their identities. Additionally, West et al. (2018) show these two factors as the most modifiable factors linked to later life employment success.

These factors of family beliefs and self-advocacy are also integral to social studies education throughout a child's school life. Part of the social studies is having children explore themselves in relation to their families, peers, and people in the community (as we pointed out related to the fifth and sixth thematic strand of the National Council for the Social Studies; that is, experiences focusing on the "study of interactions among individuals, groups, and instructions," along with "study of how people create, interact with, and change structures of power"). Children learn to consider internal and external expectations along with how dynamics of power and institutional historic structures influence personal choice. Likewise, those relationships and possible outcomes are key dimensions in shaping a teaching practice as an early childhood educator; that is, work with child–family connections and how those are influenced by societal structures and expectations. Herein again the foundational idea and tool of eco-mapping is essential.

Attention to social-emotional learning (SEL). Along with full inclusion of all children, a related strong value for Ms. Leslie is her belief in *attention to children's whole selves* as integral to successful learning. To do so, she assesses, plans, and teaches with attention to SEL while planning and implementing the content of social studies. What a natural mix, she thinks. She knows the importance of SEL connected to academics has increased over the past two decades (Weissberg et al., 2017). We now acknowledge that school success relies not only on academic successes but also and concurrently on the acquisition and utilization of skills associated with social and emotional competence (Zins & Elias, 2007). Social competency is made up of a composite of several social skills, practiced with peers and others. Effective social skills lead to positive social interactions, peer acceptance, and further reinforcement and development of adaptive social skills (Gresham et al., 2006). Denham and Burton (2003) describe the growth of social competence over time as children acquire discrete social skills beginning in early childhood. These social skills interconnect in ways that individuals can utilize within a specific context to expand what they might know and value. For example, we spend a great deal of curricular and instructional time in social studies helping children consider others' perspectives. This practice goes hand in hand with children's typical developmental trajectories toward a robust formation of empathic skills, including observation, careful listening, and wondering about the world outside themselves.

Two key ideas are critical for a teacher to devise a SEL focus to facilitate learning social skills: social learning theories, and the acquisition and performance deficit model. Social learning theory posits that children learn through watching others and ultimately seeing the consequences of those actions through a process in which children "acquire, interpret, perceive, and utilize" social information (Ladd, 2007, p. 134). Learning through watching is what Bandura (1986) referred to as vicarious experiences where another individual, adult, or peer, takes action. Through observational learning, an individual can watch and wonder, and potentially attune to modeled behavior, retain it, and then take the action when motivated to do so (Bandura, 1986). Bandura saw this cognitive process as not being outwardly observable. Rather, he posed that individuals take note of consequences for actions, and subsequently set goals and courses of action for themselves internally. For Lola, this idea might mean she observes a child sharing their marker with a peer and receiving praise from the teacher and the other child. This observation can allow Lola to model a similar action. In another instance, Lola might see her friend Xander's face change to show disappointment, then anger when spots fill up at the sensory table and he has to select another center. Lola then sees Xander self-select the use of the "calming corner." Thus, Lola has observed a self-regulation strategy that can be used when disappointment is experienced and when a learning center is at full capacity. These behaviors can be further reinforced when Lola sees Xander return to select the block center with a smile on his face. Lola observing Xander is an example of the integration of social-emotional learning and social studies shown in figure 7.3, Social Emotional Learning (SEL) Integrated With Social Studies.

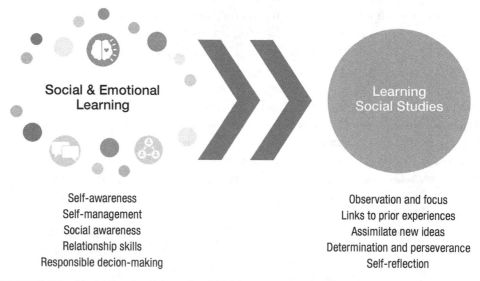

Social & Emotional Learning

Learning Social Studies

Self-awareness
Self-management
Social awareness
Relationship skills
Responsible decion-making

Observation and focus
Links to prior experiences
Assimilate new ideas
Determination and perseverance
Self-reflection

FIGURE 7.3 Social-Emotional Learning (SEL) Integrated With Social Studies. *Source*: Michelle Parker-Katz and Amanda Passmore.

When we teach ways to act, as Ms. Leslie was aiming to do with Lola, at times we might assume—even unconsciously—there is a deficit. That is, we might assume a child does not know how to perform or use a social skill with fluency (Gresham, 2010). To combat a deficit in this area, a child needs foundational knowledge and potentially a model to learn the language and skills regarding the specific social skill of concern (Fenty et al., 2008). In fact, many children, and particularly children with disabilities or children showing they learn differently, may benefit when provided explicit instruction on when and how to demonstrate a wide range of social skills (Joseph, 2016). For Lola, this might be recognizing how her body reacts to being angry. Upon recognizing this feeling, she might learn a strategy of taking ten deep breaths that she counts using her ten fingers. Then, she might look at a card she carries around, or a chart in an area of the classroom. From those visuals, she could see images reminding her of choices she can make to manage her anger. Many posters are available, so teachers like Ms. Leslie do not have to create them anew. Through vehicles like Google Images and Pinterest, teachers can find charts to show students electronically or to post on a classroom wall (see "visuals to help children manage anger").

Caution is needed here, however. Disability has long been associated with a deficit and an implicit view that people with disabilities need to be fixed. That something is missing or wrong. Many have suggested alternative views. Some talk about how disability need not be a defining marker to a person (Coomer, 2019;

Dinishak, 2016; Jung et al., 2019). Among others, Miller (2007) suggests that all children be allowed space and time to explore. They are social and cultural beings who seek to make meaning of their worlds. Teachers like Ms. Leslie are attuned to this idea. They might create class norms and expectations about how we respect all our class "pals." They might brainstorm with children explicit "ways we act," and have children agree on them and post images and words as reminders. Children can learn that while we have differences we may or may not see, we also have many similarities. This core value of acceptance of peers is a paramount learning outcome in inclusive environments, so that learning is authentic and invites individual accomplishment of outcomes. While successful adult outcomes indicate that teaching and learning with this richness in mind and in practice has great benefits, it can be hard to do. Ms. Leslie values it, but how can these values and thoughtfulness transform into effective teacher practice?

How Do Teachers Implement Planned Strategies to Help All Students Thrive?

Ms. Leslie devised three overlapping and interconnected interventions aimed at supporting Lola's learning of social studies. They are (1) partnering with Lola's family, (2) using social stories, and (3) developing a "signal system" to remind Lola about possible good choices she could choose and implement.

Like other teachers of young children, Ms. Leslie knew that an essential element to supporting Lola was working in a very close relationship with Lola's grandmother, Ms. Williams, who was raising Lola and her two older siblings. Collaborative home-to-school connections are essential to supporting and growing feelings of empowerment in caregivers, particularly caregivers of children with unique needs. Such views along with action plans can help caregivers be increasingly confident as they build practices to problem-solve around their child's specific areas of challenge. Moreover, home–school connections can help us all support children to generalize skills and maintain using them in other settings outside home and school (Barton, 2015; LaRocque et al., 2011). The avenues to designing home–school linkages will vary given that family and school funds of knowledge vary. Passmore and Zarate (2020) acknowledge variance and propose a structure they call PEAK, that is, partnerships of empowerment, accessibility, and knowledge. The goal of keeping in mind structure helps educators create active partnerships with families, while they draw on several systems concurrently to encourage caregivers to build skills and knowledge.

From their connections, Ms. Leslie knew that some of the less appropriate social skills she saw Lola use at school were something Ms. Williams saw at home, too. Through building a relationship with Ms. Williams, Ms. Leslie felt the trust between Ms. Williams and herself was growing. They both agreed they wanted to build school-based interventions so they could work at home and at school. By so doing, Lola could experience a seamless support system of expectations, ongoing feedback, and positive reactions from key persons in her life.

Eco-map. Therefore, a first intervention rested on developing connections with Lola's family and home life. Ms. Leslie began by doing an eco-map. To do this map, she planned an intentional and focused conversation (one or more, depending on time commitments) with Lola's primary family caretaker, which was her grand-mom. After making a time to meet electronically to ease the time burden for Ms. Williams, Ms. Leslie followed model scripts and resources she'd read for facilitating the discussion (see Jung, 2010; McCormick et al., 2008). During the eco-mapping process, she used a blank sheet. She started by drawing a circle in the middle with Lola's name and another circle with Ms. Williams' name. As she asked Ms. Williams questions about other family, friends, groups they belonged to (e.g., church, city park district), and wider connections such as to health-care providers, she created more circles and drew lines to show connections with the kinds of support they provided to the family and how often. As they talked, Ms. Leslie made some lines thicker to show the different strengths of support the family received. For some, the connections seemed a bit uncertain or vague; for those, she used a dotted line. When Ms. Williams indicated any tensions or stress, Ms. Leslie made a wavy line to indicate a shakiness and unstable connection. Before the conversation with Ms. Williams, Ms. Leslie practiced with a friend—especially planning how she could discuss and ask any questions to gain information about particularly sensitive topics (for example, financial support, housing conditions, emotional assistance as needed, medical issues). Figure 7.4, Early Draft Eco-Map for Lola, is the result of these initial conversations with Ms. Williams.

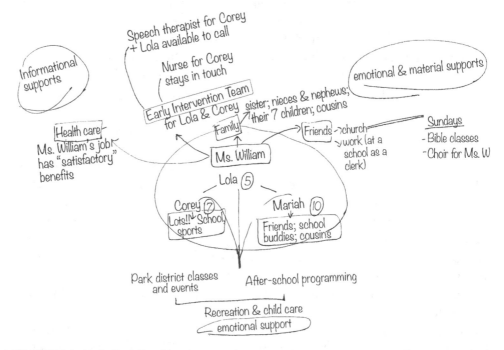

FIGURE 7.4 Early Draft Eco-Map for Lola. *Source*: Michelle Parker-Katz and Amanda Passmore.

After the eco-mapping process, which also continued to help Lola and her family strengthen their relationship with Ms. Leslie, Ms. Williams and Ms. Leslie targeted three behaviors they jointly wanted Lola to alter. They considered the resources available (like other family, friends, church, after-school programming, therapists) who could also support the plan. They decided that Lola could learn about other choices she could make, and how to make them, in order to have greater success learning at home and in school. These were the behaviors mentioned above: less screaming when not getting what she wanted, less grabbing of others' materials, and fewer tantrums resulting in Lola throwing things. Ms. Leslie observed over a two-week period with the purpose of identifying the circumstances of those inappropriate reactions. Ms. Williams did the same at home. Both Ms. Leslie and Ms. Williams filled out a log each week in which they identified one of the three behaviors, the date, the time, and what had been happening right before. They also marked approximately how long it took Lola to move out of her rage and be able to take support and redirection.

Secret code and choice cards. Meanwhile, Ms. Leslie designed a small checklist of actions they wanted to help Lola learn to use to replace those three less appropriate behaviors, both at home and in school. Then the three met; that is, Lola, Ms. Williams, and Ms. Leslie. Ms. Williams and Ms. Leslie named the behaviors they wanted to change. They modeled the appropriate behaviors, which included how Lola could use things from school also at home (see again "visuals to help children manage anger"). These strategies could help Lola choose actions that would gain her favor in the eyes of Ms. Williams, Ms. Leslie, and Lola's peers.

During the meeting, also, they all played with a free self-management app called I-Connect (see https://iconnect.ku.edu/). This app allows Lola, her grandmother, and Ms. Leslie the opportunity to mark in the times that Lola makes good choices. In this way all can see how her behavior is changing, hopefully with fewer moments when she displayed the inappropriate behaviors. Ms. Leslie found different colorful certificates Lola would receive in school each time she earned their agreed-upon checkmarks. Ms. Williams agreed that the certificates could earn special privileges for Lola at home.

Social stories. Ms. Leslie first learned about social stories and their use from a colleague. Originally started in the 1990s as an approach to helping children with autism spectrum disorder (a social disability) learn the multiple dimensions of interpersonal communication, social stories are now used in several ways. Social stories are short vignettes or scenarios, depicted in images that can be photographs, drawings, and/or graphics along with words. They emerge after teachers and/or family observe and target a particular behavior to be altered. Usually, they are individualized and depict a particular social occurrence or interaction, and how different social skills are used in the situation. As suggested by Gut and Safran (2002, p.90), social story authors typically use four sorts of sentences: descriptive (focused on what, how, where, when, and why); perspective sentences that provide information about how people feel related to certain behaviors; directive sentences that explain an expected action; control sentences that provide direction and reminders of how a person might act.

To use social stories, Ms. Leslie reads the story to Lola, a small group, or the class. She models the appropriate social skills suggested in the tale. With young children, teachers can use a social story much like a kind of extended pretend play that the teacher and child might use over time. To help the intervention be successful, teachers should monitor how it works over time. For instance, Ms. Leslie has a chart for Lola in which she marks the date and time they read the story, in what setting, Lola's reactions such as questions or participation, and any revisions Ms. Leslie tried (and when) to improve Lola's responsiveness. As Lola implements the targeted behavior changes consistently, Ms. Leslie will need to create a way to phase out using the story and also to see how Lola proceeds to generalize the learned reactions to other related social situations.

Ms. Leslie created two social stories recently, each about fifty words and using photographs from stock images and graphics. One was about a character who had just screamed, "I don't want to do that!" The other children in the small group stared at the one who screamed. In the story, the child became even more upset because she didn't like how the other children stared at her. She decided to use her "new words" and say, "I don't like you all looking at me. That makes me feel bad. Could you look away when I scream like that? I'm trying hard to make other choices." In a related other story, Ms. Leslie focused on introducing and rehearsing the use of the "calming corners" strategy. With a few pictures she downloaded and ten key words, she'd created a tale in which a child got upset. She showed how the child decided to seek out the "calming corner," including the key words she said to the other children as she walked away. The pictures also showed how she accessed and used the corner. (Ms. Leslie used an actual photo of the classroom "calming corner," which was behind a short bookcase and had a soft bean bag chair to relax, with headphones to play calming music Ms. Leslie downloaded from YouTube.)

Signal system. Another intervention Ms. Leslie developed was the use of a signal system. She introduced Lola to it by saying it was their "secret code." It's a simple idea. Ms. Leslie uses signals at moments when Lola seems about to act out or is in the moment of doing it. First, she and Lola identified three behaviors that didn't work in their classroom community: screaming, grabbing, or throwing things. Next, they identified one gesture (Ms. Leslie touching the tip of her nose and looking directly at Lola—no words, just the gesture). The purpose was to have Lola see the gesture without additional input—to stay focused on the gesture and what the secret meaning was. They practiced that when she saw it, she would ask herself: What choices could I make now instead of screaming or grabbing or throwing things? Ms. Leslie made her a "choice card" with photos of Lola doing other acceptable actions, including walking to the calming corner. Lola wore that like a necklace; she decorated the card and made the chain. She could look at the card if she needed a reminder about possible choices.

How Can Sustained Systematic Teacher Action Research Inquiry Help Teachers Support All Children in Learning Social Studies?

The answer to this question in part resides in the C3 Framework for children learning social studies; that is, *developing questions and planning inquiries* and *communicating conclusions and taking informed action*. For young children, the social studies framework and curricular topics involve children's evolving understandings of their own selves and their identities, and how they relate to family and eventually communities. Cultural expectations, norms, and routines are embedded throughout these networks of connections. To learn about these, teachers need to gather multiple sorts of information (for example, through eco-mapping), which they draw on to plan and teach children the array of ideas in the social studies curriculum. At the same time, they can draw on the information to study particular questions about teaching in order to enhance practice. We call this process teacher action research.

For example, Ms. Leslie is doing teacher action research to see how her three integrated interventions are helping Lola learn social studies with fewer interruptions happening when Lola becomes upset.

At its core, teacher action research is ongoing and cyclical in that teachers begin an investigation, see solutions, and begin the inquiry process again to explore how their hunches and responses are working (Carr & Kemmis, 2003). Cochran-Smith and Lytle (1993, p. 5) define teacher action research as "systematic, intentional inquiry by teachers." The key term "systematic" is used by many scholars to define teacher action research. It is a planned process in which educators identify the question(s) they are investigating, the information they will gather and how, and then review the information at regular intervals (for instance, Ms. Leslie's reviews of her chart about the use of social stories with Lola). At times, teachers can work together to explore similar questions or ideas and thus build change at larger levels outside their own classrooms.

Action research, done individually or in small group teacher "learning communities," can become a great source of teachers' learning while they are in practice—learning that teachers themselves can design. Moreover, a powerful byproduct of teacher action research is to move away from the bifurcated idea of teachers' knowledge dividing practical and theoretical knowing. Cochran-Smith and Lytle (1999, p. 250) propose that teachers can construct knowledge

> when teachers treat their own classrooms and schools as sites for intentional investigation at the same time that they treat the knowledge and theory produced by others as generative materials for interrogation and interpretation. (p. 250)

Adopting the idea of "inquiry as stance," they suggest, can position teachers to build a professional practice resting on the power of their ongoing inquiry in relation to multiple stakeholders in and outside schools. Making these linkages is fundamental to teaching social studies to young children, too. Yet again, we see how the C3 Framework of *developing questions and planning inquiries* and *communicating conclusions and taking informed action* is also fundamental to teachers' enhancing their social studies instruction.

Moreover, as social studies teachers situate themselves as partners who want to expand their understandings of children and families through asking questions and gathering relevant information to take action, through teacher action research they actively develop what Pine (2008) has referred to as "knowledge democracies." Pine (2008) uses words like "collaborative enlightenment, consciousness, self-affirmation and renewal" as major concepts of democracy in education—the very idea of democracy, which is at the core of teaching social studies. For teachers of social studies, teacher action research can become a way to acknowledge and act on issues of equity in their teaching.

How Can a Teacher Begin to Conduct Teacher Action Research?

In figure 7.5, Teacher Action Research as a Recursive Process, we depict ways teachers like Ms. Leslie can design, conduct, and enhance their practices from teacher action research inquiry. First, Ms. Leslie already has some questions and hunches;

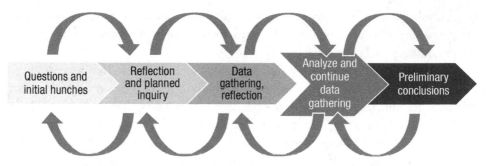

FIGURE 7.5 Teacher Action Research as a Recursive Process. *Source:* Michelle Parker-Katz and Amanda Passmore.

she has been in a way wondering and beginning an initial inquiry. Is the inquiry solely about Lola and her actions, she might wonder? Considering UDL, Ms. Leslie might ask questions about what in the environment might be barriers to Lola and other children's success. Considering an ecological frame, Ms. Leslie might wonder about her children's circles of influence from others, including friends and family. How do different networks converge and intersect, thereby helping her understand what she sees and hears in her classroom?

A next step in inquiry design is to play with questions as one clarifies and specifies the focus of the inquiry. The optimal word here is indeed "play," mirroring again what we see and support in teaching young children. This particular time in teacher action research is important. A teacher wants to leave open many possibilities, while also knowing that zeroing in on particular aspects is necessary; we cannot inquire at any one time about large swatches of our practice.

Let's look again at Ms. Leslie. To bound her inquiry and stay linked to her preferences, she might begin a journal with dates and times of when she sees and hears certain things as she teaches Lola and other children. As she talks with other colleagues, Lola's family, other children, and Lola herself, Ms. Leslie might jot down a few key words from those interactions, again with dates and times. Doing this notetaking and interacting helps Ms. Leslie be increasingly reflective. Reflection is a step toward identifying a focus for one's teacher action research.

Like other teachers, Ms. Leslie is concerned about when she will do all this "extra." Her colleagues mention improved voice-to-text software she can use. She has used her phone, too, as a notetaking device. She also carries a small notebook with her. A notebook, she realizes, allows her to draw pictures of interrelated ideas and to use graphics to help her organize her thoughts.

Teachers doing action research return often to beginning thoughts about their inquiries, reading and rereading notes to see possible patterns. That recursive process—moving back and forth as teachers gather data, look at it and make initial hunches—is pivotal to this kind of research. The practice of moving back and forth enables us to notice similar use of words or phrases, similar questions or challenges. Identifying a pattern or even a hunch can help us focus on looking more closely at a pattern, that is, holding a laser light to it. In different situations and in different circumstances, does the pattern look the same, for instance? Doing this helps us build toward identifying the particulars we want to investigate. With planned intention, we begin to shape a tighter focus and possible question of what we want to examine. As we move toward the question, we move toward developing a plan to gather data, revising it, and taking action. All along the way, we sustain an ongoing cycle of questioning, examining what we are gathering, what patterns and meaning we give to the patterns, and how it helps us respond to our inquiry. Doing this as we design and conduct teacher action research will also help us keep a focus on environment and relationships, key components in an inclusive, diverse educational setting where we recognize that all persons have strengths.

Ms. Leslie's inquiry will take some time; questions of practice are not framed nor answered in short order. Enhancing our practice of teaching all young children social studies is an ongoing effort spanning our teacher preparation, early teaching years, and advanced practice. Conducting inquiry on our practice extends our learning. It becomes a tool we have power as teachers to use to make an impact.

Ms. Leslie's inquiry results. We actually described the first "cycle" of Ms. Leslie's teacher action research results in the opening scenario of this chapter. The use of social stories and the signal system emerged in part from Ms. Leslie's partnership with Lola's family. Next up is Ms. Leslie looking at the charts she and Ms. Williams are making to see what changes may be happening to the three target behaviors they want to change at home and in school. They will look at the data to see what patterns they see: that is, which of the social stories may be helping; to what extent the signal system is working to help Lola check in with herself and self-monitor; how often, if at all, Lola looks at the visual reminders to identify choices of other actions she could do instead of screaming or grabbing or throwing. One hunch Ms. Leslie has already is to consider creating a social story about a behavior at home and how the story character makes choices there. She will then reflect on how the home and school can further work together to assist Lola's adjustment to school.

Ultimately, the purpose of Ms. Leslie's interventions and teacher action research is to improve functioning for Lola in accessing and learning the social studies curriculum, which often relies on problem-based learning that is collaborative in nature. Lola, like other young children, can succeed in doing that. But like other children as well, she may need different supports or a bit more structure to successfully navigate such an approach to learning.

Conclusion

Teaching young children social studies while highlighting inclusivity of all learners to engage in curricular study, and integrating attention to the multiple spheres of influence on children's ongoing formation of their identities, is essential in our world of exponentially growing needs for access to information and choice. Ability—and not ability or disability and the bifurcated ways we used to see those ideas, but rather all persons' abilities—intersects with the multiple aspects of a person's identity and how they choose to describe themselves at any point in life (Jung et al., 2019). As social studies teachers of young children, let us choose to take a humanistic approach to our teaching, one in which we focus on children as each having assets, dreams, preferences, and beliefs. In so doing, we focus less on "fixing" a person and more on building an understanding of who that person is (Parker-Katz & Passmore, in press) and helping all children thrive.

Activities in the Field

1. Plan a visit to a classroom serving young children in a kindergarten class. Ask the teacher if they have identified a student who may show learning, social, and/or behavioral challenges. Observe that student across different times. Notice what strikes you. What did you see? How is the teacher supporting the kindergartener? Are the techniques similar to those described here? Plan to share your notes with the learner's teacher. Talk with the teacher and compare observations you made with what the teacher has noticed. Identify any patterns over time, that is, something that you saw or heard that happened over time. Discuss your findings with the learner's teacher and your class colleagues.

2. Plan a visit to a third-grade classroom. With the teacher's permission, interview a third grader and develop an eco-map showing the connections for this young child. Share your findings with the child's teacher and your colleagues. What did you learn that will help you as you interview children that you may teach?

3. Talk with two teachers about ways they talk with families of their students and learn about the families' funds of knowledge. For example, what does the family teach their children about what to know, how, and why? How do they talk about the past, about family members' pasts and experiences? What are ways the family celebrates joyful things, and what are ways the family manages trauma? In what ways might the family be experiencing stress currently, and how can you work with the family to help ease the child's concerns?

4. Learn about and do with a colleague a SWOT analysis of the community in which a school is located. In that, you will identify strengths, weaknesses, opportunities, and threats in the community, and how children, families, and schools can work collectively to support strengths and opportunities.

Activities in the Library

1. Choose one or more learning standards for your state related to social studies. Outline a topic related to the standards, identifying topics and connected concepts. Examine the library resources, including children's literature, for teaching materials that show examples of varied ways of learning in and out of school. Share your findings with your class colleagues. Does the library have sufficient resources? What else might they need?

2. Go to the periodical section of the public library. Examine the holdings of mass-market periodicals, such as *Good Housekeeping, Sunset,* or others directed toward families. Look at parent advice columns. In what ways is the advice similar and different from what you are reading about that emphasizes collaborative family involvement with the learning needs of young children? What should the publishers of these materials add that would be of help to families?

Suggested Readings

Bronfenbrenner, U. (1992). Ecological systems theory. In R. Vasta (Ed.), *Six theories of child development: Revised formulations and current issues* (pp. 187–249). Jessica Kingsley Publishers.

Jung, L. A., Frey, N., Fisher, D., & Kroener, J. (2019). *Your children, my children, our children: Rethinking equitable and inclusive classrooms*. Alexandria, VA: Association for Curriculum Development and Supervision (ASCD).

McCormick, K. M., Stricklin, S., Nowak, T. M., & Rous, B. (2008). Using eco-mapping to understand family strengths and resources. *Young Exceptional Children, 11*(2), 17–28.

Pine, G. J. (2008). *Teacher action research: Building knowledge democracies*. Thousand Oaks, CA: Sage Publishing.

Sagor, R. D., & Williams, C. (2017). *The action research guidebook: A process for pursuing equity and excellence in education*. Thousand Oaks, CA: Corwin.

Websites for Additional Information

CAST (2018). Universal Design for Learning Guidelines version 2.2.

The Collaborative for Academic, Social, and Emotional Learning (CASEL). https://casel.org/

I-Connect University of Kansas School of Education and Human Science. https://iconnect.ku.edu/

Jung, L. A. YouTube. https://youtu.be/lWU7ofO7EmU

Kansas Technical Assistance Network. Topeka, KS. https://www.ksdetasn.org/search/resources/

How Does Social Studies Help Young Children Learn About Community and Citizenship?

Mark Newman, Ph.D.

All that society has accomplished for itself is put, through the agency of the school, at the disposal of its future members.

—*John Dewey, The School and Society*

TERMS TO KNOW

citizenship   community

Overview

This chapter answers three important questions for young children:

1. What are communities?
2. Where do I fit in my communities?
3. What does it mean to be a competent citizen?

The answers connect to three important themes of PreK–3 social studies education:

- the study of communities
- understanding how an individual fits within a community
- citizenship

Exploring communities helps young children understand what communities are, why we have them, and how they work. In learning about communities, they also learn about the various ones they belong to and where they fit in each of them. The goal of social studies is to prepare young people to be competent citizens. We practice **citizenship** within the context of belonging to a community. The learning begins in preschool and continues throughout life. Knowing what a citizen is and the rights and responsibilities that citizenship confers is an important first step for young children.

We will examine how the three themes exist as foundations of social studies. Next, the discussion moves to explore how the three themes connect to disciplinary concepts

FIGURE 8.1 Class Mascot. *Source*: Mark Newman.

of change and continuity, cause and effect, and significance. Third, we examine how studying the three themes relates to the ongoing development of the young learner.

Focus Questions

1. What do the terms "community" and "citizenship" mean?
2. How do community and citizenship connect to disciplinary concepts in social studies?
3. How do community and citizenship contribute to the overall development of the young learner?

Election years open up opportunities for PreK–3 students to learn more about themselves and how to act as citizens of a democratic community. In a kindergarten class, the teacher wanted to introduce students to voting and elections. Voting is often used in PreK–3 to make decisions affecting the class, offering students a way to experience a foundation of a democratic society.

In this instance, the election was for a class mascot for the month (see figure 8.1). First, the teacher asked the students what they knew about elections. What are elections? Why do we have them? What do people do during an election? The last query led to a discussion of voting. The teacher stressed that casting a vote does not necessarily mean that you will win, but rather that the candidate who gets the most votes will be the winner. Also emphasized was that the most important thing was to vote. Even if the result goes against you, at least you participated. If you do not participate, then your vote does not get counted and it makes it harder to win. The teacher also explained that elections occur regularly, so there are other chances to get positive results.

To show that one election is not the end of the voting process, the teacher designed the following scenario. Each month, the students would select a class mascot. They would have four choices. The first task was to have the class identify the four choices. Next, the teacher organized four teams and had each team select one of the four choices as their candidate.

Then the election campaign began. Teams supported their respective selections by conducting research and making presentations trying to persuade the class to vote for their candidate. Prior to the final election, in a primary of sorts, the students voted for two of the candidates, meaning they likely voted for their choice and another team's candidate. The selections were counted and the candidates receiving the top two choices moved on to the final election.

After the primary election, the class discussed what had happened. Through questions and probing the teacher helped the students realize that everyone has the same right to vote. The discussion also explored the idea of majority rule and that even if your candidate lost an election, you still did your best. Once the students understood how elections worked and that the majority ruled, they realized that even if they lost the election, it was not personal. They also knew that next month another election would occur and they might win that contest.

The final election led to a victor. The whole class had a victory celebration for the chosen mascot. The teacher ended the activity by asking students what they had learned about voting and elections. They made a chart to record their answers. It showed that they knew what voting was and the purpose of elections. They discussed how working well together is important and that doing your best is what counts. The students also stated that even if you do not win, there often is a next time and you might win then.

All looked forward to the next month and another election for class mascot. By participating in the election process, by voting, students learned about being members of the classroom community exercising a basic right of citizenship. They also learned that participating is important even if you do not win. In a nutshell, what the kindergarteners learned in the election is what this chapter is all about.

Why Are Community and Citizenship Foundations of Social Studies?

Before exploring community and citizenship, let's examine why they are foundations of social studies education in grades PreK–3. A good starting point is looking at the concept of children's rights. Rights and responsibilities are core aspects of community membership and citizenship. For almost a century, children's rights have been a concern for international organizations. In 1924, the League of Nations adopted the Declaration of the Rights of the Child. The United Nations ratified an extended version in 1959.

In 2006, the United Nations Committee on the Rights of the Child issued a report that discussed early childhood in ways that relate to our purposes. The report defined early childhood as from birth to age seven. It explained that these years provide the "foundation for their physical and mental health, emotional security, cultural and personal identity, and developing competencies" (Committee on the Rights of the Child, 2006, p. 3).

Young children experience rapid physical and emotional growth. During these years, a child's ability and interest, among other things, shifts. For our purposes, they become active members of families and communities. They develop their own concerns, interests, and perspectives. The UN report noted that young children have rights, with early childhood being "a critical period" for the realization of those rights (Committee on the Rights of the Child, 2006, p. 3).

The idea of rights relates directly to community and citizenship. Acting as a citizen in varied communities contributes to their own well-being and that of their communities. The concept of rights in early childhood has a long history, dating back over a century. In 1896, F. Morse noted, "Even the kindergartner at four years of age can be and is led to understand and obey the authority of his teacher, and learns readily how one child must be considered as well as another, and that all have equal rights and privileges" (p. 55).

The concept of rights is a component of a core subject area in social studies, civics education. Civics has been taught in US schools since the founding of the nation, including in the early years of schooling. Today, according to a 2016 survey by the Education Commission of the States, all fifty states and the District of Columbia have civics standards for preschool and grades K–3 (Rava et al., 2016).

Of those providing sample standards benchmarks, ten states specifically mention rights, often pairing them with responsibilities. Other states provide more specific descriptions that relate to the importance of working together (Louisiana, Maine, Michigan, Missouri, Montana, North Carolina, Ohio, Oregon) and participating in school and community improvement (Florida and New Hampshire), among other things (Education Commission of the States, 2016).

The election of the mascot activity illustrated how teachers can have young students exercise their rights as they learn more about how government works. It also helped them learn about their identity as a citizen and how to be a productive member of society by involving them in an election and voting. But, to understand their rights, young children first need to know about communities.

What Are Communities?

Community is a large, expansive term that has different meanings depending upon the context in which it is used. We will focus on the various social groupings we call communities that organize people together for certain purposes. The discussion on communities also relates to groups because young children belong to both and groups often have similar characteristics to a community.

We can define a community as an organization of people joined together to fulfill a specific purpose or purposes. For young children studying social studies, a community can be a classroom, school, neighborhood, city, or suburb, or then a state, nation, or world. A group is similar but much smaller in size and often has a narrower focus. Groups also often exist as parts of a community. Examples include teams, clubs, and even groupings of students in class to perform certain tasks.

Three questions that might be answered in PreK–3 social studies will be examined:

1. Why study communities?
2. Why do we have communities, and how do they work?
3. What does it mean to be a member of a group or community, and what does it mean not to be a member?

An important part of the discussion will be looking at how answering the above questions provides opportunities for teaching and learning.

Why Study Communities?

The study of community is basic to social studies education and plays an important role in PreK–3 grades. By studying communities, young children learn foundational social studies content and develop basic literacy skills. They also participate in activities related to their social-emotional development. In the process, students get essential life lessons in behavior and rights and responsibilities that contribute to their overall development. Studying communities brings together learning about who we are, what we can and should not do, where we do and (often) do not belong, and how we can help others, among other things.

Regarding content, the children explore how and why people organize a community to fulfill basic human and societal purposes. They examine how and why people interact as they do, as well as how we interact with the natural environment. Essential social studies themes help organize the content, including change and continuity over time and space, cause and effect, and significance.

As they study the content, students practice important skills. They develop literacy skills by reading printed texts and visuals. They learn to read and possibly construct important social studies resources such as maps, charts, and timelines. The young learners conduct research, develop projects, and present findings in varied formats. In pursuing their studies, they also develop social and emotional skills by learning to work well with others, among other things.

To sum up, studying community is basically a primer for how to live in society. It helps young learners understand the world around them, how it works, where they fit, and possibly where they can get help. It helps them develop skills and attitudes they will need later in life. Knowing why studying communities is important provides the context for exploring how to study them.

By knowing why they are studying communities, young children can see how that study is relevant to them. The place to start is the classroom. There are few communities closer to young children's lives than the classroom. By involving children in the creation of their classroom community, they get pivotal life lessons in what communities are and why they are so consequential in their lives. They also learn why studying communities is important.

In many PreK–3 classrooms, one of the first activities involves students in creating a classroom community. Depending upon the grade level and educational experience of the child, the classroom may represent their first or an early experience with peer relationships not connected to their families. Helping build the classroom community contributes to social-emotional development while involving them in learning, indeed practicing, important social studies content and skills. It also helps children gain insight into the sense of a community. What they create in the classroom binds them together for a common purpose, and it also builds relationships and commitment to ensuring the classroom works as they believe it should.

As Kane (2016) explained, creating the classroom community offers a unique opportunity for learning. She suggests young children are ready to assume responsibility and to gain some control over their world. Being actively involved in the building process empowers children and invests them in the ongoing development of the classroom. It also provides hands-on experience in being part of a group. They learn to control their emotions and to negotiate complex social interactions, including conflicts. Young children also learn that they have voices and that their voices will be heard and people will listen to them (Schneider, 1996).

A good way to continue the building of the classroom community is to have regular classroom meetings. The first meeting should focus on building the classroom community, using a question as the prompt to discussion. Foundational community functions could be part of the initial discussion, perhaps including rules and the schedule of classroom meetings. Other meetings also should use questions as prompts. For example, prompts could inquire into how things are going, what is going well, and what issues have arisen. Regarding an issue, asking how it could be solved leads to the discussion of the issue and identifying possible solutions.

The meetings have several purposes. First, they are microcosms of how a community works as the children learn to problem-solve. They also learn about rules, such as respecting the opinions of others and listening without interrupting. The meetings may involve identifying issues, gathering and examining information to pose potential solutions, and then discussing what actions to take.

Second, by having regular meetings over time, the children learn that building community is an ongoing process. The social studies themes of change and continuity and cause and effect are explored. Emerging issues can be explored to identify the cause of the issue and its effect. The solution may involve changing some aspect of the classroom community while other facets remain as is. The issues may deal with everyday matters such as sharing classroom resources or more weighty concerns including cliques that include some students while excluding others. A discussion on excluding students might lead to a new rule based on Virginia Paley's axiom, "You can't say you can't play" (Paley, 1993).

Third, as already noted, the meetings allow for the study of basic social studies themes. They also provide opportunities to build skills. As the children share ideas, they can use graphic organizers as part of the brainstorming session. Other organizers can help them categorize their ideas and represent their thinking. Depending upon literacy ability, visuals and text can be used. Seeing all the ideas in an organized fashion helps to prioritize them into potential solutions to issues.

By taking part in the building of the classroom community, children learn firsthand what a community is and how it works. They also gain insight into why studying communities is important. They are or will be members of varied communities. By studying communities, they improve the knowledge and build the skills needed to actively participate in those communities.

Studying Communities

The study of community offers rich learning opportunities for PreK–3 students. It involves children learning about what communities are, how they work, and what are the various types. They also learn who the members are and about the roles, rights, and responsibilities of membership. The young learners also gain insight into where they fit in a community and how to be a competent and responsible citizen who contributes to the well-being of their community. In the process, young learners study civics and government, economics, geography, history, and aspects of social sciences as relevant.

The various ways to study community in the PreK–3 grades are almost endless. Learning about classroom rules provides a real-world experience that easily segues to learning about laws. The way resources and supplies are organized and used, how they are shared provides a good foundation to studying needs and wants. In turn, learning about needs and wants can lead to a study of use, production, exchange, and consumption in everyday life, perhaps by looking at how stores work. That topic offers opportunities to examine where, how, and why people work. The role communities play in serving people is seen through a study of community helpers as shown below.

Using Progressive Sequential Learning to Study Communities

Because questions asked about studying one community can be applied to others, the suggestion is to connect learning about what a community is and how it works to specific examples. That way, children can follow a routine based on a progressive learning sequence. Through their studies, they can become familiar with the vocabulary and the content while building skills. The children also gain mastery over the method of studying a community. Over time, they can assume greater responsibility and independence for their learning.

For example, in forming a classroom community, children can learn about various jobs they can perform such as line leader or monitor, materials passer, calendar leader, and so on. These jobs all involve helping the classroom community work well. A chart can be posted that uses pictures and words to list the various classroom jobs and to describe what the responsibilities are.

As the study moves to the neighborhood or local community, an important topic is community helpers including fire, police, mail carrier, and others the children may identify. Where possible, the teacher can have the children match the classroom community helpers to those of the local community. Next, by constructing a Venn diagram, the similarities and differences of the helpers can be seen, leading perhaps to a discussion on how the two communities themselves are alike and distinct. As the study of community proceeds, the children increase their understanding of what communities are and how they work.

The activities described above can be adapted for use to study other communities, creating a pattern of learning related to helpers. Over time, the children can assume greater responsibility for making the lists and the Venn diagrams, even leading the discussions. Having a pattern also allows teachers to differentiate learning so that individual styles, paces, and needs can be met.

Exploring the Different Types of Communities

Generally, the study of communities starts with the types that are closest and most relevant to young children and expands out to larger examples. Learning about the classroom community, indeed participating in forming it, can move to the school, neighborhood, local community (town, city, suburb, rural area), state, possibly region, nation, and world. When children in a class are from another state or nation, the teacher can use a community from that state or nation, perhaps that of the child, as a topic of study. A similar opportunity could exist when children had lived in a different type of community, such as a city, suburb, or rural area.

But this study is not necessarily a linear progression. In Texas, for example, first graders study classroom, school, and community. But they also study aspects of Texas and the United States as relevant to history, geography, government, and citizenship (Texas Education Agency, 2018).

How communities are studied differs by state and often by school district. The study of communities may extend over several grade levels, starting with important elements before moving on to the formal study of a specific community. In Arizona, young children learn about citizenship in kindergarten before moving to communities in first grade (Arizona Department of Education, 2018). New York follows a similar pattern, studying community in second grade (The State Education Department, The University of the State of New York, 2017).

Perhaps the most important consideration is to diversify the communities studied by types, locations, and time. In many cases, a community will fit into more than one category and that could be by design. Every community studied would be of a certain type, located in a certain place, and incorporate looking at past and present.

Studying Communities Over Space and Time

The study of communities provides teachers with opportunities to use social studies themes to help children master content and build skills. The themes include change and continuity, cause and effect, and significance. They also use important social studies learning aids such as maps, timelines, and visuals. How they go about studying communities contributes to the overall development as they brainstorm ideas and collaborate.

Maps are basic resources in social studies at all levels of schooling. They are introduced to students in grades PreK–3. A first step is defining what a map is. A map is a representation of space, not just a graphic depiction of how to get from place to place. For our purposes, a map is a representation of space. It visually depicts a designated area of the world from the entire planet to something as small as a classroom. A map can show us geographic features such as landforms and bodies of water; cities, suburbs, towns, and rural areas; streets and other transportation venues; buildings and parks. A map can also focus on climate, industry, characteristics of the population, and so on.

Two geographic themes can help young children understand what maps are and how they work: location and place. Location has two aspects. First, there is absolute location that allows children to pinpoint exactly where something is. Here is my school. Here is my home. Here is my favorite park. Second, relative location shows where things are in relation to the things. My school is here and across the street is a park. My home is here, the park is this far away and my school is this far away. Relative location helps children get a bigger picture of where things are.

An effective way to have children learn about location is to have them work with a simple map of a neighborhood. It is not always possible to get a map of the actual neighborhood or local community that is appropriate for children to use. They may be too complex or the children may commute from several surrounding areas.

Place is also a basic geographic concept. A place is a location that has special qualities that distinguish it from other locations and places (Newman & Zevin, 2016). What does that mean? A child's school is a place, as is a home. It is located in a specific spot and while the school may have many similarities to other schools of the same type, it is special to the child. Beyond the obvious educational function that is personal to the student, it has social and emotional connections. For the children, their families, the teachers, and others, that school is a place. The same can be said for a favorite place to play and the neighborhood, among others.

Let's explore some map activities related to location and place. Figure 8.2 is an example of a blank map of a neighborhood that teachers can use to design exercises for young children to use maps to explore community.

The map is similar to others that can be found in workbooks and on the Internet at places such as Pinterest. It has a street grid that makes it easy for children to draw lines from one place to another. Around a central square, there is a basketball court indicating a school or park, a fire station, a home, a religious institution, a playground, two more homes, and a fire station.

The map offers many opportunities to explore the idea of a neighborhood community and the geographic concepts of location and place. One option is to have children study the map to answer the question: What can we find in a community? First, they locate all the different places on it, recording their findings on a concept map with the community in the center. Next, the teacher can ask: What else might we find in a neighborhood that is not shown on the map? Answers could include stores, a hospital, a police station, etc. After summarizing what is on the concept

FIGURE 8.2   Neighborhood Map. *Source*: soberve/Getty Images.

map, the children could discuss what a neighborhood community is and what purposes it fulfills.

A different exercise would focus on location. Using one of the homes, the teacher could have children trace the routes to different places on the map. After the routes have been traced, ask which places are closer or farther from the home. Or, the children could find the shortest route from the home to a different place.

A third option stresses relative location. For example, using the playground as the location, have children draw a circle around the three places closest to the playground. Next, using the fire station, do the same thing. Have the children compare their findings to show how a place is defined in part by what is around it.

Once the children are familiar with maps and have shown they can use them effectively, a next step might be drawing a map. They could map out the classroom or the school. They could draw a map of a park. They could even create their own neighborhood community and draw a map of what they think should be included in the neighborhood.

Maps provide a good picture of what a community looks like at a specific time. An important social studies concept is to show change and continuity over time, or, more simply put, to compare past and present. Exploring community over time can help children understand timelines as well as learn how to use them and make them. In many cases, the timelines will include pictures of people, places, or events relevant to the specific dates.

A starting point might be to have children bring pictures of themselves from when they were younger, perhaps infants, to the present day. Each picture should depict the child at a specific year in their life. The teacher would distribute a handout of a blank timeline marked with the number of years from the child's birth to the present.

For example, in kindergarten there would be five or perhaps six lines, each one for a specific year of the child's life. The children arrange the pictures in chronological order, youngest to oldest. Then, they paste the pictures next to the appropriate age on the timeline. A discussion on how they have changed and remained the same would close the exercise.

Once the children are familiar with timelines, they could do a similar exercise with the neighborhood or local community. If they have mastered pasting pictures at specific places, the children might create their own timeline, adding dates as needed. Then they would select and paste the appropriate picture beside the correct date. Again, discussions on what changed and what looked the same would help them understand that while many things change, others do not. They could discuss why they think changes occurred in some cases but not in others.

There are other effective ways to have students learn about past and present, about change and continuity. They could compare photos of the neighborhood or local community from different time periods. A field trip to an appropriate museum might offer a hands-on opportunity to see and perhaps touch items from the past and/or present. For example, about one block away from the Children's Museum in Boston is the Boston Fire Museum. Housed in the historic Congress Street Fire Station, it has old firefighting equipment and artifacts for young children to see and touch. Other communities may have similar museums or historical societies.

Experiencing the Community

Community study opens up possibilities for experiential learning through field trips and community service. Adams (2015) shows how a field trip to a grocery store helped students learn about goods and services, mapping, and rights and responsibilities. Hartman and Kahn (2017) shared how a field trip to a museum led to a project of saving energy in the home.

Another activity is a walking tour. Often walking tours are part of a young child's orientation to a new school. Treasure hunts also serve that purpose. It also is possible to take a walking tour of the area around a school. In these instances, children can gain insight into the natural and built environment as they see and possibly compare trees, bushes, and other vegetation. They can describe houses and compare how they look. Depending upon the area, there are numerous possibilities.

Knowing what communities are, what their purposes are, and that they change and remain similar over time is one aspect of learning about communities. Young children also learn about what it means to be a member of a community. They learn how to participate as citizens.

Rights, Responsibilities, and Citizenship

In many ways, the normal activities of PreK–3 students are life lessons in belonging to a group or community. Play is a prime example, as is behavior inside and outside the classroom. Formal classroom activities supplement the life experiences, adding richness to the idea of being a citizen in a community and what that means.

In many respects, being a citizen and a member of a community is basically the same thing. Citizen is a more formal term that typically has political connotations often related to rights and responsibilities. The goal of social studies is to prepare young people to be competent citizens.

What Does It Mean to Be a Competent Citizen?

Eighteenth-century philosopher Adam Smith offered a succinct description we will paraphrase here (Smith, 1790). A competent citizen:

- obeys the laws of the community
- contributes to the betterment of the community
- speaks out when the community leadership does not promote the general welfare of the community

By adhering to the above criteria, a citizen enjoys the rights and incurs certain responsibilities related to being a member of the community. Not obeying laws and working against community improvement may have consequences regarding the enjoyment of certain rights. Citizens also have the right and responsibility to seek change if the community is not working as it should.

So how does Smith's description relate to teaching and learning citizenship in PreK–3 social studies? It all relates to behavior and understanding what it means to be a good citizen. Let's use the classroom as an example. Young learners must respect the classroom community for what it is and also respect the rules for what they do to make the classroom a safe, secure, and friendly place for learning. They also need to contribute to maintaining that environment through their behavior and relations with other students and the teacher.

In this instance, neither respect, behavior, nor relations is innate; it is learned. The teacher sets up the classroom so that the young learners feel comfortable and welcome. The physical layout and any decorations play an important role here, as do supplies and resources. Rules must be established so everyone knows what they can and cannot do. Hopefully, the friendly environment and the rules promote cooperation and care.

An important element is having the young learners participate in creating the classroom community (Kane, 2016). At any age, people are more respectful and revere a group or community when they have helped to develop it, gaining a sense of ownership in the process. This is our classroom because we helped construct it. In the development of the community, the qualities of good citizenship are learned and practiced. Given the age of the children, the key word is "participate."

Participation can have different connotations. The teacher can orient the children to the classroom and ask their opinions on what they like and how they think it will work. Over the next few days, as the young learners "live" in the classroom and use it, the teacher can observe to make sure all is well. If it appears things are running smoothly, the teacher can ask the students how it is working. If an issue arises, the teacher can ask the children to pose some solutions and facilitate a resolution.

Over time, the children can help change the classroom look to better fit the topic of study. They may create bulletin boards, posters, three-dimensional models, among other things to showcase elements of the topic. In chapter one, a project on taking a tour around the world was discussed. Part of the project was having the preschoolers create paper models of plants and animals. In this way, the learners actively participated in creating the classroom environment, gaining a sense of pride based on what they had done. How they participated contributed to the overall well-being of the classroom.

An equally important aspect of citizenship is understanding that having rights does not mean getting your way all the time. In some cases, everyone agrees on a course of action so there is consensus. In other instances, differences of opinion can mean the majority will rule. But the minority still retain their rights to participate in making other decisions that support their positions.

Often, compromise comes into play, providing important lessons for children in the PreK–3 grades. They learn that compromise offers a middle ground, getting some of what they want so that others having a different view receive some of their preferences. Having elections, such as voting on the class mascot, are excellent activities that help young children learn about making decisions and compromise. Learning how to compromise is a pivotal lesson in social studies for both citizenship and life.

Smith's third criterion concerns instances when the community is not fulfilling its end of the bargain. Often in grades PreK–3 an issue that arises is membership in a smaller group that is part of the classroom community. An important lesson for young learners is that membership may not necessarily be universal or a given, but certain exclusionary practices are not permitted. In these cases, children need to make their voices heard.

Being in the in-group or out-group can have a negative impact on a child. The teacher must be aware of such situations and address them. The sense of belonging or not belonging plays an important role in child development and relates to in-groups and out-groups. It connects to a child's identity and their perceptions of their status and desire to change that status (Nesdale & Flesser, 2001, pp. 507, 512).

In her 2014 article in *Social Studies and the Younger Learner*, Rosebud Elijah described a situation her six-year-old daughter faced. In telling her mother about recess, her daughter explained there are three groups during recess: the always, the sometimes, and the goodbye groups. Elijah's daughter was in the goodbye group.

Elijah explained her dilemma:

> I wanted my daughter to recognize that being told she was in the goodbye group did not make her vanish. I wanted my daughter to have a voice—a voice that not only opted out of the goodbye group, but opted out of being delimited by any of those groups! (p. 5)

Elijah wanted her daughter to speak up about the groupings and say that it was unfair. She connected this situation to the work of Vivian Paley and the idea of "you can't say you can't play" (Paley, 1993).

For our purposes, Elijah's example relates directly to the concept of classroom community membership and subgroups within that community, member rights, and speaking out about fairness. Speaking out in situations such as the one experienced by Elijah's daughter is both a right and a responsibility. But it also points out a basic aspect of community. Everyone does not belong to every community, and within a community, everyone does not belong to every group. Various factors may determine who can join and who wants to join. Some groups may exclude using pejorative terms, as Elijah's daughter experienced. Others may do so by interest or another factor that is not negative.

The lessons of community, rights, and responsibility have assumed greater importance in recent years. As this book is being written, American society is deeply divided into two groups that strongly oppose each other, to the detriment of the nation's well-being. Young children need a different example to learn from to understand community and membership. The classroom can provide such an example.

Conclusion

This chapter explored two foundational concepts of social studies education: community and citizenship. Studying these concepts connects the individual child to the larger world and supplies guidelines on ways to contribute to those groups and communities. As you read the chapter, were you able to make connections to your own education? Did you get ideas on how you would engage students to learn about who they are and where they belong? Why is citizenship education important for supporting a democratic society?

Activities in the Field

1. Visit a preschool or elementary school classroom. Examine the room to see how it is organized and decorated. Do you notice any posters or bulletin boards, any 3-D objects, or other artifacts that students produced as a part of a project? Interview the teacher regarding how students interact and work together and for what purposes. Where evidence of projects are visible, ask how they were done.

2. Interview several students. Ask about their roles in the classroom, who they play with, what they like to do. If possible, ask them to describe who they are. Ask them who their favorite superhero or princess is and why they like that character. Based on the answers, see if you can construct a profile of each student's identity. Compare the findings.
3. Interview one or more teachers in a preschool or elementary school about citizenship and what role it plays in the classroom. Ask them to explain how they instill good citizenship in students and why it is important.

Activities in the Library

1. Review websites such as iCivics for materials related to community and citizenship. What types of activities are there and for what grades? What specifically do they offer for grades PreK–3? See if you can adapt resources for grades PreK–3.
2. Examine issues of children's magazines such as *Highlights*. Can you find any stories, games, etc., that relate to identity, community, and citizenship? If so, what are they, and what do they teach young children? If you do not find any connected to identity, community, and citizenship, why do you think that is the case? Can you design a magazine for young children that would focus on these themes? What would you include?

Study Questions

1. Where do community and citizenship fit in PreK–3 social studies education?
2. Where do rights and responsibilities fit into the study of community and citizenship?
3. What are the two aspects of community? How can they be connected in the classroom?
4. What is a citizen? What are the qualities of a competent citizen?

Reflect and Reread

1. Why is it important for children in grades PreK–3 to learn about community and citizenship?
2. Where do the concepts of rights and responsibilities fit in the study of community and citizenship?
3. How does the study of community connect to the study of citizenship?

Suggested Readings

Boyle-Baise, M., & Zevin, J. (2013). *Young citizens of the world: Teaching elementary social studies through civic engagement*, 2nd edition. New York: Routledge.

Sapon-Shevin, M. (2010). *Because we can change the world: A practical guide to building cooperative, inclusive classroom communities*, 2nd ed. Thousand Oaks, CA: Corwin.

Stone, J. G. (2001). *Building classroom community: The early childhood teacher's role.* Washington, DC: National Association for the Education of Young Children.

Chapter 9

How Are Young Children Involved in Civic Engagement?

Gayle Mindes, Ed.D.

Fight for the things that you care about but do it in a way that will lead others to join you.

—*Ruth Bader Ginsburg*

TERMS TO KNOW

citizen	cultural capital
civic action	Inquiry Arc
civic agency	political
civic engagement	problem-based learning
civic space	

Overview

This chapter concludes the book. Earlier chapters contained all of the ingredients to develop social studies curricula for young children. Now it is time for young children to act—to become engaged as citizens in their school, community, and beyond. Civic action is anchored in children's lived experiences in their families, schools, and community. Young learners engage when they enter formal childcare and educational settings with rules and social conventions. They inquire and learn of the interactions among governmental actions, leadership, and citizens working to solve social-political problems. (All states have learning standards regarding this political content, i.e., the processes, rules, and laws of our society.) Children employ inquiry, informed discussion, respect for individual rights, and respectful debate. In this way, young children are involved as citizens of their school community.

Focus Questions

1. What is political for young children?
2. How do children understand civic engagement?

What Is Political for Young Children?

Young children begin a formal journey into group life with rules and expectations for personal behavior when they enter the formal structures of the classroom in childcare and school settings.

One major challenge for young children in preschool is often the expectation of following a schedule of events. Another expectation in classrooms is sharing resources and the personal attention of the adults in the room. In preschool, young children discover differences in perspectives about playing and behaving in socially constructed, teacher-directed activities. In these years, the curriculum is driven by the views of the sponsoring agency about what is important for children to know and be able to do.

As class rules are established, routines for moving around the room and school and for sharing materials, preschoolers are learning about **politics**, the way people make decisions in social life while respecting individual rights. Thus, they begin their lifelong journey as citizens in a particular social institution. For young children, becoming a **citizen** in school means they have an identity as a member of a class. In the class, they have certain rights and responsibilities as embodied in the class rules. As children move toward the formal public-school experience, their understandings of citizenship evolve to school, community, and beyond.

In addition to learning to function in a classroom society, beginning in kindergarten, the experience contains expectations for academic achievement through planned social studies curricular activities. In the best situations, the social studies activities for young children in the K–3 years are based on problem investigation, that is, a compelling question. While formal curricular use of problem investigation is part of the social studies curriculum, the idea of using the **Inquiry Arc**—starting with a question, investigating, and taking action—can be modeled in situations where social problems occur in the class. For example, Payne (2015) describes a first grader's approach to **civic agency**, acting to solve an issue:

> People don't push in their chairs, so I bump into them, "they" said. Can we have a conversation?
> Next day, "they" initiated a conversation embodying the idea of **audience**, the opportunity to be heard: What is the problem? Who can fix this? The class wrote up potential solutions.
> The conversation resulted in this resolution: post reminder sign to push in chairs at close of day.

In this way children are practicing **citizenship** every day, learning to function in a particular class at a particular time by following the formal rules and conventions for behavior set by the community of peers. As the years go by, they will build on these experiences in multiple situations and gain confidence to function as citizens in many social groups—formal and informal. Children are beginning to influence the social groups where they are members. Thus, they are practicing **civic engagement**. Identifying a problem, investigating solutions, discussing the solutions, and finally taking action, which are all pieces of civic engagement.

In social studies curriculum activities, civic engagement actions can emerge from **problem-based** or **project-based learning**. The curricular use of problem-based learning is based on projects teachers introduce, from local curricular demands and state standards. In this view of the curriculum, there is room for children to introduce particular issues of concern as well. In these ways, children acquire knowledge of laws, governments, power relationships, individual rights and responsibilities, and the distribution of resources.

As well, through these projects young children add to their **cultural capital**—the knowledge, skills, and abilities they have, and they acquire in school and elsewhere. Howard (2018, pp. 24–31) describes the multiple components of cultural capital:

- aspirational—hopes and dreams
- linguistic—language and communication skills
- familial—personal and social resources coming from home and community
- social—peers and other contacts from school and community
- navigational—skills and abilities to be successful in school and other institutional situations
- resistance—capacity to secure equal rights and freedom

As teachers who are aware of these various views of cultural capital, we have opportunities to facilitate the development of the components of cultural capital so children can be actors in their own interest. In this way they learn citizenship skills to enable them to tackle civic engagement in the classroom, school, and community.

With support to our young citizens, then, as well as our own self-awareness, children are in a good position to apply the Inquiry Arc to schoolwork through problem-based learning, which starts with a question to investigate. The questions can lead to civic engagement through exploring issues and problems children bring to the table for action. Helm (2004) describes young children's projects as having three phases: identifying the project in the questions to be asked; collecting the answers to the questions and developing new ones as the project proceeds; and, last, displaying knowledge acquired in charts, plays, drawings, photos, and in other ways children can show what they have learned. While this is keyed to the model most often used in preschool with child-initiated questions, it is a clear example of the Inquiry Arc in action with the expectation for questions to lead investigations and action-based solutions.

How Do Children Understand Civic Engagement?

In classrooms where children are involved as citizens of a particular social group, teachers empower them to be everyday actors with rights and responsibilities. The class has rules, individuals are expected to respect each other; speaking, listening, and learning are valued throughout the day. One common example of respect shared and understood begins with opportunities to share their experiences as individuals and members of other social groups. Regular opportunities for sharing personal experiences show interest and offer an opportunity for the potential to catch issues before they become problems.

Scheduling sharing opportunities regularly throughout the day can facilitate understanding of family celebrations and larger school and community issues. As well, you can work with children for any necessary follow-up of issues raised. For example, a new baby in a family may result in greeting cards from the class or individuals. A house fire may result in a drive to collect clothes for the family. A bully on the playground may be discovered. The sharing experience models respect for individuals and offers an opportunity for greater understanding of the diversity of understanding and thought. Through informal sharing, without the higher stakes of academic knowledge expected, children have the opportunity to speak and learn.

To handle special issues children bring to the sharing experience, or for those arising during the day, many teachers include discussion of peacemaking skills by creating a structure and corner for handling interpersonal disputes arising in the classroom, halls, playground, cafeteria, etc. Structured conflict resolution is promoted with listening, voice level, vocabulary, and respect for diversity of perspective built into the structure (Dixon, 2016).

For schoolwide and community issues that may be controversial, you may wish to create a reflective discussion circle (McGriff & Clemons, 2019). The ideal way to structure such a discussion will be in teacher-created small groups where the rules for convening include:

- sharing views
- listening
- identifying new ways to view or solve
- critical evaluation of the topic or issue
- drafting an action plan

Small groups, then, share with the whole class. A final action plan is drawn up, recognizing that not everyone's ideas will be incorporated. There may even be a minority report created for additional reflection on another day, perhaps with some fact-finding investigation by class members. Through this discussion, children are learning the ways school boards, park districts, and other community entities establish civic action priorities.

In making space for sharing and social issue discussions, wise teachers ensure there is enough time for thoughtful engagement. Advice from the Center for Responsive Schools (Tilley, 2020) includes the following important principles:

- Name the issues—children may come to the discussion with different perspectives, based on their prior lived experiences.
- Help children identify real feelings—anxiety, empathy.
- Allow children to opt out of participation in particular issues of their choice.
- Consider partner discussions rather than small or large group discussions.
- Remind children that agreement does not have to be reached, but respect for various opinions and thoughts must be maintained.

In this way, you are assuring children that diverse opinions about issues can be discussed and may or may not lead to civic engagement at the moment. However, the discussion will remain a background to a greater understanding of self, classmates, and community.

Current Events

As children share stories from their lives with classmates, the social studies investigations often relate to current events. For example, Paris Williams, age six, created an initiative to feed the homeless in St. Louis, beginning with handing out 600 care packages decorated with messages and drawings by Paris. This child-initiated **civic action**—an individual act of service to one's community—resulted in the formation of the Paris Cares Foundation (Katz Keating & Grossman Kanter, 2020). While this civic action did not emerge in the classroom, it shows how young children are thinking about their world and the capacity they have to understand community needs. Other recent examples emerging from the pandemic experience are shown in Textbox 9.1, Recent Examples of Civic Action by Children.

TEXTBOX 9.1

Recent Examples of Civic Action by Children

- Two six-year-old boys in London set up a lemonade stand to raise money for people in war-torn Yemen. Ayaan Moosa and Mikaeel Ishaaq were surprised recently by Angelina Jolie, who supported their effort with a grant of $25,000. (*People*, October 12, 2020)
- Nine-year-old Robbie Bond of Hawaii was concerned about the disappearance of national monuments. He set out to visit twenty-eight endangered monuments with his family and created Kids Speak for Parks. (*Mental Floss*, September 22, 2020)
- Eight-year-old Amariyanna "Mari" Copeny wrote a letter to the White House in March 2016 about the water in Flint making kids sick. President Obama met her when he visited Flint. Since that time, Mari has spearheaded a backpack collection for children. (*Mental Floss*, September 22, 2020)
- Carver, five years old, while shopping for snacks for volunteer firefighters in California, chose a Yoda figure as a friend for the firefighters and wrote a note: "Thank you, firefighters. Here is a friend for you in case you get lonely. Love, Carver." The Yoda traveled to other fire sites and a Facebook page was created to show the travels. (*Washington Post*, October 1, 2020)

This child-initiated civic action emerged from a current event in this child's life. The importance of paying attention to sharing and current events, which may lead to civic engagement, is underlined by the recent NCSS Board of Directors. On July 16, 2020, the National Council for Social Studies Board of Directors affirmed the ethical responsibilities of social studies teachers for educating and empowering "America's youth for informed and engaged civic life in a pluralistic democracy" with emphasis on three of the six principles in its Revised Code of Ethics for the Social Studies Profession (NCSS, 2020). The principles are shown in Textbox 9.2, Three Ethical Responsibilities for the Social Studies Profession.

TEXTBOX 9.2

Three Ethical Responsibilities for the Social Studies Profession

It is the ethical responsibility of social studies professionals

- To provide to every student the knowledge, skills, experiences, and attitudes necessary to function as an effective participant in a democratic system.
- To foster the understanding and exercise of the rights guaranteed under the Constitution of the United States and of the responsibilities implicit in those rights in an increasingly interdependent world.
- To cultivate and maintain an instructional environment in which the free contest of ideas is prized.

"NCSS also advocates the teaching of social studies that includes multiple approaches, including fact-based curriculum, facing hard history, addressing controversial topics, and confronting false narratives" (NCSS, 2020).

These ethical principles are illustrated in the following classroom example of civic action emerging from current events when a group of fifth graders were concerned about the school lunch. They researched nutrition requirements, investigated dietary restrictions of peers, and took action through a letter to the school lunch manager. The issue began with children who could not eat the salad, in some cases, because of the bacon bits automatically served and in other cases because of the cheese automatically served. While ten-year-olds are more advanced in writing position statements, we can imagine other situations where younger children might take action to protect the religious principles and health needs of their peers with pictures or recorded statements.

In another class, the children were curious about Veterans Day. In general, our social studies activities should not be driven by holidays, because the holiday curriculum creates an oversimplified view of our society. That is, curricula focus on surface, sometimes trivial aspects of holidays and lead to stereotypical views of cultures and celebrations. In fact, such curricula often consist of celebrations of minor or secular holidays such as Halloween instead of Día de los Muertos; Valentine's Day; St. Patrick's Day; Cinco de Mayo instead of Mexican Independence Day; Hanukkah, instead of Rosh Hashanah and Yom Kippur; ignoring Ramadan, etc. Such holidays are often not observed by everyone and in particular not by those of Jehovah's Witness faith who only celebrate religious holidays. Wise teachers know the families and community and offer opportunities to bring artifacts, pictures, oral histories, and conversation to class when their family holidays and events are current.

However, national holidays, such as Veterans Day, deserve attention to assure young children begin to acquire historical knowledge. As well, they learn why the "day off" from school is considered an important example of ways men and women sacrificed for the greater good of the country. After investigation of the history of the holiday, beginning with Wilson's Declaration of Armistice Day in 1919, the children can propose ways to take civic action for veterans' issues. They may also collect oral histories from veterans by interviewing them or by inviting them to the classroom. At the conclusion of learning the history and importance of Veterans Day, as well as the current needs of veterans in their community, the class may write letters to support advocacy efforts for veterans, collect warm socks for the homeless, or in other ways celebrate veterans' sacrifice for democracy.

Additional ideas for linking past civic action that may lead to historical understanding and stimulate civic engagement in the present may come from children's literature included in the curriculum. Libresco (2018) identifies many ways to consider the use of books featuring the historical participation of young children in societal change. These examples may spark thoughtful consideration of possibilities for the here and now or ideas for future endeavors.

Problem-Based Curricular Examples

Whether we are teaching children to participate in civic engagement by starting with the issues they wish to solve, or those we introduce as part of the planned social studies curriculum, the problem-based projects lead to the curricular illustration of thoughtful civic engagement. To illustrate the ways teachers can implement such an approach to civics in the social studies, the following examples are listed for your review:

- For Women's History Month, the third grade investigated: "Women are as important as men" (Hubbard et al., 2020). The class examined historical materials, created exhibits, and shared their findings with a wider audience.
- In a community partnership, a class combined science learning and social studies around the issue of the effect of plastic bags on the environment.
- Another possible problem-based science and social studies investigation might include the question: "Why do some people in our community go hungry?"
- In a community with many migrant worker families, the children were curious about the history of working conditions for migrants. The investigation led to a further study of worker rights and workplace safety.
- A field trip to the community grocery store (Adams, 2015) led children to answer the questions: "What does the grocery store sell?" and "Where does food come from?"

In each of these experiences with the civic life of the classroom, children are developing an understanding of the principles of productive civic engagement. Such engagement "requires knowledge of the history, principles, and foundations of our American democracy, and the ability to participate in civic and democratic processes" (NCSS, 2013, p. 31). In these ways, they are learning that civic engagement addresses "public problems individually and collectively" (NCSS, 2013, p. 31). Children are learning how to investigate questions, beginning with their class peers—skills they will apply to an evolving social world as they progress in school. They are practicing rudimentary citizen action behaviors such as arguing, debating, voting, and volunteering. These activities foster children's capacity to understand **civic space**, "the space for people to organize, participate, communicate, and act as individuals and as members of civil society . . . the bedrock of any open and democratic society" (CIVICUS, 2017).

To support their learning, we show them how to use primary sources, including pictures and digital media. Children produce products to demonstrate understanding and inform their school friends with timelines, songs, plays, murals, and producing news for the school community. Perhaps they draft a public service announcement to foster interest in a civic concern in their community, plan a social media campaign, or develop key points for an op-ed, or create a movie starting with a storyboard.

The key for understanding and action for young children is that the issues must be local, that is within the children's world of experiences. Engagement begins at the classroom level, continuing to school and community. In recent years, we have seen examples of the ways young children are engaged in problem-solving for their communities. They are identifying specific needs in the classroom, school, and community. They are drawn to action by the concern for individuals, issues, and needs. Young children march, respond to disasters, collect toys and T-shirts, produce poems, songs, plays, and in many other ways show their understanding of democratic society. Along the way, as teachers, we foster skills for investigation, debate, consulting experts, and finding historical materials to bolster arguments. We are always mindful of the potential for diverse perspectives, based on cultural capital, and of the need to foster an atmosphere of respect for classmates and school colleagues. This critical work is not easy but is a valuable component for our work to nurture the skills children will need for civic engagement, civic action, and democracy.

Activities in the Field

1. At a field visit in a PreK–3 class, interview three children to ascertain their understanding of what it means to be a citizen. Ask them what social or civic engagement they have taken recently. Record notes to share with your colleagues. How do the children's understandings match your reading of this chapter? What are the next steps in teaching?

2. Interview three children of various ages in a community-based setting. Ask what they remember about civic engagement activities. Which experiences were most meaningful and why? Record notes to share with your colleagues. What are the teaching implications for your future curricula?

Activities in the Library

1. Consult recent issues of *Social Studies and the Young Learner* and *Young Children* to find examples of civic engagement in PreK–3. For a school of your choice, identify ways the examples could be modified and incorporated in problem-based learning to accomplish curricular standards.

2. Read the recent edition of community newspapers and magazines. Identify current events calling for civic engagement. Is there space for young children to be involved? How might the involvement fit into the civics standards for your state? Make a plan for introducing the project to a grade level of your choice.

Study Questions

1. How do young children understand politics at various ages? What is your role as a teacher in elucidating the concept?

2. Why is problem-based learning an ideal way for children to learn social studies? Where does inquiry fit into this model for delivering curricula?

3. How do young children understand civic engagement at various ages? How can you make the concept accessible to children?

4. Why are current events an important aspect of civics education? How will you incorporate them into your lesson plans?

5. Why must the understanding of civic action be focused on local issues? How does the local perspective fit with the ideal of developmentally appropriate practice?

Reflect and Reread

1. Think about your experiences in K–12 education. How were politics and civic action a part of your education? What civic action did you participate in as a young child and adolescent? What would you say to your former teachers about what you wish you might have learned then?

2. In the past year, we have seen many changes to our society. We have also seen many people being involved in civic action. How does your experience of the past year or so shape your views on your role as a teacher?

Suggested Readings

Januszka, D., & Vincent, K. (2012). *Closing circles: 50 activities for ending the day in a positive way.* Turner Falls, MA: Center for Responsive Schools.

Problem-Based Learning Examples and Project Design Template, PBLWorks https://www.pblworks.org/

Websites for Additional Information

Center for Responsive Schools https://www.responsiveclassroom.org/about/crs/

CIVICUS https://www.civicus.org/

Common Sense Media https://www.commonsensemedia.org/

Educator Resources: National Archives https://www.archives.gov/education

Edutopia: https://www.edutopia.org/article/civics-elementary-classroom

Forty Kids Who Have Changed the World https://www.goodhousekeeping.com/life/inspirational-stories/g5188/kids-who-changed-the-world/

GeoInquiries https://www.responsiveclassroom.org/about/crs/

Kid Citizen https://www.kidcitizen.net/

Learning for Justice https://www.learningforjustice.org/

National Association for Media Literacy Education https://namle.net/

Problem Based Learning: Make a Difference Examples https://www.pblworks.org/

Ryan's Recycling https://ryansrecycling.com/

Teachers: Library of Congress https://www.loc.gov/programs/teachers/about-this-program/

Time for Kids https://www.timeforkids.com/

Want to rebuild public trust? Focus on Civic Education, December 7, 2020 https://www.rand.org/blog/articles/2020/12/want-to-rebuild-public-trust-focus-on-civic-education.html

Zinn Education Project https://www.zinnedproject.org/

Appendix A
General Lesson Planning
Amy Clark, Ph.D.

Age/Grade:
Content/Curricular Area(s):

Reflect as You Plan	Preparation
• *Identify connections to national social studies curriculum theme(s).* • *Identify connections to community resources, locations, guest speakers.*	**Learning standards:** **English language proficiency standards:** **Prior knowledge and cultural-experiential knowledge related to lesson concepts:** *How will you assess children's prior knowledge, including their cultural experiential knowledge, related to the lesson content and concepts? This includes families' funds of knowledge, such as knowledge and experiences related to gardening or farming, construction, sewing, cooking, navigating immigration processes, interpreting and translating across languages; and children's daily and frequent experiences, such as taking public transportation and reading bus or train routes, completing household chores and caregiving for siblings, memorizing religious texts or prayers, and using language(s) and dialect(s) strategically and effectively according to context and conversation partners.* **Possible/anticipated misconceptions about lesson concept(s):** **Opportunities to integrate social-emotional learning:** **Opportunities to integrate multiple perspectives:**
• *What language do you want children to process and produce?*	**Opportunities to connect learning to the home in community:** **Key language functions, phrases, and/or vocabulary:** **Learning objective(s):**

Reflect as You Plan	Preparation
	Language objective(s): *Each learning objective should have a language objective that states how the child will produce and/or process key language to participate and demonstrate understanding.*
	Language frames: *Clear and differentiated phrases that facilitate children's use of key vocabulary and language function(s) during the lesson.*
• *How will you make content accessible to all children?*	**Instructional and learning supports:** *Instructional materials and resources, environmental supports, classroom arrangement, learning formats (small group, whole group, partners, etc.), technology tools, visual, tactile, and graphic supports to ensure all children, including children with a range of abilities and emergent bi/multilingual children categorized as DLLs or ELs, have opportunities to meet or exceed the objective(s).*
• *Are there any culturally relevant materials that can be used to connect new learning with children's sociocultural knowledge?* • *Describe multiple ways in which children can demonstrate understanding and meet or exceed the objective(s).*	**Assessment task and plan:** *What will the children do, say, create, perform, complete, etc., to demonstrate that they have met or exceeded the objective(s)? Assessment tasks should be as authentic as possible and include a range of options for children to demonstrate learning and achievement of the objective(s). Include: (i) how you will provide children with multiple ways to demonstrate that they have met or exceeded the objective(s); (ii) how you will collect evidence of children's learning; (iii) what will you collect as evidence; (iv) clear and concise assessment criteria; (v) how you will analyze the evidence collected to inform and differentiate instruction; and (vi) how you will share feedback from the assessment with children and families.*
• *Engage children in thinking about and articulating their learning.*	**Opportunities for self- and peer assessment:**
	Instruction
A T-chart that identifies what the teacher says and does and what children say and do is helpful. <table><tr><td>Teacher says/does</td><td>Children say/do</td></tr></table> • *How will you support children in working in collaboration with each other and/or independently to achieve the objective(s)?*	**Introduction:** *Describe how children will initially engage with the lesson topic. For example, will children examine an artifact or photo, observe a scenario, listen to a recording, or interpret and respond to an open-ended question related to the objective and concepts?* **Learning activities:** *Describe step-by-step what the teacher will do and what the children will do to meet or exceed the objective(s).* *Include the modeling process and plans for guided and partner, small group, and/or individual practice.* *Specifically address how instruction:* • *includes multiple opportunities to provide specific feedback to children throughout the lesson* • *affirms, normalizes, and builds on children's range of abilities, languages, dialects, and cultures* • *makes input comprehensible for children with different abilities and from diverse linguistic backgrounds* • *promotes oral language development and children's use of language for authentic purposes in relation to the content and concepts*

Reflect as You Plan	Instruction
• *Will children be able to monitor their progress toward meeting the objective(s)?* • *How will you provide children with feedback during the lesson?* • *How will you document your observations of aspects of children's engagement and understanding?* • *How will you support children to serve as resources for each other?*	• *provides multiple opportunities for children to:* ○ *connect new learning to prior experiences and to authentic and "real world" experiences* ○ *engage with content through multiple modalities* ○ *listen to and build on the ideas of their peers* ○ *process key concept(s) in different ways* ○ *process and use the key language, phrases, and/or vocabulary* ○ *create* ○ *engage in critical thinking about the content and concept* • *provides children with multiple ways to demonstrate understanding and new learning, including product and/or demonstration options*
	Closure
	• *Consider opportunities for children to synthesize new learning in collaboration with peers, assess their understanding and products in relation to the objective(s), and/or pose questions that emerged during the lesson.*

Reflection and Analysis
Describe:
- *strengths and limitations of the lesson*
- *changes you would make to enhance any aspect of the lesson*
- *next instructional steps and opportunities for differentiation based on your observations and analysis of assessment data*

Appendix B

Integrated Unit Outline Planning Template

Amy Clark, Ph.D.

Unit of Study Title:

Preparation	
• Age and developmental level/grade of children (PreK through three to five years or K–2 through five to eight years):	**Consider opportunities to:** • engage families and community members • connect learning to the home and community • integrate social-emotional learning • integrate multiple perspectives • connect to National Social Studies Curriculum Theme(s) • normalize and build on different abilities, languages, and dialects (of children in the classroom and beyond) • make connections to learning across the curriculum • integrate with the arts (e.g., dance and movement, dramatization and tableau, music and song, sketching and painting, photography, etc.) • assess children's prior knowledge related to the unit topic and concepts in the weeks and days before the unit launch
• Home language(s) and cultural backgrounds:	
• Different abilities:	
• Literacy Learning Standard:	
• Social Science/Social Studies Learning Standard:	
• English language proficiency standards:	
• Duration of unit of study:	
• Child and family cultural-experiential knowledge related to the learning standards:	
• Possible/anticipated misconceptions related to the learning standards:	
• Materials and primary and secondary resources (denote those that need to be procured):	

Big-Picture Planning

- Identify one to two generative guiding questions that will promote curiosity, multiple interpretations, and debate throughout the unit of study.

- Determine how you and the children will document and display new discoveries, questions, and products throughout the unit of study.

Key Concepts Related to Learning Standards	**Key Skills Required to Achieve Standards**
• literacy	• literacy
• social studies	• social studies

Vocabulary, Phrases, and Language Function(s)	**Language Frames**
	• to promote the use of vocabulary and meaningful discussions about key concepts related to standards

Culminating Performance Task and/or Product That Demonstrates Achievement of Standards/ Identified Components of Standards

- multiple accessible options for a culminating performance task or product that provide opportunities for children with different abilities and levels of English proficiency to achieve the standards and demonstrate new learning

Performance Assessment Criteria

- four levels of criteria (e.g., emerging, approaching, meets, exceeds)

Celebration of Learning

- Consult with children to design a culminating celebration of learning and consider options for performances and presentations, potential audiences (e.g., other classrooms, families, community members), gallery and display options (e.g., local library or community organization), and online publishing opportunities.

Instructional Plan		
Instructional and Learning Supports • to ensure all children, including children with a range of abilities and emergent bi/multilingual children categorized as DLLs or ELs, have opportunities to meet or exceed the objective(s). **Instructional Strategies**	**Learning Tasks and Experiences** • Organized by day or week • Facilitate and build toward successful completion of the performance task/product and achievement of standards. • Pay careful attention to the sequence of tasks and experiences and ensure that each task builds on the knowledge and skills taught and learned in the previous task. • Include how tasks and experiences tap into and engage children in using multiple modalities to process information, generate and express ideas, and produce artifacts. • Remember that children need to be **actively engaged** in **developing oral language** and **using language for authentic purposes with each other** (rather than only with the teacher) and actively **engaged in higher-order thinking throughout the unit of study**.	**Opportunities for Formative Assessments** • Outline: (i) what you will observe/collect, when, and why; (ii) the assessment approaches, tools, and formats (e.g., individual, small group); (iii) documentation and analysis procedures; and (iv) how you will share feedback with the children. • Remember: the data collected will inform decisions related to adjusting instructional and learning supports, creating partnerships and groupings, enhancing language and technology supports, etc. **Opportunities for Child Self- and Peer Assessments** • to provide children with tools to monitor their progress and learning and to provide and receive constructive feedback from peers.
Reflection and Analysis • strengths and limitations of the unit of study • changes you would make to enhance any aspect of the unit of study		

Appendix C
Investigation Planning Guide
Amy Clark, Ph.D.

Title of Investigation:

Reflect as You Plan	Preparation

• *Identify connections to national social studies curriculum theme(s).*
• *Are there opportunities to integrate movement such as total physical response (TPR) to teach and review key vocabulary and tableau and dance to interpret and/or present findings?*
• *Are there opportunities to integrate aspects of social-emotional learning, such as developing relationship skills through teamwork and fostering social awareness by examining multiple perspectives?*
• *Are there opportunities to integrate the arts, such as music and song, sketching and painting, and photography, etc., to interpret and/or present findings?*
• *Consider teaching and learning the key vocabulary and all of the languages spoken by children in the classroom.*
	• Identify a topic that addresses the content learning standard.
	
	• Topic:
	
	• Content standard:
	
	• Literacy standard:
	
	• English language proficiency standards:
	
	Describe:
	• how the topic relates to children's daily experiences
	• how it relates to the children's community and community resources
	• how it can promote questioning, interpretation, and debate
	• opportunities to authentically integrate the four language domains (listening, speaking, reading, and writing)
	• opportunities to make additional cross-curricular connections
	• instructional and learning supports that provide all children, including children with a range of abilities and emergent bi/multilingual children categorized as DLLs or ELs, with ongoing opportunities to actively investigate, analyze, collaborate, etc., in order to achieve the standards
	• primary and secondary resources related to the topic that:
	  o are accessible to all children and in particular to children with a range of abilities
	  o represent and tap into the cultures, languages, abilities, histories, and experiences of the children and families in your classroom and of children and families not represented in your classroom, setting, or community

Reflect as You Plan	Preparation
	<ul><li>○ were created by Black, Indigenous, and/or persons of color</li><li>○ promote questioning, interpretation, and debate</li><li>○ tap into and engage children in using multiple modalities</li><li>key language functions, phrases, and vocabulary that children need to understand and apply in order to investigate the topic and analyze findings in collaboration with peers</li><li>potential options through which children of all abilities and linguistic backgrounds can demonstrate achievement and present findings (keep in mind that children should play a role in designing and selecting the options)</li><li>potential opportunities to provide children with consistent feedback throughout the investigation</li><li>key assessment criteria that are accessible to children and that can guide your instruction and formative assessments throughout the investigation, as well as guide the children's work throughout the investigation</li><li>how you and the children can document the phases of the "living" investigation so that children and families can track and review the ongoing process</li><li>when and how frequently children will work on the investigation (e.g., daily for thirty minutes or twice a week for sixty minutes at a specific time of day) and the approximate duration of the investigation (e.g., two weeks, one month, or a quarter)</li></ul>
	Introduction
<ul><li>*Consider using an artifact, photo, painting, video, song, speech, guest speaker, oral story, etc., to introduce the topic and elicit children's curiosity, predictions, and questions.*</li><li>*Identify effective graphic organizers that can support children in generating and sorting questions by importance.*</li></ul>	Describe how you will introduce the investigation to the children. Describe:<ul><li>how you will introduce the topic to the children</li><li>how you will model generating questions and support children in generating questions about the topic<ul><li>○ opportunities for children to report their questions to peers and to listen to and consider questions generated by their peers</li></ul></li><li>how you will guide students to analyze and sort their questions by levels of importance</li><li>opportunities for children to build consensus on the most important one or two questions that will guide the investigation</li><li>opportunities to discuss and select sub-questions to investigate in collaboration with groups of peers</li><li>opportunities for children to discuss and investigate how they can find answers to the most important question(s)<ul><li>○ describe how you will engage families and/or community members in this process</li></ul></li></ul>
	Primary and Secondary Resources
<ul><li>*Remember to evaluate primary and secondary sources based on the criteria listed in **Preparation**.*</li><li>*Consider including some resources in different languages, including languages not spoken by children in the classroom and in the community as this may stimulate further investigation.*</li></ul>	Describe:<ul><li>the primary and secondary resources that will be used to investigate answers to the questions</li><li>how the resources are accessible to all children, including children with a range of different abilities and emergent bi/multilingual children at different levels of English proficiency</li><li>how you will teach children to distinguish between primary and secondary resources</li><li>how you will know that they are able to distinguish between them</li><li>how children, families, and/or community members will participate in the process of identifying and locating primary and secondary resources related to the topic</li></ul>

	Investigation
Consider a range of documentation options and tools for children to use, such as components of technology platforms used in your setting, reporter's notebooks, sketch pads, digital cameras, digital audio recorders, etc. • *Consider providing the children with differentiated language frames to promote the use of key vocabulary and phrases and to facilitate conversation and debate about sources, evidence, and findings.* • *Consider opportunities for cross-age/grade collaboration by establishing investigation buddies (similar to reading buddies) with older students in your settings.* • *Consider inviting family and community members and/or seeking a partnership with a local school, community college, or university to provide investigation mentors for the children.*	Describe how you will facilitate children's investigation to answer the questions. Describe: • specific strategies and techniques you will use to support all children in analyzing evidence and information found in a range of different primary and secondary resources • how the facilitation promotes maximum comprehensibility, access, and participation for all children, including children with a range of abilities and emergent bi/multilingual children with different levels of English proficiency • fieldwork, community explorations, field trips, and/or guest speakers as resources that support the investigation • how you will model and facilitate children's analysis of sources and interpretation of information ○ how you will support children in distinguishing between reliable and less reliable sources and between important information and minor details • how facilitation promotes peer-to-peer conversations and debate about the sources examined and the evidence and information collected • multiple ways in which children will collaborate to document, analyze, and organize evidence and information from a range of sources • all daily instructional routines that will be implemented during the investigation (e.g., teacher modeling, guided practice—small group practice with teacher facilitation—and whole group synthesis and review)
	Findings
	Describe how children will synthesize information and evidence collected from multiple sources to generate answers to the questions. Describe: • how you will model drawing on and synthesizing evidence collected from multiple different sources to construct possible and plausible responses to the questions • how you will support children to draw on and synthesize evidence collected from multiple different sources to construct possible and plausible responses • multiple opportunities for children to collaborate and engage in peer-to-peer conversations throughout this phase of the investigation ○ multiple opportunities for children to examine key supporting evidence and to compare different findings and responses • whether and how children will come to a consensus on key findings and key supporting evidence • opportunities for children to generate further questions and discuss implications or next steps related to their findings in collaboration with peers

	Demonstration and Dissemination

• *Consider opportunities for multimodal presentations. Can children demonstrate their learning through movement, art, and other creative expressions and in different languages and dialects?*
• *Consider recruiting family members, older students, and/or community members to support emergent bi/multilingual children in creating bi/multilingual presentations.*
	Describe how children will demonstrate their learning by applying and presenting their findings.
	Describe:
	• multiple different options through which children with a range of abilities and levels of English proficiency can effectively present their findings
	• how you will engage children in planning and designing the dissemination process
	  ○ How will you and the children determine with whom they will share their findings?
	  ○ Will findings be shared beyond the classroom? Beyond the school or center? Are there opportunities to report findings to community members?
	  ○ Are there opportunities to disseminate findings to a wider audience through social media and the Internet, for example?
	• opportunities for children to practice presenting their findings to peer groups and opportunities to provide and receive supportive peer feedback
	• opportunities for children to articulate and assess their own learning and presentations
	• opportunities for whole group reflection and synthesis of learning at the end of the investigation

Reflection and Analysis
Describe:
- *strengths and limitations of the investigation*
- *changes you would make to enhance any aspect of the investigation*
- *opportunities for future investigations based on your observations and analysis of assessment data*

Appendix D
Lesson Planning Template
Megan Schumaker-Murphy, Ed.D.

This template shows both an example of a plan and questions to ponder as you plan. The thinking prompts are shown in italics.

Basic Lesson Plan Content:
How would you describe this lesson in one sentence?

This is a social studies read-aloud of *Our Favorite Day of the Year* that immediately precedes a writers' workshop drawing/writing activity.

Lesson Plan Context:
How does this lesson fit into your broader context? Is it part of a unit? Does it combine content areas? Who are the students you are teaching? What are their cultural, language, and instructional needs? What accommodations will you use to support student learning needs? What other information do you need to keep in mind as you plan this lesson?

This lesson is one of the first lessons of the school year in an integrated first-grade classroom. This lesson is intended to help the teacher learn more about the students' home cultures. There are twenty-two students. Two students are English language learners who speak Arabic at home and two other students speak English and Arabic at home. Two students speak Spanish at home. Four students have IEP accommodations for reading, writing, and attention, and three students have accommodations for math.

Standard(s):
What are the learning standards that you will address in this lesson?

Massachusetts History and Social Science Standards:

Topic 3. History: unity and diversity in the United States [1.T3]
Supporting Question: What does the motto, "Out of Many, One" mean, and why is it a good motto of the United States?
1. Provide evidence to explain some of the ways in which the people of the United States are unified (e.g., share a common national history) and diverse (e.g., have different backgrounds, hold different beliefs, and have different celebrations, cultural traditions, and family structures).

Massachusetts English and Language Art Standard:
Grade 1 Writing Standards [W]
Text Types and Purposes
1. Write opinion pieces that introduce the topic or book they are writing about, state an opinion, supply a reason for the opinion, and provide some sense of closure.

Grade 1 Speaking and Listening Standards [SL]
Comprehension and Collaboration
1. Participate in collaborative discussions with diverse partners about grade 1 topics and texts with peers and adults in small and larger groups.

Lesson Objective:

Based on the standard, what will the students be able to do after the lesson? There should be one objective per standard.

1. Students will learn about how different holidays, celebrations, and family traditions are significant to their peers (relates to the history and social science standard identified above).
2. Students will participate in a conversation with a peer in which they give and seek information about their favorite days of the year (related to the speaking and listening standard above).
3. Students will draw a picture of and describe in writing their favorite day of the year using the prompt: My favorite day of the year is _____ because _____ (relates to the writing standard above).

Assessment(s):

What informal and/or formal formative and summative assessments will you use to determine if the students meet the objective(s)? How will you accommodate learning and language differences in your assessments?

Objective 1 assessment: This is an informal, formative assessment of observations of what students say during the read-aloud and turn and talk discussion. During the read-aloud, the teacher will ask questions such as "Do any of you celebrate Eid? What do you know about Eid?" After the read-aloud, the teacher will ask, "What do all of the students' favorite days have in common?" and "How are their favorite days different?"

Objective 2 assessment: This is an informal, formative assessment of observations during the turn and talk portion of the lesson. The teacher will listen to conversations and scaffold some groups as needed.

Objective 3 assessment: This is an informal, formative assessment. The teacher will review the pictures and writing produced during writers' workshop.

Materials:

What materials will you need to prepare for this lesson? What visual supports will you use? Will you need materials to help students regulate and attend? What materials will you need to cue students to have ready?

Our Favorite Day of the Year by A. E. Ali (extra copies if possible)
Whiteboard and markers
Sentence strips with conversation prompts "What is your favorite day?" "What do you do on your favorite day?" and "What do you like about your favorite day?"
Sentence strips with writing prompt "My favorite day is _____ because _____."
Teacher example
Student writing implements
Paper with writing prompts provided

Time	Procedure	Differentiation/Learning Supports
How long will part of the lesson take?	*What will you say and do during this part of the lesson? How will you incorporate your assessments?*	*How will you support learning for children with language and learning differences throughout this lesson?*
Read aloud: ten minutes Group discussion: five minutes	Beginning: *How are you going to transition into and introduce this lesson?* This lesson begins on the carpet. Students will have just transitioned in from gym class. The teacher will ask them to go straight to the carpet from when they enter the classroom. Once the children are on the carpet and the teacher is seated, the teacher will use the "if you can hear me clap your hands" then "if you can hear me touch your nose" strategy to make sure students are quiet and looking at her.	*What will you already have in place to support students with learning and language differences?* Transitioning from specials to a read-aloud is a daily routine that students are used to completing. There is a visual schedule in English and Arabic with photos on the wall of the classroom. One student brings his chair to the carpet as part of the routine, and there is a fidget basket available on the carpet for students who would like a fidget during the read-aloud.

Time	Procedure	Differentiation/Learning Supports
	The teacher will introduce the book *Our Favorite Day of the Year* by telling them that they are learning about how everyone has a special or favorite day, but that our favorite days are all different. She will remind the class that today was gym day, which is many of the students' favorite day of the week, and that today, she will read a book about a classroom community where students celebrate their favorite days of the year with their classmates. During the read-aloud, the teacher will ask questions like "Do any of you celebrate Eid like Musa?" "What do you know about Eid?" and "Do any of you celebrate Los Pasados?" "What does your family do to celebrate Los Pasados?" After the end of the story, the teacher will ask the students "How are the students' favorite days the same?" and "How are the students' favorite days different?"	Students that receive English language support will have pre-read the book with the ELL instructor. Students that need support for reading comprehension will pre-read the story the day before. All students receiving supports will practice the questions for the turn and talk after this pre-read. If available, students will be able to follow along with a copy of the book they hold.
Turn and talk example: three minutes Turn and talk: six minutes	Middle: *What is the middle part of your lesson? What are you going to do and say to teach the content and keep students engaged?* After the group discussion, the teacher will cue the students that now that they know about favorite days, they will be writing about their favorite day for writers' workshop and that to get their brains ready to write, they will turn and talk with their classmates about their favorite day. The teacher will display the conversation prompt sentence strips and model with the teacher assistant how they will listen to each other and then ask each other one or more of the three questions on the sentence strips. The teacher will tell the students that they have three minutes each to talk about their favorite day.	*What will you do if assessments show students aren't understanding the content? What will you do if informal assessments show students have mastered the content?* *How will you support English Language Learners and students with learning differences?* The teacher will use the observational assessment from the large group discussion to determine if she needs to scaffold the turn and talk discussion. During turn and talk, she will walk around and listen to students' conversations and scaffold as necessary. The Arabic speakers who are learning English will be paired with the children that speak both Arabic and English. The Spanish speakers will be paired. Students will be encouraged to speak the language they are most comfortable speaking with their partners. The teacher will offer sticky notes with the prompts on them for students who need them. The prompts will be displayed at the front of the rug. The teacher will use a three-minute visual timer and give the students a verbal cue to change partners when the timer goes off.

Time	Procedure	Differentiation/Learning Supports
Writers' workshop: twenty minutes	End: *How will you wrap up the lesson and transition to the next activity?* After the turn and talk, the teacher will ask if two children want to share what they learned about their partner's favorite day. Once the students have shared, the teacher will tell the students that they will be drawing and writing about their favorite day. She will show them an example of her drawing of her birthday, which is her favorite day, and read the writing that goes with it that says, "My favorite day is my birthday because I get to hear from lots of the people that I love when they call or text me to say 'Happy birthday!' On my birthday, my daughter decorates a cake for me, and then my family lights a birthday candle and sings *Happy Birthday.* When they are done singing, I make a wish as I blow out the candle and then we eat the cake!" Then the teacher will put her example on the whiteboard. She will tell the students they are going to draw their favorite days and then write about them for the writers' workshop. The teacher will say, "Once you get your paper from [student name], you will get up and find your writing spot for today and start your picture!" Once the students are dismissed and settled into their writing spots, the teacher will walk around to determine who needs scaffolding.	*How will you support students with language and learning differences to transition from one activity to the next?* The students regularly transition from a read-aloud to readers' or writers' workshop tasks and know the routine. One student, who needs assistance during transitions, will be asked to pass out the papers to her peers. Students are able to choose where they sit for the writers' workshop. They can sit at their desks, sit or lay on the rug with a clipboard or lap desk, or stand at the tall table in the room. A variety of writing implements are available for students at their tables including fat and skinny markers, pencils, colored pencils.

anti-racist one who promotes racial justice by working against racist policies and ideas

anti-racist pedagogy a pedagogy that calls for teachers to highlight the perspectives of marginalized groups, invite children to critically examine issues with power structures, and critically examine instruction and assessment to identify potential linguistic and cultural biases

audience the opportunity to be heard

baseline what must be considered for any curricular implementation

big ideas ideas that anchor child investigation

C3 Framework a framework (2013) created by the National Council for the Social Studies with standards to guide the instruction of social studies understandings

childcare also called daycare; a system historically used by low-income families in order to work

citizen a member of a community

citizenship how and why we participate in our various communities

civic action an individual act of service to one's community

civic agency acting to solve an issue

civic engagement identifying a problem, investigating solutions, discussing the solutions, and taking action

civic space space for people to "organize, participate, communicate, and act as individuals and as members of civil society" (CIVICUS, 2017)

civics a subject area that examines political systems and citizenship

class meeting a practice that serves as a vehicle to share and discuss information and advance personal interactions in the classroom

classroom library curation the careful, weighted selection of children's books into social studies teaching

Common Core State Standards standards (2010) adopted by most states to guide the instruction of math and English Language Arts

community an organization of people joined together to fulfill a specific purpose or purposes

cultural capital the knowledge, skills, and abilities young children have and acquire in school and elsewhere

culturally grounded honoring strengths of individual's cultures and integrating aspects of home cultures into curriculum and interactions

culturally responsive teaching pedagogical practices to help children achieve academic success and cultural competence

culture the artifacts, behaviors, and belief systems of a people

developmentally appropriate practice the idea that in curricular development, plans should be age appropriate, individually appropriate, and culturally and linguistically appropriate

digital divide having limited or no access to cell phones, tablets, and computers, streaming entertainment subscriptions, or broadband Internet

digital literacy experiences and facility in using digital communication methods

digital native a member of a generation that has never known a world without Internet, video streaming, cable TV, and computers in all forms

documentation panel a visual presentation to summarize knowledge

economics a subject area that explores how resources are created, distributed, and used; needs and wants; and financial literacy

emergent bilinguals children from diverse cultural and linguistic backgrounds who are in the process of not only learning English but also developing proficiency in another language(s)

emergent curriculum the idea that educational activities in the classroom are based upon children's interests, issues in their families and community, activities in the learning centers, and in outdoor experiences

equity being able to access materials without obstacles such as language or special needs

evidence based problem-solving approach to childcare and education, integrating research, child data, and appreciating family values

funds of knowledge the information and experiences children have based on family and community living

geography a subject area that uses a spatial perspective to study the natural and human-built environment

global literature books set in and featuring people and how they live in parts of the world outside the United States

Head Start a preschool program started in 1965 to meet the needs of the "whole child" by improving their cognitive, social, emotional, and physical health as well as engage with parents and communities

history a subject area that employs a time perspective to study the past, present, and, at times, the future

inquiry an investigatory process based upon what the learner identifies as most salient and personally relevant in answering a deep question

Inquiry Arc an inquiry approach involving 1) developing questions and planning inquiries, 2) applying disciplinary concepts and tools, 3) evaluating sources and using evidence, and 4) communicating conclusions and taking informed action

interculturalism a disposition toward actively working to live *in* diversity, not merely *with* it

International Baccalaureate (IB) a program implemented in schools around the world that "aims to develop inquiring, knowledgeable and caring young people who help to create a better and more peaceful world through intercultural understanding and respect" (2014)

language stores children's vocabulary breadth and depth

linguistically responsive teaching pedagogical practices that focus on identifying and activating all linguistic and non-linguistic resources to provide comprehensible content

literacy the ability to listen, read, think, and communicate

media literacy the ability to access, analyze, evaluate, create, and act using all forms of communication

mirror books books that offer children ways of seeing themselves and their experiences represented

multicultural literature books portraying the experiences of people whose linguistic, racial, ethnic, class, sexual orientation, and/or gender identities are not widely depicted in the children's literature published by companies marketing to schools, libraries, and bookstores

new literacies the interconnected concepts and skills needed to process as well as create digital, multimedia, and multimodal (c.g., audio, video) products

Next Generation Science Standards (NGSS) standards (2013) based on an inquiry approach to education

political having to do with the processes, rules, and laws of our society

politics the way people make decisions in social life while respecting individual rights

problem-based learning learning based on projects teachers introduce, from local curricular demands and state standards; there is room for children to introduce particular issues of concern, as well

project-based learning an approach that relies on the inclusion of both teacher-initiated topic investigations as well as child-inquisitiveness; it offers opportunities to connect and enhance literacy acquisition, mathematical thinking, and application of science principles

sliding glass door books books that offer children ways to see others and situations they don't know or won't ever experience personally, offering opportunities to change perspective (see also *window books*)

social-emotional learning the knowledge, skills, and attitudes for functioning interpersonally in school with peers, teachers, and other adults

social justice everyone deserves equal economic, political and **social** rights and opportunities

social studies a subject area that explores the social aspects of human society so students can better understand the world

social studies literacy the breadth of academic vocabulary knowledge in civics, economics, geography, and history, and the ability to create and interpret the ways social studies professionals communicate their research perspectives

springboard books books that facilitate classroom discussions and deliberations, sparking children to think about matters that matter

translanguaging the notion that bilinguals draw from one linguistic repertoire rather than having two distinctly separate languages

understanding by design (UDL) an approach that advocates starting with end goals, moving backward to determine the important steps along the way to culmination of yearly goals

window books books that offer children ways to see others and situations they don't know or won't ever experience personally (see also *sliding glass door books*)

workforce those who are paid to care for and educate children

An Introduction to the Book

Allen, D. (2020). Harvard EdCast: The role of education in democracy. https://www.gse.harvard.edu/news/20/10/harvard-edcast-role-education-democracy

Common Core State Standards. (2010). Common Core State Standards Initiative. http://www.corestandards.org/

Dewey, J. (1916). *Democracy and education.* New York: Macmillan.

Frobel, F. (1876). Garden of children, p. 118. In Morrison, G. S. (2018) *Early Childhood Education today,* 14th edition. New York: Pearson.

Guskey, T. R. (2020). *Get set, go! Creating successful grading and reporting systems.* Bloomington, IL: Solution Tree.

Guskey, T. R., & Bailey, J. M. (2001). *Developing grading and reporting systems for student learning.* Thousand Oaks, CA: Corwin Press.

Mindes, G. (2015). Pushing up social studies from early childhood to the world. *Young Children.* July. (Co-editor of the Social Studies Section of this journal issue; with Derry Koralek)

Mindes, G. (2016). Standards based curriculum and assessment. Invited entry for Couchenour, D. and Chrisman, K. *Sage encyclopedia of contemporary early childhood education.* Thousand Oaks, CA: Sage Publishing.

Montessori, M. (1912). *The Montessori method.* New York: Schoken books.

National Council for the Social Studies. (2013). *College, Career, and Civic Life (C3) Framework for Social Studies State Standards: Guidance for enhancing the rigor of K-12 civics, economics, geography, and history.* Silver Springs, MD: author.

Next Generation Science Standards. (2013). https://www.nextgenscience.org/

No Child Left Behind (NCLB). (2001). Public Law 107-110.

Piaget, J. (1923). *Language and thought of the child.* New York: Routledge.

Rand Corporation. (2018). Countering truth decay: A RAND initiative to restore the role of facts and analysis in public life. https://www.rand.org/research/projects/truth-decay.html

Teaching Strategies Gold®. (2011). https://teachingstrategies.com/solutions/assess/gold/

Vygotsky, L. (1934). *Thought and language,* Rev. edition. Cambridge, MA: MIT Press.

Chapter 1: Why Is Studying Social Studies Important for Young Learners?

American Economic Association. (2019). What is economics? https://www.aeaweb.org/resources/students/what-is-economics

California State Board of Education. (2017). *History-social science framework: Chapter three: Learning and working now and long ago.* Sacramento, CA: California State Board of Education, 31.

Center for Civic Education. (1998). Basic facts about the Center for Civic Education: Goals. https://www.civiced.org/campaign-to-promote-civic-education/resources/the-role-of-civic -education-an-education-policy-task-force-position-paper-with-policy-recommendations -september-1998

Cole, B., & McGuire, M. (2011). The challenge of a community park: Engaging young children in powerful lessons in democracy. *Social Studies and the Young Learner, 24*(1), 24–28.

Colorado Department of Education. (2012). *Colorado Preschool Social Studies Academic Standards in High Quality Early Child Care and Education Settings.*

Davey, L., & Elijah, R. (2015). Writing our way to the post office: Exploring the roles of community workers with four-year-olds. *Social Studies and the Young Learner, 28*(1), 4–7.

Derman-Sparks, L., & Edwards, J. (2020). *Anti-Bias education for young children and ourselves,* 2nd edition. Washington, DC: NAEYC.

Georgia Department of Education. (2016). *Social studies: Georgia standards of excellence.* Atlanta, GA: Georgia Department of Education.

Golston, S. (2010). The civic mission of schools. *Social Education, 74*(1), 4–6.

Gonser, S. (2018). How social studies can help young students make sense of the world. *Chalkbeat.* https://www.chalkbeat.org/posts/ny/2018/07/12/how-social-studies-can-help-y oung-students-make-sense-of-the-world/

Helm, J., & Katz, L. (2016). *Young investigators: The project approach in the early years,* 3rd edition. NY: Teachers College Press.

Illinois State Board of Education. (2016). Illinois social science inquiry standards, grades K–2. Springfield, IL: Illinois State Board of Education.

Little Minds at Work. https://littlemindsatwork.org/social-studies-curriculum/ Massachusetts Department of Elementary and Secondary Education. (2018). *History and social science framework.* http://www.doe.mass.edu/frameworks/hss/2018-12.pdf

National Council for Geographic Education. (2012). *Geography for life: National geography standards,* 2nd edition. http://ncge.org/geography-for-life

National Council for the Social Studies. (2013). *The College, Career, and Civic Life (C3) Framework for Social Studies State Standards: Guidance for enhancing the rigor of K–12 civics, economics, geography, and history.* Silver Spring, MD: National Council for the Social Studies.

National Council for the Social Studies. (2019). Early childhood in the social studies context. https://www.socialstudies.org/early-childhood-social-studies-context

Newman, M., & Ogle, D. (2019). *Visual literacy: Reading, thinking, and communicating with visuals.* Lanham, MD: Rowman & Littlefield.

Swan, K., Lee, J., & Grant, S. G. (2018). *Inquiry Design Model: Building inquiries in social studies.* Silver Spring, MD: National Council for the Social Studies and the C3 Teachers.

Wiggins, G., & McTigue, J. (2005). *Understanding by design,* 2nd expanded edition. Alexandria, VI: ASCD.

Chapter 2: How Are Literacy and Social Studies Inextricably Linked?

An, S. (2020). First graders' inquiry into multicolored stories of school (de)segregation. *Social Studies and the Young Learner, 32*(3), 3–8.

Andrä, C., Mathias, B., Schwager, A., et al. (2020). Learning foreign language vocabulary with gestures and pictures enhances vocabulary memory for several months post-learning in eight-year-old school children. *Educational Psychology Review, 32,* 815–850. doi:10.1007/s10648-020-09527-z

Barnes, D., & Brantley-Newton, V. (illus.). (2019). *The king of kindergarten.* Nancy Paulsen Books.

Battelle for Kids. (2019). *21st century learning for early childhood framework*. Author. https://www.battelleforkids.org/learning-hub/learning-hub-item/21st-century-learning-for-early-childhood-framework

Brackett, M. A. (2019). *Permission to feel: Unlocking the power of emotions to help our kids, ourselves and our society thrive*. Celadon Books.

Derman-Sparks, L., Edwards, J. O., & Goins, C. M. (2020). *Anti-Bias education for young children and ourselves* (2nd edition). National Association for the Education of Young Children.

Donovan, M. A. (2020). Mirrors, windows, and springboards: Choosing and using quality literature with the young children we know. In Mindes, G. (Ed.), *Contemporary challenges in teaching young children: Meeting the needs of students*, 170–183. Routledge.

Hamilton, L. S., Kaufman, J. H., & Hu, L. (2020). *Media use and literacy in schools: Civic development in the era of truth decay*. RAND Corporation. https://www.rand.org/pubs/research_reports/RRA112-2.html

Herdzina, J., & Lauricella, A. R. (2020). *Media literacy in early childhood: Framework, child development guidelines, and tips for implementation*. Erikson Institute, Technology in Early Childhood Center. https://tcccenter.erikson.edu/publications/media-literacy-report/

Illinois State Board of Education. (2017). *Illinois social science learning standards*. Author. https://www.isbe.net/Documents/K-12-SS-Standards.pdf

Illinois State Board of Education. (2004). *Illinois social/emotional learning standards*. Author. https://www.isbe.net/Pages/Social-Emotional-Learning-Standards.aspx

Kansas State Board of Education. (2020). *History, government, and social studies standards*. Author. https://www.ksde.org/Agency/Division-of-Learning-Services/Career-Standards-and-Assessment-Services/Content-Area-F-L/History-Government-and-Social-Studies

Lee, J. L., & Swan, K. (2013). The C3 framework and the Common Core Standards. In *Social studies for the next generation: Purposes, practices and implications of the College, Career, and Civic Life (C3) Framework for Social Studies Standards. NCSS Bulletin 113*. National Council for the Social Studies.

Massachusetts Department of Elementary & Secondary Education. (2018). *History and social science curriculum framework*. Author. https://www.doe.mass.edu/frameworks/hss/2018-12.pdf#search=%22history%20social%20science%20framework%22

Michigan Department of Education. (2019). *Michigan K-12 standards: Social studies*. Author. https://www.michigan.gov/documents/mde/Final_Social_Studies_Standards_Document_655968_7.pdf

Moll, L. C., Amanti, C., Neff, D., & Gonzalez, N. (1992). Funds of knowledge for teaching: Using a qualitative approach to connect homes and classrooms. *Theory into Practice, 31*(2), 132–141.

National Association for the Education of Young Children (NAEYC). (2020). Developmentally appropriate practice: A position statement of the National Association for the Education of Young Children. Author. https://www.naeyc.org/resources/developmentally-appropriate-practice

National Association for Media Literacy (NAMLE). (n.d.). Our mission. https://namle.net/about/

National Council for the Social Studies (NCSS). (2013). *The College, Career, and Civic Life (C3) Framework for Social Studies State Standards: Guidance for enhancing the rigor of K–12 civics, economics, geography, and history*. Author. https://www.socialstudies.org/sites/default/files/2017/Jun/c3-framework-for-social-studies-rev0617.pdf

Nebraska State Board of Education. (2019). Nebraska State Learning Standards. Author. https://cdn.education.ne.gov/wp-content/uploads/2019/11/Nebraska-Social-Studies-Standards-Final-11-2019.pdf

Neuman, S. B., & Wright, T. S. (2014). The magic of words: Teaching vocabulary in the early childhood classroom. *American Educator* (Summer), 4–13.

Penn, A., & Gibson, B. (illus.). (2011). *A kiss goodbye*. Tanglewood.

Pennsylvania Department of Education. (2014). *Pennsylvania Academic Standards*. Author. https://www.stateboard.education.pa.gov/Regulations/AcademicStandards/Pages/default.aspx

Sims Bishop, R. (1990). Mirrors, windows, and sliding glass doors. *Perspectives, 1*(3), ix–xi.

Swan, K., Lee, J., & Grant, S. G. (2018). *Inquiry Design Model: Building inquiries in social studies*. National Council for the Social Studies.

Tyner, A., & Kabourek, S. (2020). *Social studies instruction and reading comprehension: Evidence from the early childhood longitudinal study*. Thomas B. Fordham Institute. https://fordhaminstitute.org/national/resources/social-studies-instruction-and-reading-comprehension

Visual Thinking Strategies. (n.d.). What's going on in this picture? Author. https://vtshome.org/daily-image/

Washington Office of Superintendent of Public Instruction. (2019). *Washington K-12 social studies learning standards*. Author. https://www.k12.wa.us/sites/default/files/public/social studies/standards/OSPI_SocStudies_Standards_2019.pdf

Chapter 3: How Can Social Studies Anchor the Curriculum?

American Montessori Society, https://amshq.org Accessed 08/07/2020.

Bailey, R., Stickle, L., Brion-Meisels, G., & Jones, S. M. (2019). Reimagining social-emotional learning: Findings from a strategy-based approach. *Phi Delta Kappan, 100*(5), 53–58.

Berry, C., & Mindes, G. (1993). *Theme-Based curriculum: Goals, themes, activities, and planning guides for 4's & 5's*. Glenview, IL: Goodyear Press.

Bruner, J. (1966). *Toward a theory of instruction*. Cambridge, MA: Harvard University Press.

California Department of Education. (2016). Chapter Five: History Social Science Framework for California Public Schools Kindergarten through Third Grade. https://www.cde.ca.gov/ci/hs/cf/documents/hssfwchapter5.pdf

Collaborative for Academic, Social, and Emotional Learning (CASEL). (2020). *CASEL'S SEL FRAMEWORK: What are the Core competence areas and where are they promoted?* Chicago, IL: author. https://casel.org/wp-content/uploads/2020/10/CASEL-SEL-Framework-10.2020-1.pdf

Common Core State Standards (CCSS). 2010. http://www.corestandards.org/

Edwards, C., Gandini, L., & Foreman, G. (Eds.). 2011. *The hundred languages of children: The Reggio Emilia experience in transformation*, 3rd edition. Westport, CT: Praeger (Greenwood Publishing).

Epstein, A. S., & Hohmann, M. (2020). *High Scope Preschool Curriculum*. Ypsilanti, MI: High Scope®.

Ferreras-Stone, J., & Demoiny, S. B. (2019). Why are people marching? Discussing justice-oriented citizenship using picture books. *Social Studies and the Young Learner, 32*(1), 3–9.

Goodman, J. F., & Rabinowitz, M. (2019). It's not fair, I don't want to share: When child development and teacher expectations clash. *Phi Delta Kappan, 101*(1), 6–11.

Grossman, P., Pupik Dean, C. G., Kavanagh, S. S., & Herrmann, Z. (2019). Preparing teachers for project-based teaching. *Phi Delta Kappan, 100*(7), 43–48.

High Scope®. 2020. *Our practice: Preschool curriculum*. Ypislanti, MI: author

International Bacculaureate Program®. (2014, updated 2016). Mission. https://www.ibo.org/

International Bacculaureate Program®. (2014, updated 2016). Primary years programme. https://www.ibo.org/programmes/primary-years-programme/

Jorgenson, S., Howard, S., & Welch, B. T. (2018). A trip to the boiler room: An experiential approach to human geography in kindergarten. *Social Studies and the Young Learner, 30*(4), 4–11.

Kansas Department of Education. (2020). *Kansas history, government, and social studies standards*. Topeka, KS: author.

Krahenbuhl, K. S. (2019). The problem with the expanding horizons model for history curricula. *Phi Delta Kappan, 100*(6), 20–26.

Krull, K., & Morales, Y. (Illus.). (2003). *Harvesting hope: The story of Cesar Chavez*. Boston, MA: HMH Books for Young Readers.

McGuigan, K. (2018). Analyzing literary maps to bridge geography, history and english language arts. *Social Education, 82*(3), 124–127.

McTigue, J., & Wiggins, G. (2012). *Understanding by design® framework*. Alexandria, VA: Association for Curriculum Development.

Mindes, G. (2016). Standards Based Curriculum and Assessment. Invited entry for Couchenour, D. and Chrisman, K. *Sage encyclopedia of contemporary early childhood education.* Thousand Oaks, CA: Sage Publishing.

Mindes, G., & Donovan, M. A. (2001). *Building character: Five enduring themes for stronger early childhood curriculum.* Boston, MA: Allyn & Bacon.

Montesorri, M. (1912 in Italian; 2013). *The Montesorri Method.* Piscataway, NJ: Transaction Publishers.

Muller, M. (2018). Justice pedagogy: Grade 1-3 students challenge racist statues. *Social Studies and the Young Learner, 31*(2), 17–23.

National Association for the Education of Young Children. (2020). Position statement on developmentally appropriate practice. Washington DC: author. https://www.naeyc.org/

National Council for the Study of Social Studies. (2013). *The College, Career, and Civic Life (C3) Framework for Social Studies Standards guidance for enhancing the rigor of K-12 civics, economics, geography & history.* Silver Springs, MD: author.

Next Generation Science Standards for States by States. (2013). https://www.nextgenscience.org/

Patterson, T. J., & Shuttleworth, J. M. (2020). Teaching hard history through children's literature about enslavement. *Social Studies and the Young Learner, 32*(3), 14–19.

Pledger, M. S. (2018). I'm an exhibitionist of student learning: Public presentations stimulate deeper learning. *Childhood Education: Innovations, 94*(6), 20–23.

Rebell, M. A. (2018). Preparation for capable citizenship: The schools' primary responsibility. *Phi Delta Kappan, 100*(3), 18–23.

Seitz, H. (2008). The power of documentation in the early childhood classroom. *Young Children,* 88–93.

Seixas, P., & Morton, T. (2013). *The big six historical thinking concepts.* Toronto, CA: Nelson.

Sell, C. R., Schmaltz, J., & Hartman, S. (2018). We came to Colorado: Third graders inquire into the past to honor their present. *Social Studies and the Young Learner, 30*(3), 26–31.

Shatara, H., & Sonu, D. (2020). Teaching world communities as cultural translation: A third-grade unit of study. *Social Studies and the Young Learner, 32*(4), 4–9.

Smarsh, S. (2018) *Heartland: A memoir of working hard and being broke in the richest country on earth.* New York: Charles Scribner's Sons.

Steiner, R. (1922/1965). *The education of the child.* Rudolf Steiner Press. https://wn.rsarchive.org/Articles/GA034/English/RSP1965/EduChi_index.html

Swan, K., Grant, S. G., & Lee, J. (2013). The inquiry arc of the C3 Framework. In *Social studies for the next generation: Purposes, practices, and implications of the college, career, and civic life (C3) framework for the social studies state standards.* Silver Springs, MD: National Council for the Social Studies.

Swan, K., Grant, S. G., & Lee, J. (2019). *Blueprinting an inquiry-based curriculum: Planning with the Inquiry Design Model.* Silver Springs, MD: National Council for the Social Studies.

Swan, K., Grant, S. G., & Lee, J. (2013). The inquiry arc of the C3 Framework. In *Social studies for the next generation: Purposes, practices, and implications of the College, Career, And Civic Life (C3) Framework for the Social Studies State Standards.* Silver Springs, MD: National Council for the Social Studies.

Teaching Strategies®. (2020). *The Creative Curriculum®,* 6th edition. Bethesda, MD: Teaching Strategies ®.

Chapter 4: Children's Literature for Children's Social Studies

Antonsich, M. (2016). Interculturalism versus multiculturalism—the Cantle-Modood debate. *Ethnicities, 16*(3), 470–493.

Donovan, M. A. (2020). Mirrors, windows, and springboards: Choosing and using quality literature with the young children we know. In Mindes, G. (Ed.), *Contemporary challenges in teaching young children: Meeting the needs of students,* 170–183. Routledge.

Lee & Low Books. (2016, January 26). Where is the diversity in publishing? The 2015 diversity baseline survey results. https://blog.leeandlow.com/2016/01/26/where-is-the-diversity-in-publishing-the-2015-diversity-baseline-survey-results/

Lee & Low Books. (2020, January 28). Where is the diversity in publishing? The 2019 diversity baseline survey results. https://blog.leeandlow.com/2020/01/28/2019diversitybaselinesurvey/

Sims Bishop, R. (1990). Mirrors, windows, and sliding glass doors. *Perspectives*, 1(3), ix–xi.

Templeton, M. (2019, June 24). YA Twitter can be toxic, but it also points out real problems. *Buzz Feed*. https://www.buzzfeednews.com/article/mollytempleton/ya-twitter-books-publishing-amelie-wen-zhao-social-media

Yokota, J. (Ed.) (2001). *Kaleidscope: A multicultural booklist for grades K-8*. National Council of Teachers of English.

Chapter 5: Why Is the Evidence for Equitable and Effective Early Care and Education Programs an Essential Foundation for the Early Childhood Social Studies Teacher?

Arteaga, I., Humpage, S., Reynolds, A. J., & Temple, J. A. (2014). One year of preschool or two: Is it important for adult outcomes? *Economics of Education Review, 40*(Supplement C), 221–237. doi:10.1016/j.econedurev.2013.07.009

Banks, N. (2019). Black women's labor market history reveals deep-seated race and gender discrimination, Working Economics Blog. Washington, DC: Economic Policy Institute. https://www.epi.org/blog/black-womens-labor-market-history-reveals-deep-seated-race-and-gender-discrimination/

Barnett, W. S., Carolan, M., & Johns, D. (2013). *Equity and excellence: African-American children's access to quality preschool*. New Brunswick, NJ: The State University of New Jersey, National Institute for Early Education Research, Center on Enhancing Early Learning Outcomes.

Barnett, W. S., Jung, K., Friedman-Krauss, A., Frede, E. C., Nores, M., Hustedt, J. T., Howes, C., & Daniel-Echols, M. (2018). State prekindergarten effects on early learning at kindergarten entry: An analysis of eight state programs. *AERA Open, 4*(2), 2332858418766291. doi:10.1177/2332858418766291

Bassok, D., Markowitz, A., & Michie, M. (2020). COVID-19 highlights inequities in how we treat early educators in childcare vs. schools. Washington, DC: Brown Center Chalkboard, Brookings. https://www.brookings.edu/blog/brown-center-chalkboard/2020/10/23/covid-19-highlights-inequities-in-how-we-treat-early-educators-in-child-care-vs-schools/

Bonnay, S. (2017). History of early childhood education: Then and now. Retrieved on November 8, 2020 from https://blog.himama.com/early-childhood-education-then-and-now/

Bradley, R. H., & Vandell, D. L. (2007). Child care and the well-being of children. *Archives of Pediatrics and Adolescent Medicine, 161*(7), 669–676.

Broughton, A. (2020). Black skin, White theorists: Remembering hidden Black early childhood scholars. *Contemporary Issues in Early Childhood, 1*(0), 1–16. doi:10.1177/1463949120958101

Burchinal, M. (2018). Measuring early care and education quality. *Child Development Perspectives, 12*(1), 3–9. doi:10.1111/cdep.12260

Burchinal, M. R., Lee, M., & Ramey, C. (1989). Type of day-care and preschool intellectual development in disadvantaged children. *Child Development, 60*, 128–137.

Burchinal, M. R., Roberts, J. E., Hooper, S., & Zeisel, S. A. (2000). Cumulative risk and early cognitive development: A comparison of statistical risk. *Developmental Psychology, 36*, 793–807.

Burchinal, M., Roberts, J. E., Zeisel, S. A., Hennon, E. A., & Hooper, S. (2006). Social risk and protective child, parenting, and child care factors in early elementary school years. *Parenting: Science and Practice, 6*, 79–113.

Cahan, E. D. (1989). *Past caring: A history of U.S. preschool care and education for the poor, 1820–1965*. New York, NY: Columbia University, Mailman School of Public Health, National Center for Children in Poverty.

Campbell, F. A., Pungello, E. P., Miller-Johnson, S., Burchinal, M. R., & Ramey, C. T. (2001). The development of cognitive and academic abilities: Growth curves from an early childhood educational experiment. *Developmental Psychology, 37,* 231–242.

Campbell, F. A., Ramey, C. T., Pungello, E., Sparling, J., & Miller-Johnson, S. (2002). Early childhood education: Young adult outcome from the Abecedarian project. *Applied Developmental Science, 6,* 42–57.

Caughy, M. O., DiPiteru, J. A., & Strobino, D. M. (1994). Day-care participation as a protective factor in the cognitive development of low-income children. *Child Development, 65,* 457–471.

Chaudry, A. J., & Datta, A. R. (2017). The current landscape for public pre-kindergarten programs. In D. A. Phillips et al., *The current state of scientific knowledge on pre-kindergarten effects* (pp. 5–18). Brookings and Duke University. https://www.brookings.edu/research/puzzling-it-out-the-current-state-of-scientific-knowledge-on-pre-kindergarten-effects/

Child Care and Early Education Research Connections. (n.d.). *Quality rating and improvement system state evaluations and research.* Retrieved on November 27, 2020 from https://www.researchconnections.org/childcare/resources/30046/pdf

Cui, J., & Natzke, L. (2020). *Early childhood program participation: 2019* (NCES 2020-075), National Center for Education Statistics, Institute of Education Sciences, U.S. Department of Education. Washington, DC. Retrieved November 25, 2020 from http://nces.ed.gov/pubsearch/pubsinfo.asp?pubid=2020075

Cunningham, C., & Osborn, D. (1979). A historical examination of blacks in early childhood education. *Young Children, 34*(3), 20–29. Retrieved November 26, 2020, from http://www.jstor.org/stable/42643587

Early, D., Barbarin, O., Burchinal, M., Chang, F., Clifford, R., Crawford, G., Weaver, W., Howes, C., Ritchie, S., Kraft-Sayre, M., Pianta, R., & Barnett, W. S. (2005). *Pre-kindergarten in eleven states: NCEDL's multi-state study of pre-kindergarten and State-Wide Early Education Program (Sweep) Study.* Chapel Hill, NC: University of North Carolina at Chapel Hill, Frank Porter Graham Child Development Institute.

Erikson Institute. (n.d.). Barbara T. Bowman, M.A. Retrieved November 25, 2020 from https://web.archive.org/web/20090107003352/http://www.erikson.edu/default/faculty/faclistings/barbara_bowman.aspx

Felitti, V. J., Anda, R. F., Nordenberg, D., Williamson, D. F., Spitz, A. M., Edwards, V., Koss, M. P., & Marks, J. S. (1998, 5//). Relationship of childhood abuse and household dysfunction to many of the leading causes of death in adults: The adverse childhood experiences (ACE) study. *American Journal of Preventive Medicine, 14*(4), 245–258. doi:10.1016/S0749-3797(98)00017-8

Forry, N., Iruka, I., Tout, K., Torquati, J., Susman-Stillman, A., Bryant, D., & Daneri, M. P. (2013, 2013/10/01/). Predictors of quality and child outcomes in family child care settings. *Early Childhood Research Quarterly, 28*(4), 893–904. doi:10.1016/j.ecresq.2013.05.006

Friedman-Krauss, A. H., Barnett, W. S., Garver, K. A., Hodges, K. A., Weinsenfeld, G. G., & Gardiner, B. A. (2020). *The state of preschool 2019: State preschool yearbook.* New Brunswick, NJ: The State University of New Jersey, National Institute for Early Education Research.

Gordon, R. A., Colaner, A., Usdansky, M. L., & Melgar, C. (2013). Beyond an "either-or" approach to home- and center-based child care: Comparing children and families who combine care types with those who just use one. *Early Childhood Research Quarterly, 28*(4), 918–935.

Gutman, L. M., Sameroff, A. J., & Eccles, J. S. (2002). The academic achievement of African American students during early adolescence: An examination of multiple risk, promotive, and protective factors. *American Journal of Community Psychology, 30*(3), 367–400.

Heckman, J., & Karapakula, G. (2019). *Intergenerational and intragenerational externalities of the Perry Preschool Project.* Chicago, IL: University of Chicago.

Hilliard, III, A. G. (1995). *Teacher education from an African American perspective.* Paper presented at invitational conference on Defining the Knowledge Base for Urban Teacher Education, Emory University, Atlanta, GA.

Hooper, S. R., Burchinal, M. R., Roberts, J. E., Zeisel., S., & Neebe, E. C. (1998). Social and family risk factors for infant development at one year: An application of the cumulative risk model. *Journal of Applied Developmental Psychology, 19,* 85–96.

Howes, C., Burchinal, M., Pianta, R., Bryant, D., Early, D., Clifford, R., & Barbarin, O. (2008). Ready to learn? Children's pre-academic achievement in pre-kindergarten programs. *Early Childhood Research Quarterly, 23*(1), 27–50. doi:10.1016/j.ecresq.2007.05.002

Institute of Medicine (IOM) and National Research Council (NRC). (2015). *Transforming the workforce for children birth through age 8: A unifying foundation.* Washington, DC: National Academies Press.

Iruka, I. U. (2020). High-quality child care as an effective antipoverty strategy: Emerging evidence from Canada. *Pediatrics, 146*(1), e20200483. doi:10.1542/peds.2020-0483

Iruka, I. U., & Forry, N. D. (2018, 2018/01/01). Links between patterns of quality in diverse settings and children's early outcomes. *Journal of Education, 198*(1), 95–112. doi:10.1177/0022057418800941

Jargowsky, P. A. (2015). *The architecture of segregation: Civil unrest, the concentration of poverty, and public policy.* New York, NY: The Century Foundation.

Jessen-Howard, S., & Workman, S. (2020). *Coronavirus pandemic could lead to permanent loss of nearly 4.5 million child care slots.* Washington, DC: Center for American Progress. https://www.americanprogress.org/issues/early-childhood/news/2020/04/24/483817/coronavirus-pandemic-lead-permanent-loss-nearly-4-5-million-child-care-slots/

Keating, K., Cole, P., & Schaffner, M. (2020). *State of babies yearbook: 2020.* Washington, DC: ZERO TO THREE.

Lazar, I., Darlington, R., Murray, H., Royce, J., Snipper, A., & Ramey, C. T. (1982). Lasting effects of early education: A report from the consortium for longitudinal studies. *Monographs of the Society for Research in Child Development, 47,* 1–151.

Lillard, A. S., Heise, M. J., Richey, E. M., Tong, X., Hart, A., & Bray, P. M. (2017). Montessori preschool elevates and equalizes child outcomes: A longitudinal stud. *Frontiers in Psychology, 8*(1783). doi:10.3389/fpsyg.2017.01783

Love, J. M., Kisker, E. E., Ross, C., Raikes, H., Constantine, J., Boller, K., Brooks-Gunn, J., Chazan-Cohen, R., Tarullo, L. B., Brady-Smith, C., Fuligni, A. S., Schochet, P. Z., Paulsell, D., & Vogel, C. (2005). The effectiveness of early head start for 3-year-old children and their parents: Lessons for policy and programs. *Developmental Psychology, 41*(6), 885–901. doi:10.1037/0012-1649.41.6.885

Masten, A. S., & Coatworth, J. D. (1995). Competence, reliance, and psychopathy. In D. Cicchetti & D. J. Cohen (Eds.), *Developmental psychopathy: Vol. 2, risk, disorder, and adaptation* (pp. 715–752). New York: Wiley.

National Academies of Sciences, Engineering, and Medicine [NASEM]. (2019). *Vibrant and healthy kids: Aligning science, practice, and policy to advance health equity.* Washington, DC: The National Academies Press. doi:10.17226/25466

National Association for the Education of Young Children (NAEYC). (2020). Power to the Profession. Retrieved on November 28, 2020 from https://www.naeyc.org/sites/default/files/globally-shared/downloads/PDFs/our-work/initiatives/power_to_the_profession_7-8_final_for_web.pdf

NICHD Early Child Care Research Network (NICHD ECCRN). (2002). Early child care and children's development prior to school entry: Results from the NICHD study of early child care and youth development. *American Educational Research Journal, 39,* 133–164.

Nores, M., Belfield, C. R., Barnett, W. S., & Schweinhart, L. (2005). Updating the economic impacts of the High/Scope Perry preschool program. *Educational Evaluation and Policy Analysis, 27*(3), 245–261.

Phillips, D. A., Lipsey, M. W., Dodge, K. A., Haskins, R., Bassok, D., Burchinal, M. R., Duncan, G. J., Dynarski, M., Magnuson, K. A., & Weiland, C. (2017). Puzzling it out: The current state of scientific knowledge on pre-kindergarten effects, a consensus statement. In D. A. Phillips et al., *The current state of scientific knowledge on pre-kindergarten effects*

(pp. 19–30). Brookings and Duke University. https://www.brookings.edu/research/puz
zling-it-out-the-current-state-of-scientific-knowledge-on-pre-kindergarten-effects/

Phillips, D., Austin, L. J. E., & Whitebook, M. (2016). The early care and education workforce. *The Future of Children, 26*(2), 139–158. http://0-www.jstor.org.library.unl.edu/sta
ble/43940585

Raikes, H. H., Roggman, L. A., Peterson, C. A., Brooks-Gunn, J., Chazan-Cohen, R., Zhang,
X., & Schiffman, R. F. (2014). Theories of change and outcomes in home-based early
head start programs. *Early Childhood Research Quarterly, 29*(4), 574–585. doi:10.1016/j.
ecresq.2014.05.003

Ramey, C. T., Bryant, D. M., Sparling, J. J., & Wasik, B. (1985). Project CARE: A comparison of two early intervention strategies to prevent retarded development. *Topics in Early
Childhood Special Education, 5,* 12–25.

Ramey, C. T., Bryant, D. M., & Suarez, T. M. (1985). Preschool compensatory education
and the modifiability of intelligence: A critical review. In D. K. Detterman (Ed.), *Current
topics in human intelligence, vol. 1: Research methodology* (pp. 247–296). Westport, CT:
Ablex Publishing.

Ramey, C. T., & Campbell, F. A. (1991). Poverty, early childhood education, and academic
competence: The Abecedarian experiment. In A. C. Huston (Ed.), *Children in poverty:
child development and public policy* (pp. 190–221). Cambridge, UK: Cambridge University Press.

Ramey, C. T., Yeates, K. O., & Short, E. J. (1984). The plasticity of intellectual development
insights from preventative intervention. *Child Development, 55,* 1913–1925.

Reynolds, A. J. (1994). Effects of a preschool plus follow-on intervention for children at risk.
Developmental Psychology, 30, 787–804.

Reynolds, A., Temple, J. A., Ou, S.-R., Arteaga, I. A., & White, B. A. B. (2011). School-
based early childhood education and age-28 well-being: Effects by timing, dosage, and
subgroups. *Science.* doi:10.1126/science.1203618

Robertson, H. (2003). Decolonizing schools. *The Phi Delta Kappan, 84*(7), 552–553.
Retrieved December 21, 2020, from http://www.jstor.org/stable/20440415

Rutter, M. (1979). Protective factors in children's responses to stress and disadvantage. In
M. W. Kent & J. E. Rolf (Eds.), *Primary prevention of psychopathology: Vol. 3. social
competence in children* (pp. 49–74). Hanover, NH: University Press of New England.

Sacks, V., & Murphey, D. (2018). *The prevalence of adverse childhood experiences,
nationally, by state, and by race/ethnicity.* Research brief #2018-03. Bethesda, MD: Child
Trends.

Sameroff, A. J., Seifer, R., Baldwin, A., & Baldwin, C. (1993). Stability of intelligence from
preschool to adolescence: The influence of social and family risk factors. *Child Development, 64,* 80–97.

Sameroff, A. J., Seifer, R., Barocas, R., Zax, M., & Greenspan, S. (1987). Intelligence
quotient scores of 4-year-old children: Social environmental risk factors. *Pediatrics, 79,*
343–350.

Schweinhart, L. J. (1985). Effects of the Perry Preschool program on youths through age 19:
A summary. *Topics in Early Childhood Education, 5,* 26–35.

Schweinhart, L. J. (2000). The High/Scope Perry Preschool study: A case study in random
assignment. *Evaluation and Research in Education, 14,* 136–147.

Schweinhart, L. J. (2007). Crime prevention by the High/Scope Perry Preschool program.

Schweinhart, L. J., Barnes, H. V., & Weikart, D. P. (1993). Significant benefits: The High/
Scope Perry Preschool study through age 27. *Monographs of the High/Scope Educational
Research Foundation, 10.*

Shonkoff, J. P., Garner, A. S., The Committee on Psychosocial Aspects of Child Family
Health, Committee on Early Childhood, Adoption, Dependent Care, Section on Developmental Behavioral Pediatrics, Siegel, B. S., Dobbins, M. I., Earls, M. F., McGuinn, L.,
Pascoe, J., & Wood, D. L. (2012, January 1, 2012). The lifelong effects of early childhood
adversity and toxic stress. *Pediatrics, 129*(1), e232–e246. doi:10.1542/peds.2011-2663

Shonkoff, J. P., & Phillips, D. A. (2000). *From neurons to the neighborhoods: The science of
early childhood development.* Washington, DC: National Academy Press.

Simpson, J. (2012). Oneida Cockrell: Pioneer in the field of early childhood education. *Young Children,* 58–61. Retrieved November 25, 2020, from https://www.yumpu.com/en/docum ent/read/11006700/our-proud-heritage-oneida-cockrell-national-association-for-the-

Sparling, J., & Lewis, I. (1979). *Learning games for the first three years: A guide to parent/ child play.* New York: Walker and Company.

Tout, K., Magnuson, K., Lipscomb, S., Karoly, L, Starr, R., Quick H., ... Wenner, J. (2017). *Validation of the quality ratings used in Quality Rating and Improvement Systems (QRIS): A synthesis of state studies.* OPRE Report #2017-92. Washington, DC: U.S. Department of Health and Human Services, Administration for Children and Families, Office of Planning, Research and Evaluation.

Trent, M., Dooley, D. G., & Dougé, J. (2019). The impact of racism on child and adolescent health. *Pediatrics, 144*(2), e20191765. doi:10.1542/peds.2019-1765

Urban Institute. (2019). *Segregated from the start: Comparing segregation in early childhood and K–12 education.* Washington, DC: author.

US Department of Health and Human Services, Administration for Children and Families (US DHHS, ACF). (May 2005). *Head start impact study: First year findings.* Washington, DC: author.

van Huizen, T., & Plantenga, J. (2018). Do children benefit from universal early childhood education and care? A meta-analysis of evidence from natural experiments. *Economics of Education Review.* doi:10.1016/j.econedurev.2018.08.001

Weikart, D. P., Deloria, D., Lawser, S., & Wiegerink, R. (1970). Longitudinal results of the Ypsilanti Perry preschool project. *Monographs of the High/Scope Educational Research Foundation, 1.*

Whitebook, M., McLean, C., & Austin, L. J. E. (2016). *Early Childhood Workforce Index - 2016.* Berkeley, CA: Center for the Study of Child Care Employment, University of California, Berkeley.

Whitebook, M., McLean, C., Austin, L. J. E., & Edwards, B. (2018). *Early childhood work-force index.* Berkeley, CA: University of California, Berkeley, Center for the Study of Child Care Employment.Yazejian, N., Bryant, D., & Kennel, P. (2013). Implementation and replication of the Educare model of early childhood education. In T. Halle, A. Metz, & I. Martinez-Beck (Eds.), *Applying implementation science in early childhood programs and systems* (pp. 209–225). Baltimore, MD: Brookes.

Yazejian, N., Bryant, D. M., Hans, S., Horm, D., St. Clair, L., File, N., & Burchinal, M. (2017). Child and parenting outcomes after 1 year of educare. *Child Development, 88*(5), 1671–1688. doi:10.1111/cdev.12688

Yazejian, N., Bryant, D. M., Kuhn, L. J., Burchinal, M., Horm, D., Hans, S., File, N., & Jackson, B. (2020). The educare intervention: Outcomes at age 3. *Early Childhood Research Quarterly, 53,* 425–440. doi:10.1016/j.ecresq.2020.05.008

Yoshikawa, H., Weiland, C., & Brooks-Gunn, J. (2016). When does preschool matter? The *Future of Children, 26*(2), 21–35. http://0-www.jstor.org.library.unl.edu/stable /43940579

Yoshikawa, H., Weiland, C., Brooks-Gunn, J., Burchinal, M. R., Espinosa, L. M., Gormley, W. T., Ludwig, J., Magnuson, K. A., Phillips, D., & Zaslow, M. J. (2013). *Investing in our future: The evidence base on preschool education.* Washington, DC: Society for Research in Child Development and Foundation for Child Development.

Zigler, E., & Valentine, J. (Eds.). (1979). *Project head start: A legacy of the war on poverty.* New York: Free Press.

Chapter 6: Meeting the Needs of Young Emergent Bilinguals

Alamillo, L., Yun, C., & Bennett, L. H. (2017). Translanguaging in a Reggio-inspired Spanish dual-language immersion programme. *Early Child Development and Care, 187*(3–4), 469 486. doi:10.1080/03004430.2016.1236091

Association for Supervision and Curriculum Development (ASCD). (n.d.). A whole child approach to education and the Common Core State Standards initiative. http://www.ascd .org/ASCD/pdf/siteASCD/policy/CCSS-and-Whole-Child-one-pager.pdf

Child Trends Databank. (2019). *Preschool and prekindergarten.* https://www.childtrends.o rg/?indicators=preschool-and-prekindergarten

Children of Immigrants. (2019). Urban Institute calculations using Census Bureau American Community survey data. https://www.urban.org/features/part-us-data-driven-look-chil dren-immigrants

Choi, Y. (2002). *The name jar.* Dragonfly Books.

Cummins, J. (1994). The acquisition of English as a second language. In K. Spangenberg-Urbschat & R. Pritchard (Eds.), *Reading instruction for ESL students.* International Reading Association.

Cummins, J. (2000). *Language, power and pedagogy: Bilingual children in the crossfire.* Multilingual Matters.

Cummins, J. (2011). Literacy engagement: Fueling academic growth for English learners. *The Reading Teacher, 65*(2), 142–146.

Fillmore, L. W. (2000). Loss of family languages: Should educators be concerned? *Theory into Practice, 39,* 203–210. doi: 10.2307/1477339

Fillmore, L. W. (2014). English language learners at the crossroads of educational reform. *TESOL Quarterly, 48*(3), 624–632. doi:10.1002/tesq.174

García, O., & Wei, L. (2014). *Translanguaging: Language, bilingualism and education.* Palgrave Macmillan.

González, N., Moll, L. C., & Amanti, C. (2005). *Funds of knowledge: Theorizing practice in households, communities, and classrooms.* L. Erlbaum Associates.

Guerrero, M. D. (2004). Acquiring academic English in one year. In Heath, S. B. (1983). *Ways with words.* Oxford University Press.

Hernandez, C. M., Morales, A. R., & Shroyer, M. G. (2013). The development of a model of culturally responsive science and mathematics teaching. *Cultural Studies of Science Education, 8,* 803–820. doi:10.1007/s11422-013-9544-1

Husband, T., Jr. (2010). He's too young to learn about that stuff: Anti-racist pedagogy and early childhood social studies. *Social Studies Research & Practice, 5*(2), 61–75. http://www .socstrp.org/issues/ PDF/5.2.6.pdf

Jackson, P. W. (1968). *Life in the classrooms.* Rinehart and Winston.

Krashen, S. (1982). *Principles and practice in second language acquisition.* Pergamon Press.

Krashen, S., & Terrell, T. (1983). *The natural approach: Language acquisition in the classroom.* Pergamon Press.

Ladson-Billings, G. (1995). But that's just good teaching! The case for culturally relevant pedagogy. *Theory into Practice, 34*(3), 161.

Leung, K., Ang, S., & Tan, M. L. (2014). Intercultural competence. *Annual Review of Organizational Psychology and Organizational Behaviour, 1,* 4889–519.

Lucas, T., & Villegas, A. M. (2010). The missing piece in teacher education: The preparation of linguistically responsive teachers. *National Society for the Study of Education, 109,* 297–318.

Lynch, E. W., & Hanson, M. J. (Eds.). (2011). *Developing cross-cultural competence: Working with young children and their families* (4th ed.). Brookes.

Migration Policy Institute. (2018). Children in U.S. immigrant families. https://www.migratio npolicy.org/programs/data-hub/charts/children-immigrant-families

Na, A. (2001). *A step from heaven.* Front Street.

National Association for the Education of Young Children. (2011). Code of ethical conduct and statement of commitment. https://www.naeyc.org/sites/default/files/globally-shared/do wnloads/PDFs/resources/position-statements/Ethics%20Position%20Statement2011_092 02013update.pdf

National Center for Education Statistics (NCES). (2018). Preschool and kindergarten enrollment. https://nces.ed.gov/programs/coe/pdf/Indicator_CFA/coe_cfa_2018_05.pdf

National Center for Education Statistics (NCES). (2019). *The condition of education 2019* (2019-144), English language learners in public schools. https://nces.ed.gov/programs/coe /indicator_cgf.asp

National Council for the Social Studies (NCSS). (2013). *The College, Career, and Civic Life (C3) Framework for Social Studies State Standards: Guidance for enhancing the rigor of K-12 civics, economics, geography, and history.* NCSS.

Pew Research Center. (2018). Six facts about English Language Learners in U.S. schools. https://www.pewresearch.org/fact-tank/2018/10/25/6-facts-about-english-language-learners-in-u-s-public-schools/

Ramsey, P. G. (2004). *Teaching and learning in a diverse world: Multicultural education for young children* (3rd ed.). Teachers College Press.

Short, D. J., Becker, H., Cloud, N., Hellman, A. B., & Levine, L. N. (2018). *The 6 principles for exemplary teaching of english learners*. TESOL Press.

The Annie E. Casey Foundation. (n.d.). Immigration & refugees. https://www.aecf.org/topics/immigration-and-refugees/

Thomas, W., & Collier, V. (2002). A national study of school effectiveness for language minority students' long-term academic achievement. Center for Research on Education, Diversity and Excellence.

Velsasco, P., & Fialais, V. (2016). Moments of metalinguistic awareness in a kindergarten class: Translanguaging for simultaneous biliterate development. *International Journal of Bilingual Education & Bilingualism, 21*(6), 760–774. doi:10.1080/13670050.2016.1214104

Vygotsky, L. S. (1978). The prehistory of written language. In M. Cole, V. John-Steiner, S. Scribner, & E. Souberman (Eds.), *Mind in society: The development of higher psychological processes* (pp. 103–119). Cambridge: Harvard University Press.

Chapter 7: How Are We Including and Supporting All Children, Helping All Children Thrive?

Al-Azawei, A., Serenelli, F., & Lundqvist, K. (2016). Universal Design for Learning (UDL): A content analysis of peer-reviewed journal papers from 2012 to 2015. *Journal of the Scholarship of Teaching and Learning, 16*(3), 39–56.

Bandura, A. (1986). *Social foundations of thought and action*. Englewood Cliffs, NJ.

Barton, E. E. (2015). Teaching generalized pretend play and related behaviors to young children with disabilities. *Exceptional Children, 81*(4), 489–506.

Bronfenbrenner, U. (1992). Ecological systems theory. In R. Vasta (Ed.), *Six theories of child development: Revised formulations and current issues* (pp. 187–249). Jessica Kingsley Publishers.

Carr, W., & Kemmis, S. (2003). *Becoming critical: Education knowledge and action research*. Routledge.

Cochran-Smith, Marilyn, & Lytle, Susan. (1999). Relationships of knowledge and practice: Teacher learning in communities. *Review of Research in Education, 24*. Washington, DC: American Educational Research Association. pp. 249–305.

Coomer, M. N. (2019). Deconstructing difference and inclusion in educational research: Reflections on the international journal of qualitative studies in education special edition on difference. *International Journal of Qualitative Studies in Education*, 1–5.

Crocetti, E., & Meeus, W. (2015). The identity statuses: Strengths of a person-centered approach. *The Oxford Handbook of Identity Development*, 97–114.

Denham, S. A., & Burton, R. (2003). *Social and emotional prevention and intervention programming for preschoolers*. Kluwer Academic/Plenum. doi:10.1007/978-1-4615-0055-1

Dinishak, J. (2016). The deficit view and its critics. *Disability Studies Quarterly, 36*(4).

Dunst, C. J., Sukkar, H. & Kirkby, J. (2016) Contributions of family systems and family-centered practices for informing improvements in early childhood intervention. In H. Sukkar., C. Dunst, & J. Kirkby, *Early Childhood Intervention*. Routledge.

Epstein, A. S. (2014). Social studies in preschool? Yes!. *YC: Young Children, 69*(1), 78.

Fenty, N. S., Miller, M. A., & Lampi, A. (2008). Embed social skills instruction in inclusive settings. *Intervention in School and Clinic, 3*, 186–192. doi:10.1177/1053451207312922

Florian, L. (2019). On the necessary co-existence of special and inclusive education. *International Journal of Inclusive Education, 23*(7–8), 691–704.

Ford, D. Y., Whiting, G. W., Goings, R. B., & Robinson, S. A. (2017). Students in special education: Issues, theories and recommendations to address overrepresentation. In M.

Tejero Hughes and E. Talbott (Eds.), *The Wiley handbook of diversity in special education*, 1st edition, pp. 131–148. (Chapter 7)

Gilles, C., Wilson, J., & Elias, M. (2010). Sustaining teachers' growth and renewal through action research, induction programs, and collaboration. *Teacher Education Quarterly*, *37*(1), 91–108.

Gresham, F. M. (2010). Evidence-based social skills interventions: Empirical foundations for instructional approaches. In M. Shinn & H. Walker (Eds.), *Interventions for achievement and behavior problems in a three-tier model including RTI* (pp. 337–362). National Association of School Psychologists.

Gut, D. M., & Safran, S. P. (2002). Cooperative learning and social stories: Effective social skills strategies for reading teachers. *Reading and Writing Quarterly: Overcoming Learning Difficulties*, *18*(1), 87–91.

Hartman, A. (1978). Diagrammatic assessment of family relationships. *Social Casework*, *59*, 465–476.

Harvey, M. W. (2002). Comparison of postsecondary transitional outcomes between students with and without disabilities by secondary vocational education participation: Findings from the National Education Longitudinal Study. *Career Development for Exceptional Individuals*, *25*(2), 99–122.

Hayenga, A. O., & Corpus, J. H. (2010). Profiles of intrinsic and extrinsic motivations: A person-centered approach to motivation and achievement in middle school. *Motivation and Emotion*, *34*, 371–383. doi:10.1007/s11031-010-9181-x

Joseph, J. D., Strain, P., Olszewski, A., & Goldstein, H. (2016). A consumer reports-like review of the empirical literature specific to preschool children's peer-related social skills. In B. Reichow, B. Boyd, E. E. Barton, & S. L. Odom (Eds.), *Handbook of early childhood special education* (pp. 179–1970). Springer, Cham.

Jung, L. A. (2010). Identifying family supports and other resources. In R. A. McWilliam (Ed.), *Working with families of young children with special needs* (pp. 9–24). The Guilford Press.

Jung, L. A., Frey, N., Fisher, D., & Kroener, J. (2019). *Your Children, My Children, Our Children: Rethinking Equitable and Inclusive Classrooms*. ASCD.

LaRocque, M., Kleiman, I., & Darling, S. M. (2011). Parental involvement: The missing link in school achievement. *Preventing School Failure: Alternative Education for Children and Youth*, *55*(3), 115–122. doi:10.1080/10459880903472876

Lortie, D. C. (1975). *School teacher: A sociological study*. Chicago: University of Chicago Press.

McCormick, K. M., Stricklin, S., Nowak, T. M., & Rous, B. (2008). Using eco-mapping to understand family strengths and resources. *Young Exceptional Children*, *11*(2), 17–28.

McWilliam, R. A. (2010). *Routines-based early intervention: Supporting young children and their families*. Baltimore: Paul H.

Miller, A. (2007). Rhetoric, paideia and the old idea of a liberal education. *Journal of Philosophy of Education*, *41*(2), 183–206.

Moll, L. C. (1990). Community knowledge and classroom practice: Combining resources for literacy instruction. Technical Report.

Moll, L. C., Amanti, C., Neff, D., & Gonzalez, N. (1992). Funds of knowledge for teaching: Using a qualitative approach to connect homes and classrooms. *Theory into Practice*, *31*(2), 132–141.

Neal, J. W., & Neal, Z. P. (2013). Nested or networked? Future directions for ecological systems theory. *Social Development*, *22*(4), 722–737.

Parker-Katz, M., & Passmore, A. (forthcoming). Bringing a humanistic approach to special education curriculum. In Ming Fang He & William H. Schubert (Eds.), *Oxford encyclopedia of curriculum studies*. New York: Oxford University Press. doi:10.1093/acrefore/9780190264093.013.1580

Passmore, A. H., & Zarate, K. (2020). Helping families reach their PEAK: Partnerships that promote family empowerment. *Teaching Exceptional Children*, 0040059920958737.

Pine, G. J. (2008). *Teacher action research: Building knowledge democracies*. Sage.

Rose, D., Harbour, W., Johnston, C. S., Daley, S., & Abarbanell, L. (2006). Universal design for learning in postsecondary education. *Journal of Postsecondary Education and Disability*, *19*.

Test, D. W., Mazzotti, V. L., Mustian, A. L., Fowler, C. H., Kortering, L., & Kohler, P. (2009). Evidence-based secondary transition predictors for improving postschool outcomes for children with disabilities. *Career Development for Exceptional Individuals*, *32*(3), 160–181.

Underwood, Smith, & Martin (2018). Institutional mapping as a tool for resource consultation. *Journal of Early Childhood Research*, *17*(5). doi:10.1177/1476718X18818205

Weissberg, R. P., Durlak, J. A., Domitrovich, C. E., & Gullotta, T. P. (2017). Social and emotional learning: Past, present, and future. In J. A. Durlak, C. E. Domitrovich, R. P. Weissberg, & T. P. Gullotta (Eds.), *Handbook of social and emotional learning: Research and practice* (pp. 3–19). Guilford Publications.

West, M., Sima, A., Wehman, P., Chan, F., & Luecking, R. (2018). Students at high risk of poor school-to-work outcomes: Mitigating factors. *Rehabilitation Research, Policy, and Education*, *32*(2), 78–88.

Zins, J. E., & Elias, M. J. (2007). Social and emotional learning: Promoting the development of all children. *Journal of Educational and Psychological Consultation*, *17*(2–3), 233–255.

Chapter 8: How Does Social Studies Help Young Children Learn about Community and Citizenship?

Adams, E. (2015). Civics in the grocery store: A field trip of awareness and agency. *Social Studies and the Young Learner*, *27*(4), 16–18.

Arizona Department of Education. (2018). *History and social science standards. Kindergarten-2nd grade*. Phoenix, AZ: Arizona Department of Education.

Committee on the Rights of the Child. (2006). *Convention on the rights of the child*. Geneva, SZ: United Nations.

Dewey, J. (1916). *The school and society*. Chicago, IL: University of Chicago Press, p. 19.

Elijah, R. (2014). Discovering and constructing our identities: Reading the favorite daughter. *Social Studies and the Younger Learner*, *27*(2), 5–8.

Hartman, S., & Kahn. S. (2017) Start local, go global: Community partnerships empower children as scientists and citizens. *Social Studies and the Young Learner*, *29*(4), 3–7.

Kane, K. (2016). Back to school: Why creating classroom community is so important. NAEYC blog. https://www.naeyc.org/resources/blog/why-creating-classroom-community-so-important

Morse, F. (1896). Civics in our public schools. *Journal of Education*, *53*(4), 55–56.

Nesdale, D., & Flesser, D. (2001). Social identity and the development of children's group attitudes. *Child Development*, *72*(2), 506–517.

Newman, M., & Zevin, J. (2106). *Geography as inquiry: Teaching about and exploring the earth as our home*. Lanham, MD: Rowman & Littlefield.

Paley, V. (1993). *You can't say you can't play*. Cambridge, MA: Harvard University Press.

Rafa, A., Rogowski, D., Railey, H., Brennan, J., Baumann, P., & Aragaon, S. (2016). *50-state comparison: Civic education policies*. Denver, CO: Education Commission of the States.

Schneider, E. (1996). Giving students a voice in the classroom. *Educational Leadership*, *54*(1), 22–26.

Smith, A. (1790). *The theory of moral sentiments*, 6th edition. London: A. Millar, A. Kincaid, & J. Bell.

The State Education Department, The University of the State of New York. (2017). *New York State K-8 Social Studies Framework*. Albany: The State Education Department, The University of the State of New York.

Chapter 9: How Are Young Children Involved in Civic Engagement?

Adams, E. (2015). Civics in the grocery store: A field trip of awareness and agency. *Social Studies and the Young Learner*, *27*(4), 16–18.

CIVICUS. (June 21, 2017). Civic space in the Americas. https://www.civicus.org/index.php/media-resources/reports-publications/2877-civic-space-in-the-americas

Dixon, H. (2016). Making peace in kindergarten: Social and emotional growth for all learners. *Young Children, 71*(4).

Helm, J. H. (2004). Projects that power young minds. *Educational Leadership, 62*(1), 58–62.

Howard, T. C. (2018). Capitalizing on culture: Engaging young learners in diverse classrooms. *Young Children, 73*(2), 24–33.

Hubbard, J., Moore, M. F., & Mc Fadyen Christensen, L. (2020). Women are as important as men: Third graders investigate diverse women in U.S. History. *Social Studies and the Young Learner, 32*(4), 16–21.

Katz Keating, S., & Grossman Kanter, W. (September 21, 2020) Stories that makes you smile: The first-grader started a foundation to feed the homeless, *People*, p. 28.

Libresco, A. S. (2018) And the children shall lead: Using the 2018 notable books to nurture young citizen-activists. *Social Education, 82*(3), 158–162.

McGriff, M., & Clemons, S. (2019) Reflective discussion circles: A method for promoting civic engagement. *Social Studies and the Young Learner, 31*(4), 3–8.

National Council for Social Studies. (2013). Civics. In *Social Studies for the Next Generation: Purposes, Practices and Implications of the College, Career, and Civic Life (C3) Framework for Social Studies State Standards, Bulletin 113*. Silver Springs, MD: author, p. 31.

National Council for Social Studies Board of Directors. (2020). Statement on ethical responsibilities of social studies teachers. Silver Springs, MD: NCSS.

Payne, K. A. (2015). Who can fix this? The concept of "audience" and first graders' civic agency. *Social Studies and the Young Learner, 27*(4), 19–22.

Serriere, S., Mitra, D., & Cody, J. (2010). Young citizens take action for better school lunches. *Social Studies and the Young Learner, 23*(2), 4–8.

Tilley, J. (2020). Creating space to discuss social issues. *Center for Responsive Schools*. https://www.responsiveclassroom.org/creating-space-for-students-to-discuss-social-issues/

Index

Page numbers in italics refer to figures and tables.

Printed in the USA
CPSIA information can be obtained
at www.ICGtesting.com
LVHW081642210823
755804LV00008B/206